Shakespeare and the Critics

by A. L. FRENCH

CAMBRIDGE
At the University Press
1972

Published by the Syndics of the Cambridge University Press
Bentley House, 200 Euston Road, London NW1 2DB
American Branch: 32 East 57th Street, New York, N.Y.10022

© Cambridge University Press 1972

Library of Congress Catalogue Card Number: 75–183221

ISBN: 0 521 08470 9

Printed in Great Britain by
Alden & Mowbray Ltd
at the Alden Press, Oxford

Contents

_To_
MY MOTHER
AND THE MEMORY OF MY FATHER

Acknowledgments

I am grateful to the editors of the following journals for allowing me to use material which first appeared there: *English Studies*, *The Oxford Review*, *The Cambridge Quarterly*.

There are other debts which are hard to define and impossible to repay. The late A. P. Rossiter started me thinking about Shakespeare. Frequent discussions with colleagues and students have made me question my opinions; and I am especially grateful to Mr Graeme Henry, who has time and again forced me to reconsider my views. Dr J. M. Newton has also been a valuable critic. Mr H. A. Mason's recent book, *Shakespeare's Tragedies of Love* (and the articles in *The Cambridge Quarterly* from which it is largely drawn), offered much useful stimulus; as did also the many other critics cited in the following pages.

To Mr M. H. Black, of the Cambridge University Press, I owe my thanks for his very full and searching criticism of my first draft.

To my wife I am grateful for her constant help with and at every stage of the book's evolution. Without her encouragement it would not have appeared at all.

The following ladies helped greatly by typing various drafts of early versions of the chapters: Mrs Jan Armstrong, Mrs Dorothy Johnstone, Mrs Gay Holmes. Mrs Joan Hotson typed the final draft faultlessly.

For the errors of fact, taste, and judgment which no doubt remain, I alone am responsible.

A. L. FRENCH

Note on texts

Hamlet, *King Lear* and *Antony and Cleopatra* are quoted from the current New Cambridge editions. *Measure for Measure*, *Othello* and *The Winter's Tale* are quoted from the New Arden editions. All other quotations from Shakespeare plays are taken from *The Complete Works*, edited by Peter Alexander.

When [Mr Casaubon] said "Does this interest you, Dorothea? Shall we stay a little longer? I am ready to stay if you wish it," – it seemed to her as if going or staying were alike dreary. Or, "Should you like to go to the Farnesina, Dorothea? It contains celebrated frescoes designed or painted by Raphael, which most persons think it worth while to visit."

"But do you care about them?" was always Dorothea's question.

"They are, I believe, highly esteemed. . . . if you like these wall-paintings we can easily drive thither; and you will then, I think, have seen the chief works of Raphael, any of which it were a pity to omit in a visit to Rome. He is the painter who has been held to combine the most complete grace of form with sublimity of expression. Such at least I have gathered to be the opinion of conoscenti."

– George Eliot, Middlemarch, chapter XX

1. Introduction: What do we Bring to Shakespeare?

I

SHAKESPEARE is nowadays pretty well beyond criticism. By 'criticism' I don't necessarily mean downright adverse judgment: I mean any sort of discussion that doesn't start from the premise, and work on the assumption, that his works (or almost all of them) are perfect, and that the task of criticism is simply to find out, in each case, that principle in a play which ensures it is so and not otherwise. Such a principle, people believe, exists in every Shakespeare play just because it is a Shakespeare play. All we're doing is looking for something that is bound to be there; and all that is required is hard work, patience, and an indefinite suspension of judgment.

The making of this assumption can have some rather unfortunate consequences. For one thing, it means that we – readers, teachers, students – are reduced to illustrating perfections, and inhibited from asking whether they are really perfect. All sorts of interesting questions about Shakespeare cannot then be posed, because if they are we may find that the answers aren't at all reassuring, or even that there aren't any answers. Our minds are not free; our attitudes are restricted to undifferentiated deference. And of course by putting all of Shakespeare on the same plane of excellence, we may be not only manacling our minds but also promoting poor writing and loose feeling beyond their merits; so that we shall be doing a grave disservice to the very excellence we are concerned with. What is more, if we bring bad writing up to the level of good, we shall by the same token be bringing down the good things, not to mention the great ones, to the level of the rest.

1

I'm not saying Shakespeare is a bad writer, of course. All I'm doing at the moment is to ask the reader to grant the possibility, not the fact, of inequalities and unevennesses in Shakespeare's plays: the object being to free our minds from assumptions about his perfection and allow us to ask all kinds of questions which, if we think he never nodded, sound merely impudent. And to ask such questions doesn't mean that we shall – or that we shan't – find answers to them; it is indeed essential to what I am suggesting that we should make no assumptions of any sort about what we're going to discover.

Perhaps I should now be more specific and ask the reader to ponder some queries about the plays I am going to discuss in this book. Is there, for example, any extant account of *Hamlet* which takes full cognisance of *all* the data of the play, leaving nothing out and not getting anything in by distorting it? Different people will give different answers, naturally; but if you talk to the answerers you find that they disagree flatly and finally about what the data are; so the reason why they cannot agree about how to organise them is that they are talking about organising different things. The extraordinarily various and (often) wildly contradictory things people have found in *Hamlet* may lead us to suspect that a play which has provoked so many responses can't be said to have *an* ascertainable meaning; and perhaps the first problem is not so much to decide whether all the data can somehow be fitted in to an account of it, as to see whether it has anything that can properly be called data. Later in this chapter I shall be suggesting that Shakespeare had a great deal of freedom when he wrote his dramas; at the moment I want to suggest that we, as critics, must claim our freedom of action too.

Again, we might ask a naive question about *Othello*: why does the hero become jealous of his wife? (I leave on one side the question of where exactly he does so; and by asking 'why?' I don't mean we should look for some ultimate cause – I just mean a plausible proximate cause.) Now, some people say he gets jealous because of Iago's insinuations; others that he does so because he is a jealous sort of man whose interest in Desdemona is largely possessive. Others again take an intermediate position, and say that Othello is, because of his colour, alienated from the society he is living in and therefore particularly liable to the insecurity upon which jealousy feeds. (This last notion is popular among students, who are understandably worried about race-relations in their own society.) It may be that there are in the play hints of all these views and that Shakespeare never commits himself to any one of them; but what seems to me to be lacking from the published critiques (or most of them) is a full consideration of the evidence. Even Dr Leavis's classical essay at times makes its points rather too easily, particularly about the temptation scene, and doesn't ask whether a play that shows a man becoming jealous with no more pretext than his own egotistical temperament isn't perilously close to being a melodrama (and it may be a melodrama – that also is a possibility). Bradley, on the other hand, quibbles about the *word* 'jealousy' and in any case projects all the evil onto Iago – thus making the play a melodrama of another kind. It seems to me significant that whereas Bradley sentimentalises Desdemona and makes her into the worst sort of Dickens heroine, Leavis barely mentions her at all: that is, neither critic asks whether her part in the relationship mightn't be a factor of some importance in making Othello rise to Iago's improbable bait. Both critics leave me feeling that the jealousy is inadequately motivated in dramatic terms; that may be the play's fault, but we ought to take a searching look at it before saying so. And of course we have to be careful about what we mean by 'adequately motivated' and 'in dramatic terms'.

There are naive questions too that we might ask about *King Lear*. For example: does the play show us Lear being thrown out into the storm, or does he on the contrary leave out of injured pride? If the reader objects that these questions are altogether too naive, I can only point out that the conventional account simply assumes the first of them to be purely rhetorical. If, however, we think of them as genuine alternatives, with neither calling for a simple answer which is wholly 'right', isn't it possible that we shall have to revise our notions about what we are to make of Lear in Acts III, IV and V? It is also possible that we shall find the play to have been offering us one view of Lear up to a certain point, and quite another later on; so that we shall be forced to ask whether the play itself has any consistent attitude to the events within it. And mightn't it be argued that some parts of the sub-plot (particularly in the last two Acts) have usually been read and written about in a very abstract way, as though all they were doing – and all they needed to do – was to work out a thematic 'pattern'? If we find that they are doing no more than working out such a pattern, we may still say that Shakespeare is fully aware that they're functioning in this way; the fact that they're inadequate is precisely their point. But we couldn't reach this conclusion without first having asked some searching questions about whether or not they succeed in the same way as the parts of the last two Acts which concern Lear and Cordelia – on the assumption that we think *they* succeed.

In the case of *Antony and Cleopatra*, we obviously need to ask questions about the mode of the play, in particular the relation of the many comic moments to the interest in love and military honour. We may or may not end up feeling, with Mr H. A. Mason, that the moments of obviously great poetry in the play have too little to do with the characters we have been seeing, and wonder whether the official hero isn't at some moments offered as a great man and at others, with equal plausibility, as a mere buffoon. But we can hardly find satisfactory solutions to such problems (assuming there are answers) if we don't ask the questions first.

It may be that we shall end up, in all these cases, by finding that our questions turn out to be unanswerable – which is no reason for not asking them. Or we may find that conventional answers don't work, and that we can only give satisfactory accounts of the plays by seeing them differently from the conventional ways of looking at them. And, in any case, if we approach them without the usual deference we are not very likely to find them faultless. We may find our reactions rather mixed; and, if we do, we ought to say so. Why we 'ought' to say so is suggested by Matthew Arnold's comment on a remark of Sainte-Beuve:

"In France," says M. Sainte-Beuve, "the first consideration for us is not whether we are amused and pleased by a work of art or mind, nor is it whether we are touched by it. What we seek above all to learn is, whether *we were right* in being amused with it and in applauding it, and in being moved by it." Those are very remarkable words, and they are, I believe, in the main quite true. A Frenchman has, to a considerable degree, what one may call a conscience in intellectual matters; he has an active belief that there is a right and a wrong in them, that he is bound to honour and obey the right, that he is disgraced by cleaving to the wrong.

('The Literary influence of Academies')

II

A good many of the problems that arise in reading Shakespeare come about, as I have said, because critics habitually start from the assumption that there must be a way of 'explaining' everything that happens in a play: if there are things we can't explain that is the fault of our incompetent reading and not of Shakespeare. Put so nakedly, the assumption is obviously absurd because it prejudges every conceivable issue. And we may get rather different results if we approach the plays without any preconceptions about their faultlessness.

There are other assumptions that people also make about Shakespeare. Some of them are also questionable. For instance, it is easy and useful to think that Shakespeare shared 'Elizabethan' notions about moral, political, and psychological issues; and that we can find out what these notions were by reading the works of Elizabethan moralists, psychologists, and statesmen. Well, of course it would be dubious to assume that Shakespeare felt and thought on all matters exactly as we do – even supposing that we (whoever 'we' are) rejoiced in perfect unanimity about all moral, political and religious issues. Still, the scholarly study of 'background' may give us a sense of the possible modes of feeling, the available sentiments, that existed in Shakespeare's day – on the assumption, of course, that some modes were possible and some weren't. Background study is therefore likely to be useful and may even be indispensable.

Yet one might be pardoned for wondering whether there aren't dangers in the study of background which are at least as great as those resulting from its neglect. An obvious danger is that we may be allowing Elizabethan divines or statesmen to read Shakespeare for us, thus putting him on a level with them. One reason, I suspect, why the *Henry VI* plays have been neglected is that they are believed to be no more than illustrations of Tudor political orthodoxies, derived from not very interesting chroniclers like Hall. So firmly established is this interpretation of the plays that few critics have troubled to take a careful look at the evidence. Or again, take *Hamlet* – which is admittedly a difficult play. Some people read it in the light of Elizabethan notions of Melancholy, as set out by Timothy Bright, for example; and they make it into a mere illustration of some rather crude theories about human behaviour. One can't help feeling, whatever one makes of the play in the end, that it is more complex and interesting than that. Other critics see the interest of *Hamlet* as centring upon the ethics of Revenge: some say that the Ghost is proved to be a disguised devil by the very fact that it commands Hamlet to take private revenge; others claim that, while the Elizabethan attitude to revenge was certainly disapproving, a man was allowed to pursue it if the crime to be avenged was sufficiently grave and if no other way was open to him – Hamlet, in effect, is at war with Claudius. Other critics, again, make out Elizabethan notions about ghosts to be very important; and most readers, over the incest between Claudius and Gertrude, are happy to take Hamlet's and the Ghost's word for it that it is indeed incest. Now, all of these matters are important; and if we can discover what his patrons might have expected of Shakespeare, so much the better – though a good artist is presumably a man who is constantly breaking down established habits of thought. There is no excuse for our ignoring information if it is available, but equally there is no excuse for applying it lazily and unintelligently.

Othello and *Antony and Cleopatra* both involve our thinking about love, marriage, and war, all of which bring us to various notions of what is meant by that complicated word 'honour'. But it seems to me to be throwing up the sponge if we go to *Othello* expecting that it will move within 'known' Elizabethan views about the rights of women and the behaviour of husbands. Indeed, the argument cuts the other way: to a man accustomed to think of his wife as a chattel, *Othello* would probably have seemed deeply subversive and highly offensive. And both *Othello* and *Antony* raise awkward questions about 'love'.

Lear makes us think about the duties of children to parents and of subjects to kings; armed with what we take to be Elizabethan notions about The Family, and with the Commandment 'Thou shalt honour thy father and thy mother', it is easy enough to reduce the play to a homily. Or, armed with a mixture of Elizabethan and modern Christianity, it is not difficult to see Lear as being on a pilgrimage to redemption, a pilgrimage during which he discovers many important truths. But it is worth at least seeing what happens if we approach the play without easy assumptions as to what Shakespeare thought and what his audience expected. There is, as I've said, no reason to suppose that 'the Elizabethans' all thought the same thoughts, any more than 'the English' today are like-minded about war or sex. If we aren't careful, we may when reading Shakespeare find ourselves taking only one of the possible views as being 'representative', and crediting Shakespeare with it to the exclusion of all others; so that we may end by being quite as wrong about his plays as we could be if we hadn't looked into the background at all.

Some people will object that this kind of anti-historicism is actually rather orthodox; the historicists, it will be said, were pretty thoroughly defeated some years ago, and we nowadays take it more or less for granted that we have to read Shakespeare's plays as we find them instead of importing dubious assumptions exhumed by scholars. I can only envy such people the company they keep and the books and journals they read. And I should like to teach the students they teach and have my students read the same books as their students. It may be true that, among some academics, historicism has had its day; but among students it is still rife because they read what is written for them by the editors of paperback editions or included by the compilers of paperback anthologies of critical essays. I take down from my shelves the Penguin *Three Jacobean Tragedies*, and on the first page of the Introduction I read about a 'whole genre of plays, sometimes called Revenge Tragedy (itself a subdivision of a wider group, "the tragedy of blood") which appeared during the last few years of the sixteenth century and the first decade or so of the seventeenth'. Or I take down the Signet Classics edition of *2 Henry IV* and read in the introduction (p. xli): 'Today...we recognise that Shakespeare's histories embody Elizabethan political views...' I open John Holloway's *The Story of the Night* and learn, of Othello, that his 'affronted indignation should be seen against the background of the Elizabethan prayer-book, where in the marriage service the husband promises to cherish and comfort his wife, but the wife to serve and obey the husband' (p. 39). Evidently, the Elizabethan World Picture, though banished from the stage, still mutters audibly in the cellarage. One could go on for pages accumulating evidence of this kind, but that would be merely tedious. What I would rather do is to look at a couple of Shakespeare plays which appear to invite us to make conventional assumptions, and to decide whether and in what spirit we ought to accept the invitation.

Suppose, for example, that we could find some act which was, beyond question, considered deeply sinful in Shakespeare's day; and suppose we could show that Shakespeare in fact treats it in a variety of ways, running the whole gamut from disapproval through indifference to approval. Shouldn't we then not merely have cast doubt on whether, on that issue, there was *any* one 'Elizabethan' attitude, but also have gone some way further in our grasp of how vital it is not to approach Shakespeare with preconceptions? For 'historical' assumptions are only a type of any and all assumptions, and if I can convince the reader on this score I may have laid the groundwork for some of the more curious things I'm going to say later in the book. I may have suggested both Shakespeare's freedom, and also what I think should be our freedom, from received ideas.

Take suicide. Everyone knows that in the seventeenth century it was thought sinful; not till 1823 did Parliament abolish the practice of burying suicides at the crossroads under a pile of stones. In Shakespeare's day the Church of England, like the Catholic Church, rigidly forbade the burying in consecrated ground of anyone who had taken his own life. Now in Shakespeare there is a sharp contrast between the view taken of suicide in the Roman plays and what we find in plays whose background is more or less Christian. In the Roman plays there is no superstitious horror of suicide and frequently, indeed, it is thought of as being rather honourable (Brutus, Cassius; Antony). Elsewhere, however, a very different note is sounded. In *Hamlet*, for example, we have the 'doubtful death' of Ophelia, and the whole scene in which she is buried (v.i) is filled with references to the conventional Elizabethan abhorrence of suicide. The Church authorities have apparently been dubious about accepting the coroner's finding of 'accidental death' and will only bury her with 'maiméd' (much truncated) rites. The officiating cleric grumbles that Ophelia really, he thinks, ought to have been buried as a suicide, under a heap of 'Shards, flints and pebbles' (v.i.225). We recall that earlier in the play Hamlet himself has talked about how the Almighty has 'fixed / His canon 'gainst self-slaughter' (I.ii.131). There is a good deal of eschatological terror in *Hamlet*, too, about where a man goes after death if he hasn't made a proper end.

The background in *Romeo and Juliet* is also straight-forwardly Christian and, as befits a play set in Italy, it is Catholic. The Friar, who marries the lovers and gives Juliet the potion, is a Franciscan, and Juliet twice goes to him ostensibly for 'shrift' (confession). Romeo, hearing he has been banished for his killing of Tybalt, says:

> There is no world without Verona walls,
> But purgatory, torture, hell itself. (III.iii.17)

Banished, he says, is a word that 'the damnéd use... in hell' (47). On the other hand, the Friar remarks of Juliet's supposed death, 'Now heaven hath all' (IV.v.67), and on the same subject Balthasar believes that 'her immortal part with angels lives' (V.i.19). Romeo calls the Friar 'a divine, a ghostly confessor, / A sin-absolver, and my friend professed' (III.iii.49). And there are plenty of references to common Christian ideas like sin and the honourable estate of marriage. The Friar will not leave the lovers alone together

> Till holy church incorporate two in one. (II.vi.37)

It is against this backdrop that we must see the catastrophe of the play.

Now, the catastrophe is not unprepared for: both Romeo and Juliet have earlier threatened, in the violence of their passion, to take their own lives. Romeo offers to stab himself at III.iii.108 but is restrained by Friar Laurence, who cries

> Hold thy desperate hand...
> Hast thou slain Tybalt? Wilt thou slay thyself?

He goes on to argue that, after all, Romeo has only been banished, so he and Juliet may well be reunited later on. Juliet, after her father has been pressing her to marry Paris, goes to the Friar's cell.

> If, in thy wisdom, thou canst give no help,
> Do thou but call my resolution wise,
> And with this knife I'll help it presently... (IV.i.52)

Again the Friar interposes:

> Hold, daughter; I do spy a kind of hope,
> Which craves as desperate an execution
> As that is desperate which we would prevent.

In both these cases Friar Laurence describes the intended
act as 'desperate', a word which meant literally 'without
hope'. To be without hope was to have turned away from
God altogether, so it is fitting that the Friar, playing
Comforter, should say 'I do spy a kind of hope' and should
go on to talk in terms of a scheme which will be 'desperate'
in quite another sense – 'reckless', or perhaps 'extravagant'
(see *OED*).

But in the end both lovers commit suicide – Romeo by
drinking the poison he bought from the apothecary, and
Juliet by stabbing herself with her husband's dagger. The
Friar, in his long speech to the Prince at the end, deduces,
quite rightly, that Juliet killed herself:

> she, too desperate, would not go with me,
> But, as it seems, did violence on herself.   (v.iii.262)

We note the significant recurrence of the word 'desperate'.
The Prince a little later opens Romeo's farewell letter to his
father:

> here he writes that he did buy a poison
> Of a poor pothecary, and therewithal
> Came to this vault to die, and lie with Juliet.   (287)

In other words, all the characters on the stage know that the
lovers took their own lives. One of these characters is a
Friar, to whom such an act would have been especially
abhorrent. Yet where is there a single word of blame, or
even of doubt? There is none. Indeed, while the Friar was
earlier horrified by the very idea of suicide, he now says
nothing about it; his chief emotions are regret about what
has happened coupled with sorrow that, however uninten-
tionally, he should have helped to bring it about. Moreover,
no-one objects when Montague offers to erect a golden
statue of Juliet; the play ends in a general atmosphere of
sad reconciliation.

All this is very curious, to say the least. We could argue ourselves out of the predicament by claiming that Shakespeare is writing a play about a Catholic society for a rabidly Protestant audience, so that the whole piece is designed to show how wickedly Catholicism encourages the very sins it condemns; this would make Friar Laurence into a Machiavellian figure like Jacomo and Barnardine in *The Jew of Malta*. Or we could say that the story of Romeo and Juliet is, as in Bandello, an essay in ethics, demonstrating the dreadful effects of unregulated passion; at the end we are meant to think of the lovers as being eternally damned for their transgression. But I take it that such arguments are too obviously unacceptable for me to have to counter them. It is perfectly plain that we are not meant to blame the lovers, or the Friar, at all.

But notice that our predicament arises from our expectation that Shakespeare will both conform with Elizabethan notions about suicide and will also remain entirely consistent throughout a given play. In view of what actually happens, it must be that these expectations are themselves wrong. I think they are. In this case at least, Shakespeare uses the conventional notion about suicide when it suits him (in III.iii and IV.i) and forgets it when it doesn't (in the final scene). He could, if he wished, rely upon ideas that would be in the audience's mind because they were part of the moral fabric of life at the time: equally, he could ignore or inhibit them. He could, after all, scarcely have explored fully every moral issue that raised itself, so he availed himself of this essential artistic freedom.

It's obvious, though, that freedom of this kind might lead, at the hands of a man who was irresponsible, confused, or merely tired, to something we could only call an evasion of the issues. With this proposition in mind I shall look at one of the problems I find in that difficult play *Measure for Measure*. (Let me stress that I'm not offering an *account* of the piece; I am only looking briefly at one problem that would have to be thought about if I were.) Shakespeare, in his freedom, can introduce us to a society in which whatever he likes can happen, without our being bound to feel that things which don't happen as they do in seventeenth- (or twentieth-) century London could never have happened anywhere. The Duke's temporary abdication, for instance, and his return in disguise, are quite frankly a piece of theatrical contrivance: the end – the analysis of justice and mercy – may be held to justify the means. And the anti-sex law that Angelo resurrects and puts into operation, though it seems absurd, can be accepted by the audience as a postu- late or *donnée* which enables Shakespeare to focus our atten- tion where he really wants to. We can deal with the objection that these contrivances make the play look rather rigged, even dehumanised, by saying that, after all, without the contrivances we shouldn't have had the particular insights that these circumstances, and these only, yield.

But the difficulty arises, pretty soon, that we don't really know in this play what *is* a datum. Of course, there are some inconsistencies that are obviously inconsistencies and, equally obviously, don't matter: for example, Mistress Overdone's being told something she herself has mentioned a few moments before but has apparently forgotten (see I.ii.77f.). This is trivial. But larger problems arise when we subject the play to a not specially rigorous inspection as to the fidelity with which it sticks to its own postulates in less indifferent matters. Take, for example, the anti-sex law the enforcement of which is the efficient cause of most of the action. Where does this law come from, and what does it say?

We aren't to think that the Duke absconds with the intention that Angelo shall revive this law in particular. He first deputes the government to Angelo and Escalus with the words:

> Your scope is as mine own,
> So to enforce or qualify the laws
> As to your soul seems good. (I.i.64)

Here, 'qualify' (as generally in Shakespeare) means 'modify' or even 'diminish'; so the Duke is suggesting that

Angelo might even, if he feels inclined, lessen the severity of the laws. After the Duke has left, Escalus says

> A power I have, but of what strength and nature
> I am not yet instructed. (79)

To which Angelo replies "Tis so with me'. This 'power', I take it, is the formal written confirmation of their commission, adumbrated in the Duke's lines just quoted – a confirmation that their power as justiciars is indeed the same as his.

The Duke was not telling the truth, we discover, in saying that he had to leave hastily. To the Friar he confides his real purpose: he wants a hatchet-man to enforce the 'strict statutes and most biting laws' which have been 'let slip' for years (I.iii.19); but, rather inconsistently, he adds a little later that

> Lord Angelo is precise;
> Stands at a guard with Envy; scarce confesses
> That his blood flows; or that his appetite
> Is more to bread than stone. Hence we shall see
> If power change purpose, what our seemers be. (50)

Both reasons cannot be true: if, as the last lines seem to imply, Angelo is not going to be a good magistrate, because of personal failings of one kind or another, then the Duke cannot be serious in expecting him to administer the laws harshly but scrupulously. Neither the Duke, nor the play in which he appears, attempts to reconcile these flagrantly different statements of intent; nor is it clear whether the inconsistency is a hit at the Duke or simply an oversight.

This is the more confusing in that we have just heard about the new law which has been proclaimed as soon as the Duke's back is turned. Claudio is to have his head chopped off within three days, 'for getting Madam Julietta with child' (I.ii.66); this is apparently in agreement with the 'proclamation' mentioned a moment later (73), which has also announced that all suburban brothels are to be pulled down (88). Claudio, when he appears, remarks that

> this new governor
> Awakes me all the enrollèd penalties
> Which have, like unscoured armour, hung by th' wall
> So long, that nineteen zodiacs have gone round,
> And none of them been worn; and for a name
> Now puts the drowsy and neglected act
> Freshly on me: 'tis surely for a name. (154)

Apparently, then, this Act was perfectly legal: all Angelo has done is to revive it. Now, to discover what the Act said about sexual relations, we have to be clear what the state of affairs between Julietta and Claudio actually was. He tells Lucio that

> upon a true contract
> I got possession of Julietta's bed.
> You know the lady; she is fast my wife,
> Save that we do the denunciation lack
> Of outward order. (I.ii.134)

The Arden editor tells us what this means: the pair have entered a contract known as *sponsalia per verba de praesenti*, a common-law contract which was absolutely binding whether followed by a church ceremony or not.[1] This piece of background information makes it clear that Shakespeare intends the revived law to be thought of as extremely harsh, in that it must have forbidden, on pain of death, all sexual intercourse outside a formally consecrated marriage. He is thus drawing our attention to the rigorousness of the law in order that we shall pay close attention to the various characters' responses to it. Claudio, in reply to Lucio's query 'Whence comes this restraint'? has just said:

> From too much liberty, my Lucio. Liberty,
> As surfeit, is the father of much fast;
> So every scope by the immoderate use
> Turns to restraint. Our natures do pursue,
> Like rats that ravin down their proper bane,
> A thirsty evil; and when we drink, we die. (I.ii.117)

This mood of bitter self-condemnation is, as has often been

---

[1] J. W. Lever, in the New Arden *Measure for Measure*, introd., pp. liii–liv; cp. the note on I.ii.134.

remarked, quite inconsistent with what Claudio says only a few lines later; 'Lechery?' asks Lucio, and Claudio says 'Call it so' (129), seeming to imply that one would be pretty silly to call it anything of the kind, since, as he then goes on to explain, his engagement to Julietta was a 'true contract'. Leavis comments: 'Claudio has committed a serious offence, not only in the eyes of the law, but in his own eyes. No doubt he doesn't feel that the offence deserves death; nor does anyone in the play, except Angelo (it is characteristic of Isabella that she should be not quite certain about it).'[1] The trouble with this is that the only law in whose eyes the offence looks serious is precisely the law that condemns Claudio to death; while to say that Isabella isn't quite certain whether he deserves death is to ignore her normal, natural – her truly human – reaction to the news Lucio brings: 'O, let him marry her!' (I.iv.49). Thus Claudio is not guilty of lust, except in terms of a grotesque law that makes no distinction between the consummation of a marriage which lacks only formal sanctification, and the grossest promiscuity.

But actually this is not true; and here we come in sight of yet another puzzle about our intended assumptions. For the fact is that this law, when revived, is applied with remarkable haphazardness to the prostitutes and procurers whom one supposes it was disinterred to deal with. If we grant that, according to the law, Claudio must lose his life, what are we to think when Pompey, Mistress Overdone and the rest suffer no such penalty? What are we to think when no-one, not even Angelo, even suggests they ought to? J. W. Lever, the Arden editor, notices this oddity and remarks: 'Significantly, neither Pompey nor Overdone is regarded as meriting death';[2] but *of what* this is significant the editor does not divulge. Nor do the 'professionals' (as Leavis aptly calls them) escape just because they are handled by the more humane Escalus. The constable Elbow accuses Pompey, and in Angelo's presence, of being

1 F. R. Leavis, *The Common Pursuit* (1952), Peregrine edn 1962, p. 162.
2 Lever, edn cit., p. lxxi.

A tapster...; parcel bawd; one that serves a bad woman; whose
house...was, as they say, plucked down in the suburbs; and now
she professes a hot-house; which I think is a very ill house too.

(II.i.62)

Angelo doesn't, as we might have expected, jump in and
have Pompey condemned to death, or even arrested; in
fact he says nothing, and after seventy lines of cross-
examination by Escalus, which gets nowhere, Angelo leaves,
saying merely that he hopes 'you'll find good cause to whip
them all' (136). Admittedly, both Pompey and Mistress
Overdone are later arrested (III.ii); but this is because they
have reverted to their procuring, and in any case they are
only going to be imprisoned, not executed. (Nor, incidentally, do we hear of anyone else in Vienna being executed
for sexual offences.) Thus, the law treats Claudio as
promiscuous when he isn't, and the professionals as not
promiscuous when they are. It is impossible to make sense
of this.

But notice that our efforts at making sense of the play
have broken down after we have made a certain assumption,
an assumption derived from scholarly investigation into
the nature of Elizabethan marriage contracts. The assumption we made was that Claudio's words at I.ii.134 refer to
the *sponsalia per verba de praesenti*: he is telling the truth
when he implies that Julietta and he have entered into this
contract, so that they are as good as married. But if we
look at what the play tells us, instead of trying to make it
conform to what we think we know about its background,
we find a very different state of affairs, as I shall now try to
show. Claudio told Lucio that it was a 'true contract' and
that Julietta was 'fast [his] wife'; but Claudio is a character
in a play, and there is no reason to accept automatically
anything he says as being gospel truth. And when we look
at the play again, we notice what should have been obvious
from the very first – that *only* Claudio ever claims that he
and the girl are to all intents and purposes married already.
He has an axe to grind: it is in his interest to persuade himself and others that this is the case. Yet if it were the case,

17

he would have had no reason to feel bitterly self-reproachful
a little while before. His explanation in fact has the air of
having been invented on the spur of the moment, in order
to convince Lucio, so that the convinced Lucio will transmit
to Isabella a plea which will appeal to her legalistic mind.
If what Claudio says is true, it would have to count heavily
in his favour when Lucio tells Isabella and when Isabella
talks to Angelo; it would at least be worth mentioning.
That it isn't true at all is shown, I think, by the fact that
Lucio doesn't say a word about any 'true contract' when he
is talking to her. Indeed, his terminology suggests rather
that he doesn't believe Claudio. With Isabella his first
reference to the affair is to say that her brother 'hath got his
friend with child' (I.iv.29) – 'friend' meaning 'mistress'.
He characterises Angelo as being

> a man whose blood
> Is very snow-broth; one who never feels
> The wanton stings and motions of the sense... (57)

He wouldn't talk in this strain if his point were not that
Claudio was one who *did* feel the wanton stings and motions
of the sense, which is why Angelo can't be expected to
sympathise with him. If Lucio were trying to convey that
Claudio was virtually married, the implied comparison
would be pointless.

At the beginning of II.ii the disinterested Provost refers
to Claudio's act as a 'vice' (5), though he thinks the young
man shouldn't 'die for 't'. Clearly, then, he has no notion
of any true contract. Angelo calls Julietta a 'fornicatress'
(23), so he has no inkling either. Yet these terms are
echoed by Isabella herself as soon as she comes in:

> There is a *vice* that most I do abhor (29)

and

> Who is it that hath died for this *offence*? (89)

These words harmonise with Angelo's further description of
the act as an 'evil' and a 'foul wrong' (92, 104). Not once
does Isabella play what, given Claudio's account of the
situation, should be her strongest card; not once does she

represent the act as anything but fornication. Obviously we are not to suppose that in the interval between I.iv and II.ii Lucio has told her what her brother said. Unless we want to elaborate the fantastic theory that Lucio, while ostensibly trying to help his friend, is actually trying to get his sentence confirmed, by suppressing material evidence, we can only suppose that he, who (as his part of prompter to Isabella shows) is no fool when it comes to deciding which arguments are plausible and which the reverse, knows that Claudio's claim about the true contract is pure moonshine.

What makes this conclusion inevitable, for me at least, is that Julietta – who surely ought to know – makes no reference to any contract when she is being interrogated by the disguised Duke. 'Repent you, fair one, of the sin you carry?' he asks (II.iii.19); and a little later the response comes:

> I do repent me as it is an evil... (35)

She has confessed that the 'most offenceful act' was 'mutually committed' (27), but she has no explanation, let alone excuse. And Isabella, even in the very last scene of the play when she is giving the returned Duke as objective an account of what has happened as she can manage, still calls her brother's crime 'the act of fornication' (v.i.73).

It is perfectly plain, then, if we read *Measure for Measure* with moderate attention, that Claudio's claim is not true. He is the only one to make it, and it is not repeated by his friend, his sister, or even his fiancée. Consequently, he is condemned quite justly, if the law itself is just. So we have once again seen the extreme danger of an approach through 'background'. Such an approach reduces this play to gibberish, because Angelo's resurrected law is thereby turned into what is in effect a law in restraint of matrimony itself; and it is hard to see how what Rossiter calls a 'damaging analysis of the shortcomings of law and justice as social institutions'[1] could result from such a ridiculous situation.

[1] A. P. Rossiter, *Angel with Horns* (1961), pp. 155–6.

Nevertheless, even if we leave 'background' out of account, I'm not sure we can completely dispose of the difficulties. However little we take the lovers to be affianced, and even if we take them not to be affianced at all but just passionately in love, the fact remains that a law which condemns Claudio but spares the professionals is hard to swallow even as a *donnée*, because it is simply self-contradictory. Nothing can get round the objection unanswerably made by the Arden editor (though whether he quite grasps it as an objection isn't clear), that 'the offences of Claudio and Pompey are judged by wholly incompatible standards'.[1]

To my mind the consequences of this incompatibility are disastrous. It's not as if Shakespeare were concentrating our attention on an issue in one place and in another inhibiting it. He does this, as we saw, in *Romeo and Juliet*, over suicide. There, we don't worry about our being expected to drop abruptly all our normal expectations about suicide in the last scene; the play is a highly conventional one and, however constricting we may finally think the convention, Shakespeare is so firmly in control of it that one can have known the play for years without realising that, from a strictly 'logical' point of view, it is inconsistent. But *Measure for Measure* is precisely about the moral/legal issue as to which we find so gross an inconsistency; hence our attention is not inhibited in the crucial respect, but focused on just that respect. *Measure for Measure* is a profoundly puzzling play, but the effect of introducing background information is to make it more puzzling, not less.

From this brief glance at a couple of Shakespeare plays we must conclude that background information can be, and often is, extremely misleading. When Shakespeare is clear about his assumptions, he makes it clear in the play itself what they are. The importation of assumptions from outside the play can, as we have seen, reduce a straightforward piece like *Romeo and Juliet* to nonsense. Or such assumptions

[1] Lever, edn cit., p. lxvi.

may push an already difficult play, like *Measure for Measure*, further towards total unintelligibility.

But to say that background information is sometimes misleading doesn't mean that we can afford to disregard it altogether. The question is to know how to use it intelligently, and to try and decide how far, in any given play, Shakespeare is merely, for the sake of simplicity, taking a contemporary belief for granted, and how far he is setting up a quite new one of his own. We mustn't fall into the trap of assuming that 'background' is useless; indeed it is my whole point that we mustn't start by assuming anything at all. If we do, we are liable to take away from a play not what is in it but what we should like to be in it. Assumptions about 'background' are merely a particular instance of the general assumptions about Shakespeare which one finds everywhere in modern criticism – not the least of which is, as I claimed earlier, that his plays make perfectly good sense, or can be made to make it.

What happens, then, if with such thoughts as these in mind we look at four of Shakespeare's tragedies – *Hamlet*, *Othello*, *King Lear* and *Antony and Cleopatra*?

2. Hamlet

I INTRODUCTORY

FIRST FOR SOME CONSIDERATIONS which are so elementary that they are always getting overlooked. Each of Shakespeare's plays (like other plays and like novels) presents various points of view. Each point of view is fully dramatised; and in any given piece the points of view add up to a total vision of human behaviour which is not identical with the vision that any one character has. There are occasional exceptions: Prospero in *The Tempest*, and (perhaps) the Duke in *Measure for Measure*, are outside – beyond – their plays; we take their attitudes as more or less corresponding with what the plays as a whole are trying to convey. As a rule, though, no single character in a Shakespeare play should be taken as the author's representative; even in the case of Tragic Heroes like Othello or Lear, their view of themselves and their respective worlds is not identical with the plays'.

All this is obvious. But it is only natural for the critic to want to project his own beliefs and values on to what he is criticising; in Shakespeare's case the sensibility that informs the plays is so free and open that the critic can all too easily twist them to suit his own predilections. If you want to glamorise Othello, for instance, it is not hard to make your view of him coincide with his view of himself – which, as F. R. Leavis showed, is precisely what Bradley (among others) did. To follow Bradley here is rather like believing Emma's notions about herself in Jane Austen's novel, a novel which is about the very painfulness of learning to see oneself truly. Few people now, perhaps, simply 'believe' Othello; yet in other Shakespeare plays critics still fall into the trap of identifying the play's 'truth' with the 'truth' granted to one of its personae.

22

In the case of *Hamlet* at least three totally contradictory readings are current. (In summarising them I shall have to simplify drastically.) In one view Claudius is a good man and Hamlet is the something that is rotten in the state of Denmark (Wilson Knight). In another Claudius and his court are corrupt; Hamlet, initially good, is infected by the very evil he sets out to destroy (L. C. Knights,[1] H. D. F. Kitto). In Dover Wilson, on the other hand, Hamlet really is a sweet prince, and there is practically nothing to be said against him; Bradley's reading is along the same general lines save that he sees Hamlet has nasty streaks, thus avoiding Dover Wilson's disastrous need to tamper with the stage directions.[2] What these commentators have all done is to identify one persona's view of things with the play's. Dover Wilson sees Hamlet as presumably Horatio sees him. Knights and Kitto see Claudius and the court as Hamlet sees them. Wilson Knight sees Claudius and the court and Hamlet as Claudius sees them. Each critic assumes that the persona he chooses is telling the disinterested truth, the *play's* truth, so anything other personae say is more or less prejudiced and untrustworthy.

Thus we have several readings of *Hamlet*, each claiming it is the one right reading, but each contradicting and being contradicted by all the others. Now we can only conclude one of two things. Either the play is hopelessly ambiguous (which it may quite well be), or else the various critics have gone badly wrong. If they have gone wrong, they may have done so in the 'point of view' way suggested above; because, I suspect, they want not merely to project their moral values on to the piece but actually to rack it to them. Of course a critic's moral sensibility is bound to influence his reading of a play, and of course Shake-

---

[1] I refer to Knights's later work on the play, first published as *An Approach to "Hamlet"* in 1960 and reprinted together with *Some Shakespearean Themes* by Penguin Books in the Peregrine series (1966). My references are throughout to this composite volume.

[2] Principally the notorious 'early entrance' of Hamlet at II.ii.159; but also throughout the play-scene, where the stage-directions compel the reader to accept Dover Wilson's own interpretation of what is happening instead of allowing him to make up his own mind. Examples could be multiplied.

speare's plays do speak to the moral sense; but there is all the difference in the world between letting a work speak to one and torturing it to say what one wants to hear. Many of *Hamlet*'s critics have done the latter.

They have done so, I think, because *Hamlet*, having a unique collection of problems, offers unique temptations to the reader. There are at least three very perplexing obscurities: (i) What are we to think of Claudius and his court? and are Claudius and Gertrude meant to be seen as committing incest, which Polonius and the others tacitly condone? Then (ii) What are we to make of the Ghost? – closely linked with this being (iii) What are we to make of the obligation the Ghost lays on Hamlet to revenge his murder? What is the play's attitude, if it has one, to private revenge?

There are of course all sorts of answers that critics have offered to these questions. What critics mostly have in common is that they assume there *are* answers. Well, let us see first whether the play gives us a coherent picture of the life of the Danish court. If we can find some clarity here, we might have at least a basis for giving reasonable answers to the other questions.

II   THE DANISH COURT

Shakespeare never intended us to see the king with Hamlet's eyes, tho', I suspect, the managers have long done so.   (Coleridge)

By seeing what two distinguished modern critics have said about the Court we may be able to see how coherent Shakespeare is being. L. C. Knights and H. D. F. Kitto both take Shakespeare to have a very firm – not to say stern – attitude here. As to Professor Knights, the point at which I find myself parting company with him comes pretty soon after he has started talking about the play proper (his first twenty-odd pages being rather peripheral). He says that in the *Hamlet*-world there is a basic antinomy – between death on the one hand and on the other 'life lived with a peculiarly crude vigour of self-assertion' (p. 183). This

'life' is that of the Court, and Knights goes on to expand
what was implied by 'crude':

This is the man [Claudius, as we see him in I.ii] whose accession to
the throne, and whose indecently hasty – and, in an Elizabethan
view, incestuous – marriage with his dead brother's wife has been
"freely" endorsed by the "better wisdoms" of the Council. In the
whole Court of Denmark there is no one, Hamlet apart, to utter a
breath of criticism. How should there be? The ethos of the place –
so we are told, or directly shown – is made up of coarse pleasures –

> This heavy-headed revel east and west
> Makes us traduced and taxed of other nations;
> They clepe us drunkards, and with swinish phrase
> Soil our addition;

it is made up of moral obtuseness (Polonius), sycophancy (Rosencrantz and Guildenstern), base and treacherous plotting (Laertes)
and – since Shakespeare didn't introduce Osric at the climax of the
tragedy for the sake of a little harmless fun – brainless triviality. This
is the world that revolves round the middle-aged sensuality of Claudius
and Gertrude. "Something is rotten in the state of Denmark"...
(pp. 183–4)

Hamlet himself, Knights argues, is corrupted by this
rottenness in the very act of trying to destroy it, because it
calls forth a corresponding corruption in him. Now what
strikes me as odd about this long comment on the court is its
tone. Is the court presented by Shakespeare's play as having
an ethos to which the audience ought to feel so superior?
Hamlet has (we know) a strongly prejudiced view of the
court, but even from this view Knights makes a pretty
tendentious selection. It is especially odd that he should
take this tone, and see things from Hamlet's viewpoint,
when he has alleged that he is considering 'the action of the
play, so far as possible, as directly presented, without
reference to what Hamlet himself may say about it' (p. 181;
Knights devotes the whole of part II, §3 to this attempt). In
his earlier essay on *Hamlet*, on the other hand, he was
critical of people 'who like to feel wholehearted sympathy or
antipathy for the characters of a play, and who like to feel
assured that they are safely following clear moral judgments
imposed by the author'.[1] The passage I have just quoted

[1] L. C. Knights, *Explorations* (1946), Peregrine edn 1964, p. 86.

from the later essay reminds one oddly of the Victorian moral
fervour of Edward Dowden:

On the throne... reigns the appearance of a king; but under this
kingly appearance is hidden a wretched, corrupt, and cowardly soul,
a poisoner of the true king and of true kingship, incestuous, gross and
wanton, a fierce drinker, a palterer with his conscience, and as
Hamlet vehemently urging the fact describes him "a vice of kings,"
"a villain and a cut-purse," "a paddock, a bat, a gib." Such is kingship
in Denmark.[1]

Noting, then, Professor Knights's general bias, we can have a
look at some of his specific charges. What about Polonius?
He is morally obtuse, says Knights, who refers us to
Professor Kitto[2] for a full account of how Polonius is
symptomatic of the corruption that permeates the Danish
state. Turning up Kitto, we find he also thinks 'Polonius,
like everything else in Denmark, is rotten' (p. 250). Is this
true?

Polonius' dramatic presence begins to make itself felt
strongly in I.iii, when he starts by giving worldly-wise advice
to Laertes and then (after his son has sailed) forbids Ophelia
to have anything more to do with Hamlet. Now, Polonius'
caveat about Hamlet has been anticipated by Laertes right
at the start of the scene; he too tells his sister to be dubious
about the Prince's intentions. Kitto slights Laertes'
motives as being mere 'worldly prudence', and from the
lines he quotes (I.iii.5–10, 39–43) it certainly looks as
though that is a fair description. But he doesn't quote the
lines which give this prudence its point. Laertes says to
Ophelia:

> Perhaps he loves you now,
> And now no soil nor cautel doth besmirch
> The virtue of his will. But you must fear,
> His greatness weighed, his will is not his own,
> For he himself is subject to his birth.
> He may not, as unvalued persons do,
> Carve for himself, for on his choice depends
> The sanity and health of this whole state,

[1] Edward Dowden, *Shakespeare: His Mind and Art* (1875), 1962, p. 136.
[2] H. D. F. Kitto, *Form and Meaning in Drama* (1956), 1960, ch. 9.

And therefore must his choice be circumscribed
Unto the voice and yielding of that body
Whereof he is the head. Then if he says he loves you,
It fits your wisdom so far to believe it
As he in his particular act and place
May give his saying deed, which is no further
Than the main voice of Denmark goes withal.   (I.iii.14)

Laertes is explaining very carefully to his naive sister that since Hamlet is now heir-apparent – we heard him declared so at I.ii.109 – his marriage is a matter of more than merely personal concern; he cannot simply go ahead and marry any woman he loves. Laertes makes this point no less than four times. Ophelia is not of the blood-royal; Hamlet is. I do not see why a twentieth-century audience should find Laertes unpleasantly prudential or in any way peculiar: royal marriages are not a simple matter even nowadays, and to Shakespeare's audience Laertes' point probably seemed so obvious that he could only have been labouring it out of a genuine fear for his sister's safety.

And it is this obvious point that is presumably in Polonius' mind when he echoes his son. He says of Hamlet:

Do not believe his vows, for they are brokers
Not of that dye which their investments show,
But mere implorators of unholy suits,
Breathing like sanctified and pious bonds
The better to beguile.   (I.iii.127)

But Kitto (who ominously keeps the eighteenth-century emendation 'bawds' for 'bonds') proceeds to comment:

[Polonius] hears that his daughter is on affectionate terms with a young man, of whom we know no ill, except perhaps that his spirit is too fine for this "unweeded garden"; and these are the thoughts, and this the language, to which he naturally turns. Is it not perhaps a little over-generous to speak, as Granville-Barker does, of Polonius' "meddling"? Would it not be fairer, both to Polonius and to Shakespeare, to call him a disgusting and dirty-minded old man?   (p. 261)

Yes, it would certainly be fairer, if this were all Polonius said, and if we hadn't been alerted by Laertes' earlier warning. Polonius has started the episode by speaking these lines, which Kitto ignores:

'Tis told me he hath very oft of late
Given private time to you, and you yourself
Have of your audience been most free and bounteous.
If it be so – as so 'tis put on me,
And that in way of caution – I must tell you
You do not understand yourself so clearly
As it behoves my daughter and your honour.   (1.iii.91)

Polonius has been listening to court gossip, which has it that
Ophelia and Hamlet have been seeing too much of each
other: this has been 'put on' (impressed upon) him, and he
has been 'cautioned' not to let things go any further. His
reason for taking this line is the same as Laertes': Hamlet,
being a prince, cannot choose for himself whom to marry.
And Polonius is afraid of what may happen if the affair is
not stopped. If we have any lingering doubts about what he
is driving at, his words thirty lines later make it trans-
parently clear:

> for Lord Hamlet,
> Believe so much in him that he is young,
> And with a larger tether may he walk
> Than may be given you: in few Ophelia,
> Do not believe his vows . . .   (1.iii.123)

(These lines carry on to the extract Kitto mentions, which I
quoted a little while ago.) Polonius assumes that Hamlet
realises his special position and so can't possibly be sincere in
his dealings with Ophelia. Polonius is not to know – neither
are we, at this stage – that Hamlet hasn't given it a thought;
nor that Gertrude (as she says very much later, at v.i.237)
would have approved of the match.[1] I suppose that if
Polonius had not tried to stop the affair he would have been
thought cynically ambitious.

Thus it is silly to call Polonius a 'disgusting and dirty-
minded old man': Kitto is applying ruthlessly simple moral
standards to a play one of whose intended points is the
difficulty, delicacy and complexity of the very process of
moral discrimination. And he is doing this because he wants

---

[1] I take it that Gertrude's rather vague words at iii.i.38–42 only mean 'I hope
you can calm Hamlet down and restore his sanity.' And cf. Dover Wilson's
note to ii.i.115–16.

to show that *Hamlet* is, like some Greek tragedies, a religious drama, and thus has to show that – as he says more than once – 'evil is abroad'. But to predicate 'evil' (which must surely have a metaphysical overtone) of Polonius and the court is to misuse the word completely.

Kitto's comments on the Polonius/Reynaldo scene (II.i) have more justice – at first glance, anyway. The essence of his case here lies in this question: 'what would we naturally think of a man who spoke *to* his son like that [Polonius' advice in I.iii], and then *about* his son like this?' (p. 265). The upshot is that Polonius is not only dirty-minded but also 'treacherous' (p. 266). But what we would naturally think of such a man depends, surely, on our sense of his motives. Polonius, in getting Reynaldo to keep an eye on his son, is acting unpleasantly but clear-sightedly, and we need to take both impressions. We know he said

> to thine own self be true
> And it must follow as the night the day
> Thou canst not then be false to any man.　(I.iii.78)

But a father who seriously expected his spirited young son to follow such coldly sensible advice when abroad would be ridiculously optimistic. Why is it not 'natural' for a man to worry about his absent son's behaviour? His method of ensuring that he knows exactly what Laertes is up to is meant to strike us as underhand, Polonius emphatically not being a thing enskied and sainted, but it is the only method open to him. Moreover the episode is thematically and tonally relevant. Polonius does not know what his son is going to do, and to that extent doesn't know what he is; similarly, we spend a good deal of the play speculating about what Hamlet is and what Claudius is; they, in turn, spend much time wondering about each other and arranging tests which, they think, will provide evidence to support their theories. Polonius tries to cross-question Hamlet, but is outwitted; Rosencrantz and Guildenstern try the same thing, but Hamlet's answers are various and ambiguous; Ophelia is used to assay Polonius' theory, and elicits a violent but quite enigmatic response. Likewise, Hamlet has the Gonzago play put on to test Claudius, but the results (as I shall argue later) are less conclusive than Hamlet himself supposes. And he notoriously devotes a good deal of his time, and ours, to speculating about his own motives and deeds or non-deeds.

As for the faults that Polonius expects his son to commit – gaming, drinking, fencing, swearing, quarrelling and drabbing – Kitto clearly thinks these are very dreadful vices and that it is loathsome of Polonius even to suggest his son may be subject to them. Here again, Polonius is merely being clear-headed about the facts of human nature. I think critics tend to lack Shakespeare's moral largeness – which doesn't of course mean an indiscriminate permissiveness. Knights does refer, towards the end of his essay, to Shakespeare's 'generosity, his outgoing feeling for life in all its forms'. I think this insight admirable, and what I regret is that the critic doesn't see the 'feeling for life' extending to Polonius and Claudius and Osric and everybody else.

I pass now to the scene where Polonius reads Hamlet's love-letter aloud to Gertrude and Claudius. Shakespeare, says Kitto, contrives to 'make it as revolting as possible'; it is 'shockingly indecent' that 'a love-letter, extorted from Ophelia, should be bandied about between people such as these' (p. 273). This is a fair comment, given Kitto's view of the three people.

We have already seen that Polonius can't be reduced to a nasty old man; and what we need to ask, in the scene under discussion (II.ii), is – once again – why he reads out the letter, why the episode takes place at all. Yet Shakespeare tells us unequivocally and several times. The premise from which any reading must start is given us at the beginning of the scene, when Claudius refers to Hamlet's 'transformation' (II.ii.5); and if this isn't clear enough, Gertrude later refers to 'my too much changéd son' (36). Hamlet has put on the antic disposition he talked of in Act I, and by so doing has upset and disconcerted his mother and uncle. There is no reason whatever to suspect that their concern is other than genuine: after all it is a serious matter when the heir to the throne, 'the observed of all observers', is going off his head. They speculate about the cause of his madness: Claudius blames 'his father's death', and to this Gertrude adds 'and our o'erhasty marriage' (ii.ii.8, 57); Polonius of course blames love. They spend time and ingenuity in trying to find out what the cause was, because they think that if they remove it Hamlet will return to sanity. Polonius' argument is long and rambling, but its logic is really quite simple: Hamlet was in love with Ophelia; she, following her father's instructions, rebuffed him; this was traumatic, and led to madness. He reads out the love-letter in order to establish the basic premise of his argument – namely, that Hamlet *was* in love with Ophelia. (As it happens his diagnosis is wrong, but it isn't stupid.) Now all this is pretty amateurish, but it's the best that these none too perceptive people can do; and there's no reason to talk of Hamlet's letter as being 'bandied about' out of sheer nastiness (like Birkin's at The Pompadour, in *Women in Love*). Kitto goes on very high-mindedly: '[Polonius'] daughter's happiness is at stake, and he talks in a way which shows that honesty and simple human feelings mean nothing to him' (p. 273). But it's not true, here, that Ophelia's happiness is at stake: whether or not she is really in love, Polonius doesn't for a moment suppose (as we have seen) that a match between Hamlet and her is possible. He implies precisely this to the King and Queen, and they don't contradict him:

> *Claudius.*　　　But how hath she
> 　　　　　　　Received his love?
> *Polonius.*　　　　　　　What do you think of me?
> 　*Cl.* As of a man faithful and honourable.
> 　*Pol.* I would fain prove so. But what might you think
> 　　　When I had seen this hot love on the wing,...
> 　　　If I had played the desk or table-book,
> 　　　Or given my heart a working mute and dumb,
> 　　　Or looked upon this love with idle sight,
> 　　　What might you think? no, I went round to work,
> 　　　And my young mistress thus I did bespeak –
> 　　　'Lord Hamlet is a prince out of thy star,
> 　　　This must not be.'　　　　　　　(ii.ii.128)

I don't see what can be worrying Polonius if it is not the very thing that critics deny him, a concern for people's feelings. Of course, he likes to be in the limelight, and wants to show Claudius how clever he is, but there's no need to confuse partly interested motives with revoltingly indecent ones. Moreover to talk about Polonius in such terms is to convict oneself of having no sense of humour.

Polonius is a man bred in courts, exercised in business, stored with observation, confident of his knowledge, proud of his eloquence, and declining into dotage...Such a man is positive and confident, because he knows that his mind was once strong, and knows not that it is become weak. Such a man excels in general principles, but fails in the particular application. He is knowing in retrospect, and ignorant in foresight...This idea of dotage encroaching upon wisdom, will solve all the phaenomena of the character of *Polonius*.   (Johnson)

Polonius' elaborate attempts to keep an eye on his son, guard his daughter's virtue and find out what is wrong with Hamlet, are funny – which is not to say that he comes off clean: any more than the fact that Major Bagstock in *Dombey and Son* is funny means that we are supposed to forget his bottomless vulgarity.

As I said, the use of Ophelia to find out what is the matter with Hamlet has been thought very disgraceful. But the critics have been anticipated by Ophelia's father, when he gives her the (holy) book:

> we are oft to blame in this,
> 'Tis too much proved, that with devotion's visage
> And pious action we do sugar o'er
> The devil himself.   (iii.i.46)

These words reveal, according to some critics, the rottenness in Polonius' soul; but it seems to me an odd sort of rottenness if he knows that what he is doing is underhand and dislikes having to do it. He thinks it necessary to 'loose' Ophelia to Hamlet and to spy on them, for reasons of state: this has been his attitude all along. Bradley sees this very clearly, and he also exculpates Ophelia:

Why should [Ophelia] not tell her father the whole story and give him an old letter which may help to convince the King and the Queen?

Nay, why should she not allow herself to be used as a "decoy" to settle the question why Hamlet is mad? It is all-important that it should be settled, in order that he may be cured; all her seniors are simply and solely anxious for his welfare; and, if her unkindness *is* the cause of his sad state, they will permit her to restore him by kindness (III.i.40). Was she to refuse to play a part just because it would be painful to her to do so? I find in her joining in the "plot" (as it is absurdly called) a sign not of weakness, but of unselfishness and strength.[1]

Modern critics never say how, given the situation, they think the Danish court should have behaved towards Hamlet. I think Shakespeare shows them as behaving with reasonable good sense and decency, according to their pretty limited lights.

And so we come to Claudius and Gertrude. They have both been treated roughly by critics, largely, I suppose, because readers have been content to take what Hamlet and the Ghost say about them as being true, rather than paying attention to the play and seeing what it says. About Claudius we do eventually find out that he murdered his brother; and we gather he is in some sense (in what sense I will return to later) committing incest with Gertrude. There-fore – it has been assumed – *everything* he does must be bad; Hamlet always tells the literal truth about him. So as well as being an incestuous murderer, Claudius really is physically unimpressive, a lecher and a drunkard. Kitto, for example, slides into describing the Claudius whom Hamlet sees: 'surely the physical appearance of Claudius must be such that it makes sense to us when Hamlet, showing Gertrude his picture [III.iv.64], calls him a "mildewed ear," a "moor"' (p. 257). Perhaps it must likewise 'make sense' when Othello calls Desdemona an 'impudent strumpet'? We can also ask, What actor, assigned the role of Claudius, would – or could – play him as a paddock, a bat, a gib?

L. C. Knights falls into a similar trap. 'It is clear', he says, 'that on [Claudius'] first appearance we are intended to

---

[1] A. C. Bradley, *Shakespearean Tragedy* (1904, 1905), Papermac edn 1965, p. 131. I shall always quote Bradley from this edition.

register something repulsive.' After quoting the first seven lines of Claudius' opening speech (I.ii) he adds: 'we need know nothing of Claudius' previous activities to react to those unctuous verse rhythms with some such comment as "Slimy beast!"' (p. 183). He further calls the King's kindness to Hamlet 'ostensible'. I think such definite and damning judgments would be quite proper if Shakespeare had begun his play with the Ghost's revelations, followed these with 'O my offence is rank', and only then given us the scene in the court (which, as we shall see, is more or less what happens in the corrupt German version of the play known as *Der Bestrafte Brudermord*). That he didn't suggests he wanted us to suspend judgment about Claudius till much later; of course Knights is right to think that the unctuousness and equivocalness of Claudius' first words insinuate a doubt about him, but similarly the obsessiveness of Hamlet's first soliloquy insinuates a doubt about *him*. If we take what Shakespeare offers, we shall find Claudius to be a character whom the playwright presents with care, understanding and subtlety.

We needn't fall into Wilson Knight's opposite mistake of seeing everything through Claudius' own eyes and finding him the 'typical kindly uncle'[1] (I should like to have met some of Wilson Knight's uncles). Claudius' nature is mixed, like that of most of Shakespeare's personae, or most people in real life, and we have to find out the exact proportions of the mixture. Plays whose personae do not have mixed natures are called melodramas, and the objection to melodrama is precisely that it schematises the complexities of human life out of existence. Shakespeare's plays are not melodramas and do not work in this way.

The critics tend to sweep the inconvenient aspects of Claudius under the carpet. No doubt 'unctuous' is a reasonable description of the first few lines of his first speech, and perhaps it can be dismissed as 'elaborate and frigid rhetoric', but we shouldn't pass over the counter-impression that insistently makes itself felt during the rest

[1] G. Wilson Knight, *The Wheel of Fire* (4th edn, corr., 1954), 1962, p. 34.

of the scene: an impression not only of efficiency but also of
dignity, even nobleness. I suppose we could take the words

> You cannot speak of reason to the Dane,
> And lose your voice   (1.ii.44)

as being merely pompous; to me it seems Claudius' tone is
genial, if a little bluff – he is trying to encourage a young
man who is slightly unsure of his standing with the new
regime, and is also trying to indicate to the rest of the court
how affable the new regime is going to be. Of course,
Claudius likes people to be happy, and wants to keep
Polonius sweet: one impulse is interested, the other less so.
With Hamlet, a little later, Claudius makes the best of a
very bad job, tactfully ignoring the fact that he addresses
his reply to Gertrude alone (1.ii.120f.). Moreover he tries to
reason with Hamlet about forgetting the late king; he
thinks his secret is safe, so his motives can only be benevo-
lent. I am not forgetting that this scene follows straight on
from the sinister resonances set up by the Ghost and the
watchers' comments on it and on the 'post-haste and romage
in the land'; but I see no possibility, at this stage of the play,
of attaching the ominousness to Claudius rather than to
Hamlet. The whole structure of Shakespeare's play, in fact,
makes us suspend judgment till much later, unless we use
the hindsight given by later readings. The King, too,
averts by diplomacy the war which threatened in 1.i and
which was partly responsible for the ominous tone of that
scene. No doubt admirers of Henry V will claim that this is
meant to show what a bad man Claudius is.

The King's fondness for what Knights calls 'coarse
pleasures' isn't presented by the play as something we are
meant to feel indignant or morally fervent about, any
more than we are supposed to find Hamlet's fastidiousness
merely puritanical or finicking. Hamlet talks about Claudius'
draining 'his draughts of Rhenish down' and the Danes'
partiality to 'heavy-headed revel'; but in this episode
(1.iv, before the appearance of the Ghost) Hamlet goes on
from his particular instance to talk about human flaws in
general, ending with the 'dram of evil' lines, the gist of

which (the textual corruption notwithstanding) is that you mustn't damn a man for 'one defect'. These lines surely reflect back on to what prompted them – Claudius' revels – so that his self-indulgence, if not excused, is certainly minimised. He loves the ostentatious drinking of toasts; but Renaissance kings didn't usually write their names in water. On the stage, producers often make Claudius tope almost continuously (so Stratford 1965 – Peter Hall's production); but since the text gives no indication that the King ever wavers from perfect clarity and self-control, we have to try and accept the extraordinary spectacle of a man who is always drinking and never drunk. I find this absurd, and the absurdity arises because we try to make the Claudius we see consistent with the one Hamlet sees.

Similarly, Knights is cross about what he calls the 'middle-aged sensuality' of the King and Queen. Sensuality is wicked, of course, though understandable, in the young; but in the middle-aged – ! Yet where is there any evidence that the relationship between Claudius and Gertrude *is* primarily a sensual one? Well, there is plenty; we remember lines like these:

> Let not the royal bed of Denmark be
> A couch for luxury and damnéd incest   (.v.182)

or again when Hamlet tells Gertrude not to let Claudius

> Pinch wanton on your cheek, call you his mouse,
> And let him for a pair of reechy kisses,
> Or paddling in your neck with his damned fingers...
>   (III.iv.183)

The first quotation is from the Ghost, the second from Hamlet: only they ever talk in such terms. True, Gertrude in the closet scene sees the 'black and grainéd spots' in her soul (III.iv.90), but she is acting under extreme duress, Hamlet having already committed one murder and being furious enough to commit another. When it comes to actually presenting Claudius and Gertrude together, Shakespeare emphasises the affectionateness of their relationship; to him she is 'my dear Gertrude' or 'sweet Gertrude'

(II.ii.54; III.i.28). Their tone to each other – see for example the King's words after the mad Ophelia has gone out (IV.v. 74f.) – is that of married people who know and respect each other. They aren't shown as married fornicators.

Even after Claudius has told us he killed the old king, he is not presented as a monster of villainy; nor even after he had made up his mind that Hamlet must be killed in England (a decision he reveals at the end of IV.iii; his original decision to send Hamlet to England, in III.i, has nothing sinister about it[1]). His kindness to the distracted Ophelia and his dignified coolness with the rebellious Laertes have often been commented on. Right in the middle of his plotting with Laertes to have Hamlet killed in the fencing match, he speaks these arresting lines:

> There lives within the very flame of love
> A kind of wick or snuff that will abate it,
> And nothing is at a like goodness still,
> For goodness, growing to a plurisy,
> Dies in his own too-much.   (IV.vii.113)

That depressed and introspective tone hardly belongs to a 'slimy beast'.

Again, it is argued that Claudius must be physically unimpressive because Hamlet says he is, but you can surely argue much more plausibly that he must be shown on the stage as a presentable (perhaps fine) figure of a man, so that we can see why Gertrude should have fallen for him in the first place. In any case the verse he speaks – the verse that creates him for us – has a certain largeness of utterance (we are occasionally reminded of Othello). Hamlet's references to him are therefore violently at odds with the impression he actually produces.

Finally, if Shakespeare really wanted to present a mean-minded and submoral man, why did he give Claudius that moving soliloquy in III.iii, in which he both admits his guilt and also gains, in some degree, our sympathy for the mess he has got himself into? The speech may not be quite the 'fine flower of a human soul in anguish' that Wilson

[1] See Note A below, The 'Sealed Commission'.

Knight makes it,[1] for the moral sensibility revealed by the verse is not especially 'fine'; but then its very ordinariness is what makes it moving. The King gropes his way to some not very startling truths about himself and his world; it is the *effort* towards self-knowledge, on the part of a man whose bents are quite other, that engages our compassion.

But these arguments are really rather subversive: because we soon find ourselves wondering why, if Shakespeare meant us to take an appropriately complex attitude to Claudius, he left it so late to tell us what Claudius really is. And in this respect *Hamlet* is unique in the whole Shakespeare canon, in that no other play waits so long to put its cards on the table. What usually happens is that by the end of the first Act of a Shakespeare play (and often by the end of the first scene) we have a pretty clear idea of what leading figures have done or are going to do. The *données* about Iago and Othello, Lear and Gloucester and their children, Macbeth and Duncan, are obvious before the curtain has been up for forty minutes. But about Claudius we are for a long time given no such definite information; in fact we don't get it until he confesses his guilt in so many words in III.iii – well over half-way through the play.

This needs arguing. Some critics (Rossiter, for example[2]) say that we know Claudius to be guilty the moment we see the Ghost. But do we? Dover Wilson showed, many years ago,[3] that all sorts of different views about ghosts were current in the seventeenth century; and these views are dramatised in the play itself. If Hamlet and Horatio don't know whether they should take the Ghost's word, why should *we* assume it is telling the truth? Secondly, I don't believe that Claudius' aside, 'How smart a lash that speech

---

[1] Wilson Knight, *Wheel of Fire*, p. 36.

[2] See *Angel with Horns*, p. 183: 'The Elizabethan audience, more devoutly certain of immortality than we are, knew [about Claudius' guilt] at first sight of the Ghost.'

[3] J. Dover Wilson, *What Happens in "Hamlet"* (1935). A convenient summary can be found in the New Cambridge edn, intro. pp. l–liii. My argument is not affected (though Dover Wilson's is) by Eleanor Prosser's *Hamlet and Revenge* (Stanford, 1967), which claims that very few Elizabethans in fact believed in the likelihood of ghosts being 'good'. I discuss Miss Prosser's case later in this chapter.

doth give my conscience' etc. (III.i.49f.), should be taken as a confession of guilt or a proof that he is a murderer; he is worried about the gap between his word and his deed, but we don't know exactly what deed he has in mind, and any tendency we may have to speculate is, I think, cut short by the obscure and arresting soliloquy of Hamlet that immediately follows. Finally, Claudius' behaviour at the Gonzago play is, whatever Hamlet himself may think, not conclusive evidence of guilt. Hamlet may, as Dover Wilson thinks, want Claudius to believe he is after the crown, thus diverting his suspicions; but it is just as likely that the play has two meanings – an exoteric one for the court, and an esoteric one for Hamlet and Claudius (and Horatio). The exoteric meaning is that Lucianus/Hamlet ('nephew to the King', not brother) is threatening Player-King/Claudius' life; the esoteric meaning is that Lucianus/Claudius murdered Player-King/Old Hamlet. But – characteristically – Hamlet is far too ingenious: even if Claudius were not guilty, he would have every reason to be furious about the exoteric meaning, which is an open threat. Thus, 'Give me some light – away!' tells us no more about Claudius than that he doesn't like having his life threatened in public by the heir-apparent.[1] Shakespeare makes it quite plain that we are to think Claudius is worried only at the exoteric meaning, by making him respond not at all to the dumbshow. His failure to object, or even comment, puzzled Dover Wilson, who propounded the odd solution that Claudius does not in fact see it, being deep in conversation with Gertrude and Polonius. This, I think, misses the point, which is that Claudius, with remarkable coolness, waits until Hamlet, with his talk of the murdering Lucianus

---

[1] After working out this interpretation myself I found I had been anticipated by Weston Babcock, *"Hamlet": a Tragedy of Errors* (Purdue, Ind., 1961), p. 100. Babcock thinks 'nephew' is a slip of the tongue on Hamlet's part (p. 98); Dover Wilson, on the other hand, thinks it is meant to prepare 'the Court for the assassination of Claudius which was intended to follow' (edn cit., p. 204). While it seems to me incredible that Hamlet would make such a silly mistake at the climax of a carefully contrived plan, it seems just as stupid of him deliberately to alert everyone to his murderous intent. So as far as I am concerned, 'nephew' remains an insoluble puzzle.

as 'nephew to the king', has provided an excuse for leaving which will seem perfectly natural *to the court*, particularly when Hamlet follows up with a climactically nasty reference to second marriages. I realise of course that this explanation of the play-scene probably sounds over-ingenious; but that is really my point. *Any* interpretation of the scene which 'explains' the difficulties is bound to seem too ingenious, because the scene itself does not make any obvious kind of sense. Whether, even given my reading, it would make unequivocal sense to the first-night audience – well, that is a matter for speculation. What worries me is that the texts we have can be interpreted in various ways, so that the whole scene, including Claudius' part in it, are deeply ambiguous.

Anyhow, if we take Polonius and the King and Queen in the way I have tentatively been suggesting, some other aspects of the court become clearer. For example, we needn't sneer at Rosencrantz and Guildenstern. Kitto says they are 'suborned' by the King and Queen, and quotes the lines

> we both obey,
> And here give up ourselves, in the full bent,
> To lay our service freely at your feet
> To be commanded. (II.ii.29)

Kitto comments: ' "We here give up ourselves" – to a murderer and to his guilty wife' (pp. 252–3). Since the pair don't know Claudius is a murderer (any more than we do) and give no sign of realising that Gertrude is in any of the various senses 'guilty' (any more than the rest of the court do), the comment and implied judgment are frivolous. Claudius and Gertrude, worried by Hamlet's odd behaviour, send for Hamlet's old friends and persuade them to make him reveal what is wrong. Where is the moral turpitude? They think they are helping both their King and their friend. And where is the 'sycophancy'? The homily they deliver to Claudius about Kingship (at the beginning of III.iii) apparently strikes critics as horribly fulsome; Harry Levin, for instance, sums up their words as 'a pair of . . .

flattering speeches'.[1] The suppressed argument is presumably that since we later find Claudius is a murderer and since Rosencrantz and Guildenstern praise him, they must be connivers at usurpation or worse. But in fact they do not, and cannot, know anything to the King's discredit; no doubt they go to their death convinced he is a lawful sovereign and a good man. On the other hand, by the time we see the last of them (in IV.iv) they know a great deal to Hamlet's discredit.

When Hamlet makes them admit – they do not need much pressing – that they were 'sent for' (II.ii.296), his attitude to them doesn't immediately change: the ensuing conversation about the Players is no less courteous than the comradely joking which started the scene. It is only later – when Hamlet thinks he knows Claudius is a murderer – that he expresses distrust of them (III.iv.203). Even when he has come back to Denmark and sent them to their death, he does not, I think, suggest that they knew he was to be executed on his arrival in England (the 'commission' was 'sealed', so presumably Rosencrantz and Guildenstern didn't know it commanded the 'present death of Hamlet'). The orthodox argument is that because Hamlet suspects them, and because they do eventually die, well, they must have deserved to. This is another confusion over points of view.

Finally I shall very briefly deal with a couple of other points about the Danish court. Knights says it is characterised by 'base and treacherous plotting (Laertes)' and 'brainless triviality' (Osric). It is ungenerous to dismiss Laertes in that one curt phrase. Admittedly he plots with Claudius, and does not abandon their plan to kill Hamlet even when Hamlet has apologised to him. He has lost his father and his sister, one murdered by Hamlet and the other driven mad by Polonius' death – but no matter; Hamlet apologises, and a sober Christian gentleman should take that as closing the account. Alas, Laertes is not as meekly forgiving as all that; he is hot-headed; he even wants

[1] Harry Levin, *The Question of "Hamlet"* (1959), p. 93.

revenge, and he takes it, only realising at his last gasp that he has been Claudius' catspaw. Our sympathies are simultaneously with Laertes and against him; the feeling is a painful one, and it is not surprising that people shy away from it.

Osric is fatuous, but it is beside the point to make him typify the civilisation of the court. Knights evidently thinks of him as a Bloomsbury type, but it is amusing to remember that Hamlet himself is not above a bit of brainless (and obscene) triviality when he is talking with Rosencrantz and Guildenstern in II.ii. Perhaps this is meant to show their bad influence on him. And while the court is not a particularly cultivated place, Claudius and his entourage are prepared to spend an evening watching what promises to be a rather tedious play – a play that hardly reflects very favourably on Hamlet's own judgment.

It seems, then, that the kind of temptation *Hamlet* offers is a moral or moralistic one. Critics tend to take advantage of hindsight, and assume from the very outset that we have read the play before and know Claudius to be guilty, his 'marriage' unnatural, and his courtiers mere time-servers without two scruples to rub together. On the other hand, critics who see Claudius' attractive qualities go to the other extreme and see Hamlet as the villain; Wilson Knight does this, though he puts in a saving clause at the end.[1] Still other critics simplify the complexities (or perhaps confusions) of the play by making *both* Claudius *and* Hamlet wicked. And this leads me to talk about Hamlet. Only after discussing him at some length shall I consider what the play is asking us to think about the Ghost or the revenge he orders his son to take.

III A PRINCE AND NO PRINCE

So far I have been trying to show that Shakespeare's play doesn't ask us to see the Danish court and its ethos as

[1] Wilson Knight, *Wheel of Fire*, pp. 45–6.

wholly corrupt; that to see it like this blunts and turns the very moral discriminations that Shakespeare is apparently concerned with. Supposing I am right, we have to answer some awkward questions about Hamlet's alleged corruptness: if the court is on the whole populated by rather average specimens, Hamlet cannot have been corrupted by them, and they cannot have released something in him. Three main possibilities suggest themselves: (i) Hamlet is not corrupted at all – i.e. we have to return to the 'sweet prince' reading; (ii) he is corrupted by the Ghost; (iii) he is corrupted by himself, by his own 'foul imaginations'. And of course some combination of (ii) and (iii) is possible.

The reader will, however, have noticed that these possibilities share a common assumption: that Hamlet either is, or is not, corrupt – the epithet being assumed to indicate an absolute state. But why make any such assumption? Surely the startlingly different views commentators have taken of Hamlet suggest that his nature is as mixed as that of Claudius? Of course, this lack of unanimity about Hamlet (and *Hamlet*) may only indicate that Shakespeare is not making sense, and this is a possibility I shall return to in section IV; but for the moment it seems worth asking: What impression does Hamlet make on us as we read or see the play? And how is this impression related to the world he is part of? Our first answer is that he makes an extraordinarily different impression on us at different stages in the play's development; hence our overall impression is not likely to be such that we can sum it up in one term of moral praise or blame. No doubt in the nunnery scene and the closet scene Hamlet alienates us by his brutality and obsessiveness; whereas in the exchanges with Rosencrantz and Guildenstern (II.ii.225f.), or with the players and Horatio (III.ii), he is gentle and courteous. Each set of impressions modifies the other to such an extent that we cannot fairly say, as Kitto does (p. 270), that the pleasant Hamlet is the 'real' Hamlet; this seems to be merely a devious way of sentimentalising Shakespeare. No, the 'real' Hamlet is the Hamlet we see – all of him: decency and indecency, indecision and rashness, coarseness and fineness.

Let us look at the first scene he appears in (1.ii) and see what sorts of responses he evokes. We see him as a man in black, isolated from the court life, with its political currents, that surrounds him; and he remains completely aloof for sixty lines. It is too easy for us, in our century of alienated outsiders, to reverse the stock idea that superior men are always outsiders – to think that outsiders are always superior. Hamlet is clearly (in some sense) an outsider; therefore, it can be argued, he must be superior. But in fact Hamlet's apartness, as presented by Shakespeare, is a riddle that keeps us guessing for 130 lines, till the stage empties and he begins his first soliloquy. Not till then do we know for sure the nature of his apartness or the reason for it; but Shakespeare provides some cogent pointers in the lines Hamlet speaks to his mother where he takes up her 'seems':

> Seems, madam! nay it is, I know not 'seems'.
> 'Tis not alone my inky cloak, good mother,
> Nor customary suits of solemn black,
> Nor windy suspiration of forced breath,
> No, nor the fruitful river in the eye,
> Nor the dejected haviour of the visage,
> Together with all forms, modes, shapes of grief,
> That can denote me truly. These indeed seem,
> For they are actions that a man might play,
> But I have that within which passes show,
> These but the trappings and the suits of woe.   (1.ii.76)

The point of this speech seems to have been very generally missed. Wilson Knight, for example, comments: 'his words point the essential inwardness of his suffering'.[1] And G. R. Elliott says that Hamlet 'summons the winds and rivers of the natural world to rebuke [Gertrude's] sighs and tears of unreal grief'.[2] These comments overlook the style of the speech, its artificiality and 'conceitedness'; and since Shakespeare has, even by this early stage in the play, given a convincing demonstration of his mastery over several different manners, all of them appropriate to the dramatic

[1] op. cit., p. 17.
[2] G. R. Elliott, *Scourge and Minister* (Duke U.P., 1951), p. 12.

and moral issues, it is inconceivable that he would have
given Hamlet these conceits out of mere inadvertence.
Hamlet's winds and rivers don't evoke the natural world or
point the inwardness of his suffering; rather, they recall the
conventionally literary world of Petrarchan poetic diction.
There is, one feels, a certain unreality in his grief, a certain
kind of histrionic self-regard. Though his ostensible purpose
is to deny that the 'trappings' express his grief truly, they
have a positive force because of the insistent conceits that
present them; the negatives are of the type William Empson
calls 'depraved' (see *Seven Types of Ambiguity*, chapter
VII). On the other hand, Dover Wilson sees there is something odd about the lines and says they are 'a bitter description of the mock funeral of his father, and of his mother's
behaviour thereat'[1] – that is, he sees the oddness as
sarcasm and as referring only to Gertrude. But since
Hamlet himself is obviously dressed in black, we would be
perverse not to take the speech as primarily a piece of self-
justification, whatever the ironic overtones (a moment
before, Gertrude has asked him to cast his *nighted* colour
off). Whatever the 'that within' may be, it is, even in
Hamlet's own sensibility, deeply involved with the outward
show.

The 'that within' is revealed to us in Hamlet's first
soliloquy: he is shattered by his mother's incestuous remarriage. One difficulty here, for the modern reader, is that
though scholars may tell us that Gertrude's marriage to
Claudius is incestuous, we find difficulty in feeling it to be so.
At first we may think that the notion is just one of history's
casualties, but actually the case is not so simple. Shakespeare is always making use of beliefs which, *qua* beliefs,
are unreal to the twentieth century; yet he generally
manages to give them enough imaginative reality for us to
suspend our disbelief. (An obvious example is the divine
sanction of Kingship.) Now the notion that this sort of
marriage is incestuous looks, on the face of it, like an idea of
the same kind. Why, then, is it hard to take? – is there any

1 Dover Wilson, edn cit., p. 150.

reason in the play? I think there is. Gertrude's 'incest' is never mentioned by anyone except Hamlet and the Ghost, and, what is more, neither of them (with two exceptions) mentions it to anyone else. We may vaguely remember that in the closet scene Hamlet charges his mother with incest, but on turning up the text all we find is this:

> You are the queen, your husband's brother's wife,
> And, would it were not so, you are my mother.   (III.iv.15)

Hamlet approaches the matter rather obliquely; and it is hard to tell whether Gertrude's answer,

> Nay then, I'll set those to you that can speak,

shows annoyance with the charge of incest or with Hamlet's wish that she was not his mother. A little later, when she tells him off for murdering Polonius, saying it is a 'rash and bloody deed', he answers:

> A bloody deed – almost as bad, good mother,
> As kill a king, and marry with his brother.   (III.iv.27)

Gertrude's reply to this – 'As kill a king!' – side-tracks the issue of incest; and in the rest of the scene, oddly enough, it never reappears. Hamlet doesn't repeat the charge: he argues that it must be sheer sensuality which makes her prefer Claudius to the virtuous and handsome Old Hamlet. Thus the Prince – on whose words, together with the Ghost's, the charge of incest wholly depends – emphasises not the unnaturalness of the union, but its lustfulness; even in his most brutally hysterical moments he does not bring up incest to add to the force of his indictment. The result is that by the end of the scene we have, firmly fixed in our minds, the feeling that Hamlet's savagery arises more from Gertrude's being polluted by her love for a lecherous man than from the fact that this man is her former brother-in-law. The overwhelming emphasis falls on her stepping 'from this to this' (III.iv.71). And we note that though she is eventually brought to admit her sensuality (88f.), she never seems conscious of what, according either to canon law or to commonsense, ought presumably to be much the blacker sin. When, earlier in the play, she and Claudius have been theorising about the reasons for Hamlet's madness, she says she does not doubt it is 'His father's death and our o'er-hasty marriage' (II.ii.57): no hint of incest here. Nor is Claudius' conscience sore about incest in his soliloquy (III.iii); indeed, he forgets to mention it.

Hamlet never talks about incest even to his confidant Horatio; the furthest he goes is to say that Claudius has 'whored my mother' (v.ii.64), a phrase which echoes the suggestions of sexual debauching that we found in the closet scene but carries no implication of unnaturalness. The only time he dares to use the word openly is right at the end, after Gertrude has drunk the poisoned wine and he has run Claudius through (v.ii.323). The court, including the morally cautious and stuffily proper Polonius, have evidently accepted the marriage as being nothing out of the ordinary; one might argue that their not mentioning it shows what a scandalous lot they are – an argument which very quickly commits one to the ridiculous position that the less something is mentioned the more important it is meant to be.[1] And when Shakespeare, in I.i, formally offers to create a sense of ominousness, neither Horatio nor the soldiers make any reference, however oblique, to an unnatural union; though if it was supposed to be admitted and scandalous, what better place than this to at least allude to the fact? The appearance of the Ghost is taken as boding a 'strange eruption to our state', but this is identified as probably being the impending war with Norway. Thus, only Hamlet and his father ever describe Gertrude's remarriage as incestuous, and their point of view gets no hint of endorsement from anyone else in the play.

This has carried us a long way from Hamlet's first soliloquy, but the point is a crucial one. With the best will in the world, we cannot but find his reaction to the marriage pretty excessive. Knights, who wants to show that it is the Ghost's revelation which really releases corruption in Hamlet, argues that 'there is certainly nothing unnatural

[1] Cf. Kitto, op. cit., p. 259, n. 1.

in the violence of Hamlet's recoil from' the evil in Act I. But while Claudius' attitude to Hamlet's grief is common-sensical to the point of impudence, Hamlet's attitude errs at least as far in the other direction; we cannot be seriously intended to think his mother's hasty remarriage an adequate pretext for his desire to die or to commit *suicide* – the sin against which the Everlasting has fixed his canon (and cf. the implications about suicide at v.i.1–31, 213–36). Hamlet is irrevocably caught in the past. The soliloquy is placed between the bustling (if insensitive) worldliness of the court and the friendly exchange with Horatio that follows it, so that its very positioning looks as though it is meant to imply some sort of placing judgment. The whole of the soliloquy, too, is built up on a series of antitheses between the absolutely good and the absolutely bad. The present state of Denmark is corrupt – and not only Denmark, the whole world too: 'things rank and gross in nature / Possess it *merely*'. Old Hamlet, compared to Claudius, is 'Hyperion to a satyr'. It is not only his mother who is frail: 'frailty thy name is *woman*!' By such means Shakespeare establishes an essential datum about Hamlet's sensibility – that it sees everything in terms of extremes: a human being, in Hamlet's eyes, is either a god or else a 'beast that wants discourse of reason', and there is no middle way. This datum about Hamlet is firmly established before he sees (and before we hear) the Ghost; at this stage he doesn't even know of its existence; so we can't blame what later happens to his mind purely on an external stimulus, as Knights and Kitto would like to.

When the Ghost appears to Hamlet, he addresses it in characteristically exclusive terms:

> Be thou a spirit of health, or goblin damned,
> Bring with thee airs from heaven, or blasts from hell,
> Be thy intents wicked, or charitable . . .　　　　　(I.iv.40)

These alternatives are no doubt perfectly reasonable ones; but what I want to draw attention to is not the sense of the lines so much as their syntax – the way in which Hamlet seizes the opportunity to propose a sharp opposition between

two views of the Ghost's nature, one of which (he implies)
must be wholly right and the other wholly wrong.

Knights says the Ghost tempts 'Hamlet to gaze with
fascinated horror at an abyss of evil' (p. 188), but the
'temptation' is already in Hamlet's nature and the Ghost
merely encourages him. It stimulates his proclivity
to look at things in black-and-white terms; the dead King
shares this cast of mind with his son:

> But virtue, as it never will be moved,
> Though lewdness court it in a shape of heaven,
> So lust, though to a radiant angel linked,
> Will sate itself in a celestial bed
> And prey on garbage. (I.v.53)

Here we have the same sorts of brutally simple contrasts as
Hamlet habitually deals in: virtue, lewdness, heaven, lust,
angel, garbage. Hamlet thus has supernatural licence to
pursue the natural bent of his mind. That bent, as revealed
anew after the Ghost has departed (I.v.91f.), is almost comic
in some of its manifestations:

> My tables, meet it is I set it down
> That one may smile, and smile, and be a villain,
> At least I am sure it may be so in Denmark:
> So, uncle, there you are. (I.v.107)

One doesn't have to be especially unsympathetic to find this
grotesquely silly. Dover Wilson excuses Hamlet on the
ground that he is making a 'bitter jest';[1] doubtless he thinks
he is doing so, but the effect on the reader is more like
bathetic hysteria. Hamlet's response to what the Ghost has
told him is both excessive and irrelevant; and these tenden-
cies too are important data about the mind we are being put
in such close touch with. The bathos in the lines quoted
above arises from the simple-mindedness of the contrast
'...that one may smile, and smile, and be a villain': the
assumption which underlies the phrase being that if one
smiles and smiles, one ought to be a very nice man; or if one
is a villain, one ought to glower and glower. There should,
in other words, be complete consistency between the outer

---

[1] Dover Wilson, edn cit., p. 162.

man and the inner – a consistency such as Hamlet himself, with his inward grief and outward trappings, tries to achieve.

Now if we look at Hamlet's behaviour through the rest of the play in the light of the hints given in Act I, some of it, I think, becomes more intelligible than it is sometimes found. We find that his behaviour is the result of his inhabiting a particular moral universe, which the play creates in detail and in depth. When he is talking to Rosencrantz and Guildenstern, for example, Hamlet gives them a partly true account of his malaise as an explanation for his conduct; he says: 'this goodly frame the earth, seems to me a sterile promontory,...this majestical roof fretted with golden fire...appeareth nothing to me but a foul and pestilent congregation of vapours'. Of man he says that this 'paragon of animals' is only a 'quintessence of dust' (II.ii.297f.). Later in the same scene, when he is talking to the Players, Hamlet chooses a speech to be recited. His choice of the Hecuba lines has been found curious, both because their style is oddly antique and also because they have the 'slenderest imaginable' connection with the play.[1] I don't know whether the speech is meant as a parody of some other writer, but I am sure its verse is singularly bad – ludicrously melodramatic – and the fact that Hamlet has chosen it is supposed to reflect unfavourably upon his literary tastes. But its connection with the play is by no means slender, and it is not only Hamlet's literary tastes that are called into question. In the Hecuba lines every feeling, every metaphor, is keyed up to a point where the whole business becomes laughable – laughable because inhuman. Of Pyrrhus we are told:

> '...head to foot
> Now is he total gules, horridly tricked
> With blood of fathers, mothers, daughters, sons,
> Baked and impasted with the parching streets,
> That lend a tyrannous and a damnéd light

---

[1] Martin Holmes, *The Guns of Elsinore* (1964), p. 95.

> To their lord's murder. Roasted in wrath and fire,
> And thus o'er-sizéd with coagulate gore,
> With eyes like carbuncles, the hellish Pyrrhus
> Old grandsire Priam seeks'. (II.ii.460)

By the Shakespeare of c. 1600 this must have been meant to sound like burlesque; the point of the episode is that *this* is what Hamlet remembers and admires. The style of the speech is but the means whereby a particular moral world is created: a world where there are no half-lights, or gaps between appearance and reality, or moments without intense feeling. In this Trojan world, life corresponds to what Hamlet desires, and for a while he can forget the complexities of life in the real world, the Danish court, losing himself in contemplation of the simple emblematic figures of the 'hellish' Pyrrhus and the 'reverend' Priam and the god-pitied Hecuba. What is happening, in fact, is that Shakespeare is exposing Hamlet's own moral sensibility by pushing it to extremes. The Trojan world is an illusion, of course – another form of seeming or appearance: a fact that Hamlet recognises in his soliloquy at the end of the scene (552f.). But though unreal, it is not the less attractive: in the soliloquy Hamlet further reveals his sensibility by wanting to key up the actor's violence still further, to

> drown the stage with tears,
> And cleave the general ear with horrid speech,
> Make mad the guilty and appal the free,
> Confound the ignorant, and amaze indeed
> The very faculties of eyes and ears. (II.ii.565)

These lines hover near the edge of absurdity, though Hamlet is taking himself quite seriously.

Hamlet's moral sensibility appears also, of course, in 'To be, or not to be'. There, the syntactical form taken by Hamlet's questionings (either/or) once again corresponds to his limited sense of the possibilities. He sets the 'calamity of so long life' (the 'whips and scorns of time', etc.) against the terrifying 'something after death'; it is a matter of either bearing 'those ills we have', or flying to 'others that we know not of'. This is the dilemma he finds intolerable. Not surprisingly, for if these *are* the only possibilities, no-one could possibly 'be', exist fully. But the abundance of other possibilities presented in the play suggest that the kind of 'being' Hamlet desiderates is itself chimerical. He asks, in a later soliloquy:

> What is a man,
> If his chief good and market of his time
> Be but to sleep and feed? a beast, no more:
> Sure he that made us with such large discourse,
> Looking before and after, gave us not
> That capability and god-like reason
> To fust in us unused. (IV.iv.33)

One can see very clearly from such lines why Hamlet has made such a deep appeal to the moral idealism of critics.[1] What Hamlet does not see (and what critics tend not to see either) is that his terms are themselves so unreal that no satisfactory answer to his question is possible. What is Man, beast or god? Neither, of course – but the terms of the question admit of no complex answer.

Just before the Gonzago play, Hamlet generalises from Horatio and indicates his ideal of what a man should be. It is often assumed that it is not only his ideal but also Shakespeare's:

> thou hast been
> As one in suff'ring all that suffers nothing,
> A man that Fortune's buffets and rewards
> Hast ta'en with equal thanks; and blest are those
> Whose blood and judgment are so well co-medled,
> That they are not a pipe for Fortune's finger
> To sound what stop she please: give me that man
> That is not passion's slave, and I will wear him
> In my heart's core, ay in my heart of heart,
> As I do thee. (III.ii.63)

Hamlet is implicitly accusing himself, justly enough, of being too labile; but what does he oppose to his inconstancy? The ideal he puts forwards is a kind of proud stoicism which would tend either towards self-regard or towards insensi-

[1] See, for example, Levin, *Question of "Hamlet"*, pp. 59–63.

bility. He is saying that the only way out of being over-
responsive to one's environment is to be under-responsive,
or quite irresponsive; to pretend one is in the world but not
of it. Once again he is holding up two exclusive alternatives
which don't in fact cover all the possibilities; and once
again, by so doing, he is blurring the whole issue.

Another case in point is his notorious sexual obsession, his
disillusion with womankind in the persons of Gertrude and
Ophelia. In both the nunnery scene and the closet scene,
he takes the view that only two kinds of conduct are possible
for a woman: total abstinence or total depravity. Hamlet
contrasts the 'nunnery', the place of total abstinence,
with *all* forms of sex – whether being a 'breeder of sinners',
having anything at all to do with men ('arrant knaves'), or
marriage.[1] His whole tirade (III.i.121) is built upon the
simple antithesis chastity/depravity – an antithesis in
terms of which any normal person can't win. To his mother
he speaks in the same antithetical mode; when she asks him
what she has done to provoke his censure he replies:

> Such an act
> That blurs the grace and blush of modesty,
> Calls virtue hypocrite, takes off the rose
> From the fair forehead of an innocent love
> And sets a blister there, makes marriage vows
> As false as dicers' oaths, O such a deed
> As from the body of contraction plucks
> The very soul, and sweet religion makes
> A rhapsody of words; heaven's face does glow,
> And this solidity and compound mass
> With heated visage, as against the doom,
> Is thought-sick at the act.   (III.iv.40)

The pattern, though complex, is basically the same as
before; it appears at its most obvious in the juxtaposition of
'marriage vows' and 'dicers' oaths'. The development of the
imagery too is typical: Gertrude's act has destroyed the very
idea of valid human contracts (the 'body of contraction'),
has reduced religion to gibberish and, by the end of the

[1] See Note B below, where I argue that 'nunnery' doesn't have a bawdy
meaning.

speech, has corrupted even heavenly bodies. And 'the doom' implies that the Queen's act is bad enough to bring down on the world a judgment almost as complete as the Last Judgment. The cosmic imagery brings no sense of release or widening of reference: it is Hamlet's moral universe we have to inhabit here.

It seems, then, that in most places Hamlet is given us in a pretty critical way. Shakespeare's critical or ironical treatment of him becomes even harsher towards the end of the play. Indeed in v.ii it reaches such a pitch of intensity that we may well begin to wonder whether we are not simply misreading, especially when in the last sixty lines Shakespeare returns upon himself and modulates into a very remote key. I think v.ii makes us question either our reading or Shakespeare's play, so I shall look at three of its crucial episodes: (1) what Hamlet tells Horatio about his disposing of Rosencrantz and Guildenstern; (2) his apology to Laertes; and (3) the various epitaphs on him spoken right at the end – by himself, Horatio, and Fortinbras.

(1) I have already suggested that it is a mistake to see Rosencrantz and Guildenstern as Hamlet sees them – and, moreover, it was a mistake for *him* to see them as he did. When he tells Horatio the details of what he did on board ship, we find ourselves increasingly resisting his evident belief that he was perfectly justified in writing out a new 'commission' which ordered them to be put to death on their arrival in England. Some obvious questions arise: if Rosencrantz and Guildenstern were carrying a 'sealed' commission, why does Hamlet assume they knew what was in it? But if they didn't know, why was he justified in sending them to their deaths? On the other hand, if they were in fact privy to Claudius' plot, why hadn't they been ordered to get rid of Hamlet (e.g. by throwing him over-board in the dead of night)? Now of course one possible answer to questions of this kind is that they don't, or shouldn't, arise at all. Shakespeare's art is highly con-ventional, and such questions are no more relevant than Bradley's query, 'Where was Hamlet at the time of his

father's death?' (a question he has been roundly abused for posing). I shall come back to this issue; for the moment I want to insist that the question does arise: are we meant to think that Hamlet was right in sending Rosencrantz and Guildenstern to execution? If he was wrong, what effect does our response here have on our response to the winding-up of the play? If we think he was right, on the other hand, why did Shakespeare go to considerable trouble to make it plain that Rosencrantz and Guildenstern act with perfect propriety throughout and that Hamlet could have realised the fact if he had asked himself a few sensible questions? Horatio comments on Hamlet's tale: 'So Rosencrantz and Guildenstern go to't', and Hamlet indignantly (I think) replies, 'Why, man, they did make love to this employment' (v.ii.56). Horatio's rather enigmatic remark leaves a lot to the actor, but Hamlet's retort seems to suggest that his friend's tone was unenthusiastic to the point of disapproval. Of course this exchange is too brief for us to be able to argue anything substantial from it; yet it remains an odd and disturbing blur because it comes so near the end.

(2) The apology to Laertes comes even nearer the end and thus has even more influence on how we take 'Now cracks a *noble* heart'. Hamlet's apology is, I think, designed to show how stupid he is about human relationships: how can he possibly suppose that twenty lines of double-talk could begin to satisfy a person bereaved as Laertes has been? Hamlet isn't even man enough to take the blame himself: he shifts it onto a pseudo-entity entitled 'Hamlet's madness', which he, it appears, had nothing to do with. This might just be acceptable if it were true, but when we recall the closet scene where Hamlet killed Polonius, it seems pretty obvious that he wasn't in any sense mad when he did so; indeed, he wasn't even (at that point) hysterical: he thought he was killing Claudius with the maximum of despatch and the minimum of witnesses. Thus, when he speaks to Laertes, we know he is lying. Bradley (*Shakespearean Tragedy*, Note G) defends him by asking: What else could he say? – he couldn't reveal to Laertes the real

reason for his murder of Polonius. But then the trouble is that he never shows the slightest sign of genuine contrition; there is, after all, no reason for him to be secretive about being sorry. As they stand, his words strike me as being quite peculiarly callous; perhaps we are meant to recall Claudius' words to him, early in the play, about *his* father. But within a few minutes the final carnage has taken place, and we come to the epitaphs.

(3) The crucial things here are Hamlet's concern about his 'wounded name' (v.ii.342), Horatio's 'Now cracks a noble heart' (357), and Fortinbras' closing speech (393). Now, according to the logic of the evidence I've been accumulating up to now, I ought to be able to feel that these epitaphs are crowningly ironical, or at least that we are supposed to resist – and resist very strongly – taking them at face value. It is alarming to find that I can't do anything of the sort. I respond positively and without qualification to those sombrely elegiac cadences –

> Good night, sweet prince,
> And flights of angels sing thee to thy rest!

– and this, I am sure, is the way Shakespeare meant me to respond. For the first time in the play, I am being invited to share Hamlet's view of Hamlet (which coincides with Horatio's and Fortinbras'). Yet on standing back and pondering these last sixty lines, I find it impossible to accept the invitation; no doubt it was some such difficulty that caused Eliot to remark caustically that Hamlet 'dies fairly well pleased with himself' ('Shakespeare and the Stoicism of Seneca'). By this time, one can't help feeling, Hamlet is so deeply compromised that he ought not to be allowed to get off so lightly – get off, indeed, with a good deal of unction. This is doubly bewildering in that the other two episodes I have looked at in v.ii seem designed, if anything, to underline Hamlet's break with normal modes of feeling. It is not enough to say, with Fr T. J. Kelly,[1] that 'over the end of Hamlet... Shakespeare has thrown a veil of generous

---

[1] T. J. Kelly, *Hamlet* (Jacaranda Press, 1964), p. 46.

ambiguity': the veil seems to me not at all ambiguous, and generous to the point of being indiscriminately lavish.

IV ANSWERS?

We might try to explain the problem by invoking Convention: Elizabethan heroes always die in an odour of sanctity. But we must distinguish, even in the case of Shakespeare, between proper uses of convention and improper ones. Of course *Hamlet* demands that we make all sorts of conventional assumptions which, rationally speaking, are ridiculous: the time-scheme, for example, is quite preposterous.[1] But this, it will be agreed, doesn't matter. It would not be intelligent to argue that in the closet scene Hamlet knows very well that it cannot be Claudius behind the arras, because the latter has had no opportunity to get from the lobby, where he was praying, to Gertrude's bedroom. Again, it doesn't matter that Horatio is apparently a stranger in Denmark; nor that Hamlet has forgotten to tell him about the fight with the pirates before v.i and only remembers in v.ii; nor that in I.i Horatio says the Ghost was frowning whereas in I.ii he says it had 'a countenance more in sorrow than in anger'. We know that on the Elizabethan stage time and place are fluid, that important information is often conveyed to us in artificial ways, and that minor slips are to be expected of plays which are always ready to sacrifice consistency to immediate dramatic effect. Yet the point at which a minor slip turns into a major one, the point where an inconsistency becomes flatly unacceptable – these are matters that it needs critical tact and insight to determine. Of *Othello* Leavis wrote:

...the tragic theme is centred in Othello. Dramatic sleight is not cheating so long as it subserves honesty there. We do not, even when we consider it critically, quarrel with the trick of "double time", though it involves impossibilities by the criteria of actual life and yet is at the same time necessary to the plausible conduct of the intrigue;

[1] As Hermann J. Weigand shows in *The Persistence of Shakespeare Idolatry*, ed. H. M. Schueller (Detroit, 1964), pp. 137–40.

but equivalent tricks or illusions passing off on us mutually incompatible acceptances with regard to Othello's behaviour or make-up *would* be cheating – that is, matter for critical condemnation.[1]

That will help us with *Hamlet*. For example, it might be argued that the awkward questions I raised about Hamlet's treatment of Rosencrantz and Guildenstern are non-questions – that they do not or should not arise if we accept the entirely non-naturalistic convention of the play. But it seems to me that if we don't ask these questions we are simply amputating our moral sense. It would surely be absurd to postulate a convention that prevented us from asking if a man was doing the right thing or not. But then we stumble against the awkward circumstance that the very end of *Hamlet* does, in fact, ask us to put out of our minds judgments about the hero which we have been arriving at during the previous three-and-a-half hours.

I think my arguments about the supposed incest of Gertrude and Claudius also point (perversely, no doubt) to an important weakness in Shakespeare's presentation of his dramatic data. I claimed that the play only allows us to think of the incest as a piece of gratuitous defamation on the part of Hamlet and the Ghost. If this is true, it is remarkably odd. And it is also startlingly unhistorical, because there can be no reasonable doubt that an Elizabethan audience would have regarded the marriage as incestuous; in fact it would have been regarded as incestuous (in a strictly legal sense, at least) until 1917. Why then is Shakespeare so coy about telling us that the Danish court must, in their heart of hearts, have known that Claudius' marriage was morally wrong and, in fact, no marriage at all? It wouldn't after all have been hard for him to have written in a line or two expressing unease – a kind of unease similar to that voiced by Banquo and Lennox in *Macbeth* (III.i and III.vi). You may argue that he didn't do this in *Hamlet* because he wanted to show how corrupt the court

---

[1] Leavis, *The Common Pursuit*, pp. 157–8. T. S. Eliot has some immediately relevant remarks about Elizabethan conventions in 'Four Elizabethan Dramatists'.

was. But in that case we have to account not only for the silence of Polonius but also for the silence of everybody else, including Horatio who (whatever we make of the court as a whole) is scarcely a creature of the King's.

Argument by analogy with other Shakespeare plays is suggestive, though not conclusive. In other plays Shakespeare's art is, in some important respects, simple. He establishes his *données*, often by quite naive means, and then lets the play go forward from premises that have been made clear to the dullest groundling. Now, incest is not a subject that Shakespeare treats very often. It does play an important part in *Pericles*, but the first two Acts are not by Shakespeare; in any case, the incest is between father and daughter, and we are explicitly told in the opening chorus that it *is* incest.

A more interesting – indeed, very curious – situation develops in *Richard III*. In IV.iv Richard suggests to Queen Elizabeth (his sister-in-law) that it might be a good idea if he married Princess Elizabeth, her daughter. Since the girl is Richard's niece, his marrying her would in the sixteenth century have been just as incestuous as it is today. But although the Queen uses every argument that she can think of to put him off, she never says that the marriage is in any case impossible because it is within the forbidden degrees. Admittedly, when Richard tries to get her to be the go-between, she says:

> What were I best to say? Her father's brother
> Would be her lord? Or shall I say her uncle?
> Or he that slew her brothers and her uncles?
> Under what title shall I woo for thee
> That God, the law, my honour, and her love
> Can make seem pleasing to her tender years? (337)

What is curious here is that, while 'her uncle' and 'the law' seem to glance at the incestuousness of the relationship, the Queen puts this dissuasion on precisely the same level as the fact that Richard killed the girl's brothers and uncles – a fact which would no doubt make the union repugnant but doesn't make it impossible. Perhaps the explanation of this oddity is that Shakespeare wanted a long argumentative scene, which couldn't have taken place at all if there had been nothing to argue about; accordingly, he is signalling the audience to forget their normal ethical expectations: as he does about suicide in *Romeo and Juliet*. But this doesn't help us much with *Hamlet*, where the problem is to find out what *are* Shakespeare's signals, as opposed to the beliefs of individual characters.

Ordinary sexual irregularity, such as we find in *Measure for Measure*, is rather beside the point, because it is scarcely as heinous as incest and certainly isn't against nature. Perhaps murder is a useful parallel. So let us ask: Where, in Shakespeare, is a murder committed which a substantial number of the characters do not explicitly recognise as murder and condemn as such? The answer, I think, is almost nowhere. It would look like rigging the evidence to cite Macbeth, who is himself only too damnably aware of the heinousness of his killing Duncan; or Richmond (in *Richard III*), who is getting rid of an intolerable tyrant. And perhaps it is significant that the places in Shakespeare where there is no such clear recognition that murder is wrong, are precisely the places where criticism starts to feel uncomfortable: as for example when Henry V orders his troops to cut their prisoners' throats (IV.vi and vii); or when Prince John of Lancaster (*2 Henry IV*, IV.ii) gets the rebel leaders to disperse their army by swearing an equivocal oath, and then has them executed.

Again, in *3 Henry VI*, Edward IV is violently attracted by Lady Grey and, after she has refused to become his mistress, he decides to marry her, thus making her Queen of England (III.ii). Now, there is nothing morally wrong about this, but politically it is remarkably foolish, because Warwick has gone to France to sue on Edward's behalf for the hand of the French king's sister; thus by taking Lady Grey to wife, Edward makes Warwick look a fool, insults King Lewis, and destroys any possibility of an Anglo-French alliance. All this is perfectly obvious. But we are not left to infer it; Gloucester and Clarence (Edward's brothers) keep up a contemptuous running commentary while the wooing takes place; the next scene shows us the effect of the betrothal on Warwick and Lewis (and Queen Margaret); while in the next scene (IV.i) Edward's relatives and supporters tell him to his face and at length what an ass he has made of himself. Someone will say that all this is terribly primitive, and certainly Shakespeare's presentation of the matter is expansive to the point of repetitiousness; but the point I am making is that Shakespeare habitually gives us this kind of information. Even where a Shakespeare play presents us with valuations which are at odds with each other, they are always overtly dramatised: in *Antony and Cleopatra*, for instance, Philo's view of Antony's love as 'dotage' clashes head-on with Antony's view; but both are there in the play.

Thus one singularity of *Hamlet* is that about the incest Shakespeare never makes clear his basic assumptions. This is disturbing, because on these assumptions depend our responses to Hamlet's first soliloquy, to the Ghost, and to Claudius and the whole Danish court. In this crucial respect, then, I cannot see that *Hamlet* makes sense; and what must have seemed the perversity of my earlier argumentation is not my fault but Shakespeare's.

Then there is the difficult problem of the Ghost and the closely linked question of Revenge. Eleanor Prosser's *Hamlet and Revenge* collects an impressive amount of evidence that, in Shakespeare's day, the overwhelming belief was that ghosts were usually evil spirits, and that, *pace* Dover Wilson, few people, even Catholics, were likely to jump to the conclusion that any given ghost was, so to speak, legitimate. The climate of belief in which Shakespeare was working and by which he was affected would have predisposed him, as well as his audience, to think that a ghost was much more likely to be a 'goblin damned', sent in order to entrap the soul of anyone who thought it authentic. What is more, Miss Prosser argues, there are in the play itself numerous suggestions that the Ghost is evil: for example, in the first scene it disappears as soon as Horatio adjures it 'by heaven' (49), and again when the cock crows (158) – a noise that, as Horatio explicitly says, makes it 'start'

> like a guilty thing,
> Upon a fearful summons.

And at the end of I.v (the cellarage scene), the Ghost is patently behaving demonically. Further, its wickedness is proved by the fact that it tells Hamlet to revenge its murder, revenge being, in the Christian view, wicked. Hamlet, she maintains, is thoroughly infected by this evil from the end of Act I to the beginning of Act v, most obviously when he spares the kneeling Claudius in case his soul might go to heaven.

These seem to me very strong arguments; the trouble with them, as with most strong arguments about *Hamlet*, is that they raise more questions than they solve. Let us take, for instance, Miss Prosser's arguments about the cellarage scene. The Ghost, she says, is 'acting like a devil'.

Scholars have been driven to fantastic lengths to explain this unavoidable fact. We read that Shakespeare is tricking his audience by stopping for a playful parody; the printer is tricking the reader by including a scene from the old "Ur-Hamlet"; the Ghost is tricking Hamlet; Hamlet is tricking the Ghost; Hamlet and the Ghost together are tricking the two amazed observers. The most popular explanation is the last: that Hamlet and the Ghost both pretend the voice is a devil to mislead Horatio and Marcellus. How could the audience be expected to know this? It is just as misled. And what motive could both Hamlet and a good Purgatorial spirit have for making Horatio and Marcellus think their Prince is in league with the Devil? "To terrify them into silence" is an inadequate answer. There is only one logical explanation. Shakespeare made the Ghost act like a devil because he wanted his audience to notice that it acts like a devil.[1]

What Miss Prosser doesn't notice, for all her acumen, is that the reader at once wants to ask: if the Ghost is behaving so patently like a devil, why doesn't Hamlet notice the fact? Indeed, if the Ghost's behaviour is utterly unequivocal,

---

[1] Prosser, *Hamlet and Revenge*, pp. 140–1.

why has Hamlet any doubts at all? We remember that when
he first sees the Ghost he says

> Angels and ministers of grace defend us!
> Be thou a spirit of health, or goblin damned,
> Bring with thee airs from heaven, or blasts from hell,
> Be thy intents wicked, or charitable,
> Thou com'st in such a questionable shape,
> That I will speak to thee. (I.iv.39)

He allows for both possibilities; but on Miss Prosser's
showing he should have felt (and rejected) the blasts from
hell the moment the Ghost told him to revenge the murder,
or, if not then, at least when it starts behaving like a sub-
terranean devil, shortly afterwards. But since he goes on
doubting it until he has what for him is unequivocal proof
that it was telling the truth, we can only conclude either
that we are to think of him as abnormally imperceptive or
that there is room for reasonable doubt. That there is indeed
room for doubt is suggested by Horatio's failure to identify
the Ghost as a devil at *any* point in the play – not even when
Hamlet has told him, as he clearly does offstage, that he has
been ordered to take revenge on Claudius. Nowhere is
Hamlet's reaction to the Ghost in the least like Macbeth's
to the witches; nor is Horatio's like Banquo's.

It is true that, as we eventually discover, the Ghost was
telling the truth about Claudius. But this proves nothing
neither way; as Banquo knew,

> oftentimes, to win us to our harm,
> The instruments of darkness tell us truths,
> Win us with honest trifles, to betray's
> In deepest consequence. (*Macbeth*, I.iii.123)

Nor does it seem to me that the Ghost's desire for revenge
necessarily 'places' him. No-one, not even Macbeth himself,
has ever thought it wicked of Macduff to kill Macbeth in
revenge for the murder of his wife and family; or of Lear
to kill the slave that was a-hanging Cordelia. If we assume,
as Miss Prosser appears to (p. 137), that what Hamlet
should have done was to leave Claudius as well as his mother
to heaven, it seems curious that Shakespeare doesn't present

this alternative *as* an alternative in the play's terms. Neither Hamlet nor Horatio suggest that the proper course of action is to leave God to his own devices, in the certain knowledge that Claudius will in the end have to pay for what he has done.

I may sound as though I am confident that Shakespeare meant something quite different by the Ghost from what Eleanor Prosser (and others) have claimed. In fact I am not confident at all. To me the Ghost remains quite baffling – which may, of course, have been Shakespeare's point. Yet if it was, what sort of point is it? Isn't the trouble that at times the Ghost looks like a *donnée* whereas at others it looks merely like a muddle?

These worries come to a head when the Ghost reappears in the closet scene. Even Miss Prosser calls the problem 'insoluble', though this doesn't stop her from putting forward her own solution. Briefly, what she argues is that, by appearing in III.iv just when Gertrude is on the point of repentance, the Ghost forestalls it; so that never again is she in any danger of lapsing into genuine contrition. This goes to show what a diabolical ghost it is. My objection is that you could excise the whole of the Ghost episode (lines 103–36) without thereby creating a Gertrude who inexplicably jumped from repentance to obduracy. The text could quite well run straight on, like this:

Ham.   a vice of kings,
    A cutpurse of the empire and the rule,
    That from a shelf the precious diadem stole
    And put it in his pocket.
Gert.   No more.
Ham. A king of shreds and patches! Mother, for love
    Of grace, confess yourself to heaven,
    Repent what's past, avoid what is to come . . .
           (98–101 and 144f.)

In other words, the Ghost's intervention does *not* stop Hamlet from trying to get her to repent; nor, apparently, does it stop her efforts. Within a few lines of Hamlet's renewed advice to 'repent', she is crying

  O Hamlet, thou hast cleft my heart in twain. (156)

According to Miss Prosser this cry suggests 'genuine pain at what has happened' to Hamlet rather than 'a confession of personal guilt' (p. 196n.). This seems to me a pretty desperate evasion. The fact (as I see it) is that the Ghost's intervention in III.iv makes no difference whatever to Gertrude, Hamlet, or the play as a whole; it is therefore pointless; and its presence is completely inexplicable. Yet one must suppose that, at some stage of the play's history, it did have a point: it is preserved in both Quartos as well as the Folio (not to mention *Der Bestrafte Brudermord*). But the point has been lost.

Even if we can bring ourselves to believe that the Ghost isn't very important, in the sense that it is only a piece of dramatic machinery, designed to start the story moving, we should still have to account for one very curious fact. Let us assume it to be, as it were, a given mystery; Hamlet would be quite right to be dubious about it. We should then have to say that he delays carrying out its commands for excellent reasons and that his failure to act shouldn't be explained along psychological or moral lines. But, in that case, why does Shakespeare go out of his way to insist that Hamlet is perplexed and depressed by his own inaction and can find no explanation for it? 'Who calls me coward?' he asks, and goes on:

> I should take it: for it cannot be
> But I am pigeon-livered, and lack gall
> To make oppression bitter, or ere this
> I should ha' fatted all the region kites
> With this slave's offal. (II.ii.579)

And he repeats the same charge a few lines later. At the end of 'To be, or not to be' he says:

> Thus conscience does make cowards of us all,
> And thus the native hue of resolution
> Is sicklied o'er with the pale cast of thought,
> And enterprises of great pitch and moment
> With this regard their currents turn awry,
> And lose the name of action. (III.i.83)

In the closet scene, when the Ghost comes in, Hamlet

refers to himself as 'your tardy son' and says he is 'lapsed in time and passion', a charge that the Ghost repeats –

> Do not forget! this visitation
> Is but to whet thy almost blunted purpose.   (III.iv.110)

This is only a few minutes after Hamlet has killed Polonius in mistake for Claudius![1] In his last soliloquy (IV.iv) he spends over thirty lines in reproaching himself for failing to spur his 'dull revenge'.

Thus, on the one hand we have a theory which explains Hamlet's delay, but on the other we find that the hero himself will not accept it although he is the very person who initially put it forward. You may say that Hamlet is notoriously a man of many moods, and that it is critically unfair to take a mood as being police-court evidence. Yet this doesn't resolve the dilemma: that Hamlet's reasons for delay are insistently presented in some places as good reasons, but are elsewhere suggested, with equal plausibility, to be mere excuses.

And what is true of Hamlet's delay is true, I think, of everything which involves the Ghost. It is, for example, a fact that the Ghost's intervention destroys not only Claudius but the entire Danish royal family, together with the premier and his children, as well as less important personages. Indeed, because of the Ghost Denmark passes into the hands of Norway. But is the *play* making this point or am I importing irrelevant ideas about nationalism?

The ethics of Revenge is another matter where *Hamlet* is obscure. Some critics point to things in the text which suggest that religious scruples are enlisted both in Hamlet and in ourselves; others argue that we are meant to see the Prince as being engaged in a just war. I believe both lots of critics are right, because Shakespeare is having it both ways. There are just enough references to the ethics of Revenge to start us wondering, but not enough to make us focus on it; and I myself can never decide whether Shakespeare is really interested in the whole question or not.

[1] A point made by J. C. Maxwell in *The Age of Shakespeare* (Pelican Guide, II, 1955), p. 211.

I can only conclude that *Hamlet*, in respect of the Ghost and of Revenge, is a thorough artistic muddle. We palter with our critical consciences if we try to explain these things, because in practice 'explaining' them means pretending they aren't there.

Again, I have my doubts about the way in which Shakespeare produces his catastrophe. In IV.vii Claudius convinces Laertes that the best way of getting his revenge on Hamlet is to stage a public fencing match and run him through with an unbated foil; Laertes adds that he will envenom the point; and finally Claudius suggests a further insurance in the shape of a stoup of poisoned wine. When Hamlet is killed, no responsibility will attach to anyone:

> And for his death no wind of blame shall breathe,
> But even his mother shall uncharge the practice,
> And call it accident   (IV.vii.65)

How can we take this seriously? The two men, neither of whom has been presented as abnormally stupid, assume without question that the spectators will think Laertes chose the unbated rapier accidentally; it just happened to be poisoned; and by sheer coincidence so did the cup of wine. Yet it is this incompetent and wholly incredible plan that leads to the climax of the drama ('not very happily produced' said Dr Johnson, rightly). It may once more be argued that we ought not to scrutinise Claudius' plot by normal commonsense criteria; that what we have here is another kind of dramatic convention, which Shakespeare only employs because he has somehow to bring about a confrontation between the 'mighty opposites'. But I am not willing to excuse so gross a contradiction of everything we have learnt about Claudius, who is throughout shown as characteristically (and understandably) preferring private thuggery where possible. And it is only not possible here because the catastrophe has to take place in public.

It is puzzling to notice that some of these problems find answers (of a kind) in the late German text, *Der Bestrafte Brudermord*. There is no need to discuss its provenance in any detail: it is sufficient to mention that it dates from the early eighteenth century but is thought to preserve a corrupt version of a *Hamlet* which antedates the good quarto of 1604/5 (Q.2) and which has some features in common with the bad quarto of 1603 (Q.1). Whether the version preserved in *Der Bestrafte Brudermord* is an early draft of Shakespeare's play or of the play by Kyd which preceded it (the *Ur-Hamlet*), doesn't matter: what is significant for my purposes is that it is clearly founded on a version of the story which is significantly different from Shakespeare's final thoughts as found in Q.2 and F.1. In what follows I shall not, of course, be claiming that the German piece is a better play than Shakespeare's; indeed, if it didn't throw light on Shakespeare's it wouldn't be worth reading at all.[1]

The first difference is that the German text defers the court-scene (Shakespeare's I.ii) until after Hamlet has heard the Ghost's revelations: this alters the whole tone of the exposition, because we are very much more dubious about Claudius if we are already suspecting him of being a murderer, and his address to the court then sounds more suspicious than it does in Shakespeare. By choosing a different order in which to present the incidents, Shakespeare has given a wholly different – a much less emphatic and more open – emphasis to the exposition. What is more, in the German court-scene we find a reason why Claudius doesn't want Hamlet to go back to Wittenberg: it would upset his mother. There is nothing of this in Shakespeare's text: 'It is most retrograde to our desire' (I.ii.114), leaves us guessing as to what that 'desire' might be and makes us wonder whether Claudius is being kind to Hamlet or wants to keep an eye on him. Interestingly enough, the point is also made explicitly in Q.1:

> For your intent going to Wittenberg,
> We hold it most unmeet and unconvenient,
> Being the joy and half heart of your mother.

The compiler of Q.1 (and of the German play) may perhaps

---

[1] A translation of *Der Bestrafte Brudermord*, together with the full text of Q.1, can be found in the Furness Variorum *Hamlet*, vol. II.

have confusedly remembered Claudius' much later remark
about Hamlet,

> The queen his mother
> Lives almost by his looks (IV.vii.11)

but, if so, the remembrance was used to good purpose, and
offers a clear explanation of something which Shakespeare
left obscure. We also learn in the German version, incidentally, that Hamlet has been crowned King of Norway on
Claudius' instructions; this means both that there is less
reason for him to feel ambitious and that at the end of the
play Denmark is not going to pass into the hands of a
foreign power (Fortinbras is said to be Hamlet's cousin).

Another significant difference occurs at the end of
Shakespeare's I.v (the cellarage scene). As we have seen, it
is hard to understand why Shakespeare's Ghost is so insistent
that Horatio and Marcellus should swear three times never
to tell anyone what they have seen; the episode goes on for
nearly eighty lines, and is given almost in full even in Q.1.
The German text treats the matter quite differently. The
oath Hamlet wants his friends to swear is that they should
stand by him faithfully on a matter that calls for vengeance;
the Ghost, however, objects to Hamlet's making the matter
known at all; so Hamlet tells them to go, adding that he will
tell them all 'tomorrow' – to which the Ghost raises no
objection. But no sooner has Marcellus (Francisco in the
German version) left the stage than Hamlet tells all to
Horatio. The elaborate manoeuvres of the Ghost seem,
then, to have been designed to prevent anyone other than
Horatio from being told. While this is more intelligible than
Shakespeare's handling of the incident, it is still not altogether clear why Marcellus/Francisco needed to be brought
onto the stage in the first place: if he hadn't, Hamlet could
have told Horatio and the Ghost could have rested in peace.
But by putting it in this way I may have suggested the
answer, or an answer: if Horatio was accompanied by a
supernumerary, there would be occasion for a theatrically
striking scene with the Ghost in the cellarage. And if (a
large if, of course) *Der Bestrafte Brudermord* is related to

Kyd's *Ur-Hamlet*, we have perhaps found a reason – of a
sort – for the episode's difficulties: Kyd, as any candid reader
of *The Spanish Tragedy* must admit, was quite happy to
sacrifice dramatic point to theatrical 'effectiveness' – as he
does for example in the scenes where the ghost of Andrea
talks to Revenge about matters that have a highly tenuous
connection with what is happening in the main action.
(How much my explanation really *explains* anything is a
matter I shall come back to.)

The German version places the nunnery scene differently from Shakespeare's final version, as does Q.1. In the
German play and Q.1, this encounter between Hamlet and
Ophelia comes not just before the entrance of the Players,
but in the middle of Shakespeare's II.ii, where Polonius
proposes to 'loose' his daughter to the Prince: in the
German version and Q.1 he at once suits the action to the
word. The reader will recall that I have objected strongly
to Dover Wilson's writing in a stage-direction which allows
Hamlet to overhear the plan to use Ophelia; but I must now
say that, faced with Shakespeare's text, I can easily see why
he felt he had to. As he says in his notes, Hamlet's calling
Polonius a 'fishmonger' (sc. bawd) is inexplicable unless we
suppose him to have overheard the plan that has just been
made; so also is his later reference to Jephthah (II.ii.408),
the man who sacrified his own daughter. Yet if, at some
earlier stage in the history of the text – a stage crudely
preserved in the German play – the nunnery scene had in
fact preceded Hamlet's jokes about the fishmonger and
Jephthah, no such prior knowledge of the plan would be
necessary to make Hamlet's jokes intelligible, because he
would already have seen Ophelia acting on her father's
instructions. What is more, if the nunnery scene came
earlier, we could attach some meaning to Claudius' mention of Hamlet's 'turbulent and dangerous lunacy' (III.i.4),
since in Shakespeare's text there is nothing in Hamlet's
behaviour before III.i which has corresponded to those
adjectives. (I leave aside the fact that the 'lunacy' is itself
hard to explain.) It would of course be absurd to say that in

a performance of Shakespeare's play we ought to tinker with the whole structure of the middle parts merely in order to explain a couple of trivial allusions; but the question that worries me is whether, leaving the allusions aside, such a restructuring would deeply damage the play. In other words, are we really sure that in the central scenes the structure is as it is for perfectly sound reasons? How much does it matter that 'To be, or not to be', and the encounter with Ophelia, are in III.i and not somewhere else?

The German play includes a version of *The Murder of Gonzago*, but there is no dialogue – only a dumb-show. The problem of the duplication in Shakespeare is thus avoided: so is the producer's problem of what to get Claudius to do during the dumb-show.

In the prayer scene (Shakespeare's III.iii) the German version, by diverging widely from the English ones (including Q.1), throws a quite different light on Hamlet's reasons for sparing Claudius. *Der Bestrafte Brudermord* places Claudius, not in an ordinary room, but in a temple, before whose altar he is kneeling when Hamlet comes upon him. There is no implication that Hamlet, by killing a praying man, would ensure his salvation; indeed, Hamlet says that by stabbing him he will send him, like his own father, to Hell. What makes him hold his hand is neither a Revenger's nor a Christian's scruple: it is a purely selfish act, in that he is afraid he will take Claudius' sins upon himself. In Shakespeare, of course, Hamlet spares the King because he might go to heaven instead of to the other place; and it is curious that in none of the texts does Hamlet offer a reason which reflects much credit on himself, although this is more perplexing in the Shakespearean versions because it bespeaks a cruder mind than we have come to expect from Hamlet. At some stage of the play's evolution, the point of setting this scene in a church may have been that, by committing murder, Hamlet would also have been committing sacrilege;[1] but if that ever was the point, it

---

[1] An inference made by A. A. Jack in *Young Hamlet* (Aberdeen, 1950), p. 81. A number of points in my discussion of *Der Bestrafte Brudermord* derive from this almost unknown book.

has been lost. It may be that Claudius felt he could relax his guard because he was on sanctified ground, whereas at other times in the German play he is, according to Hamlet, surrounded by guards: the hero mentions this fact twice as a reason for the difficulty of getting at him. Shakespeare's Hamlet never mentions any such external difficulties, and indeed the security precautions at Elsinore seem to be scandalously lax even after Claudius is on his guard against his nephew: he is alone during the prayer scene, and in IV.v, when the King orders his 'Switzers' to guard the door, Laertes has no trouble in forcing his way into the room a dozen lines later. That is, Shakespeare has not merely altered the emphasis to be found in the German text but has embodied in his text an exactly opposite emphasis.[1]

Two other matters are also much clearer in the German play than they are in *Hamlet*: they concern Rosencrantz and Guildenstern and Gertrude. In *Der Bestrafte Brudermord*, the two courtiers know of Claudius' plan to have Hamlet killed and are themselves to be his executioners: what is more, Hamlet neatly arranges that they should kill each other and does not change their sealed orders. He walks between them and ducks as they fire simultaneously – an incident that occurs in none of the sources but which is no more inherently absurd than, say, Barabas' falling into his own cauldron or D'Amville's knocking his own brains out with the axe he was about to use on Charlemont. As to Gertrude, she reveals in the middle of the German piece that she married Claudius after obtaining a papal dispensation, so that incest never becomes an issue.

---

[1] Curiously enough, Professor D. R. C. Marsh has recently stressed the importance of Hamlet's external difficulties in getting at Claudius, and he uses as an analogy the security precautions that have surrounded American presidents since the assassination of Kennedy: see *Shakespeare's "Hamlet"* (Sydney, 1970), p. 64. I can't find any evidence for such a belief, and I shouldn't have thought it could have survived Bradley's reasoned dismissal in *Shakespearean Tragedy*, pp. 74–6. Elsewhere, in his eagerness to defend Hamlet, Marsh claims that it is not wrong for him to kill Polonius and not wrong for him not to kill Claudius (pp. 91–2 and 86–7); just as he argues that it is wrong of Laertes to be Machiavellian towards Hamlet but not wrong of Hamlet to be Machiavellian towards Rosencrantz and Guildenstern (pp. 99–100, 93–5).

J. M. Robertson, many years ago, noticed that a number
of the moot points in Shakespeare could be cleared up by
reference to the German play, and concluded that Shakespeare had fallen between two stools in handling a story
which was basically barbarous but whose hero he decided
to make a 'supersubtle Elizabethan'.[1] Robertson's explanation of the problems, then, is that Shakespeare was working
with intractable material and trying to turn it into something very different; T. S. Eliot, in his notorious essay,
took very much the same line. Yet what is utterly baffling
is that, on certain points, Shakespeare left behind in his
sources – and thereby, in effect, suppressed – material which
was not barbaric, which would have fitted well into his
play, and which would have made it less ambiguous
without making it any less subtle. It would for example have
cost Shakespeare no trouble at all to make Claudius give a
reason for not wanting Hamlet to go back to Wittenberg; to
be clearer about the incest; or to implicate Rosencrantz
and Guildenstern in Claudius' plot. And these are only the
most obvious of the points I have been discussing. It seems
oddly perverse of Shakespeare to have neglected his sources
at precisely the points where they could have given him
most help and to have followed them sedulously at the points
where they were a hindrance.

Similarly, we are sometimes told that certain oddities in
Hamlet result from the expectations of the audience –
expectations both about the story and about the 'revenge'
convention. Both were well-known: Shakespeare had to be
careful not to disappoint his patrons. D. R. C. Marsh gives
this as an explanation of why Hamlet, as a Revenger, must
delay acting until Claudius makes a move which threatens
his life: Claudius will then be hoist with his own petard.[2]
What this argument doesn't explain is why Shakespeare
was able to ignore his patrons' wishes in other matters
where his departure from the story and its convention as
known to them must presumably have been no less dis-

---

[1] J. M. Robertson, *The Problem of "Hamlet"* (1919), p. 74.
[2] Marsh, op. cit., p. 64; cf. pp. 51, 96.

concerting. Of course, the whole business is made highly speculative by the fact that, the *Ur-Hamlet* having perished, we don't know exactly what Elizabethan playgoers might have expected;[1] but in so far as Shakespeare's version is not merely *identical* with the Kyd play (a position which nobody defends), it must have given the spectators continual surprises. I dare say that part of the interest was in seeing how Shakespeare would in fact change a well-known story. In any case, the argument does not hold up for a minute if we think of other Shakespeare plays where the dramatist is drawing on tales or earlier plays which, unlike the Kyd *Hamlet*, are still extant. The old play of *King Leir*, for example, ends with Leir being restored to his throne and living happily ever after; Shakespeare may even be using this expectation in his last scene, where there are continual teasing suggestions that things may still turn out happily; in no sense does he see himself as bound to follow the earlier play and merely satisfy expectation. Even in the English History Plays, the sources of which have a quasi-factual basis, Shakespeare habitually rewrites the stories to such an extent that it is often quite impossible to conjecture, from the plays, what the chroniclers really said. Thus the critics who explain away the difficulties in *Hamlet* by saying Shakespeare was sticking to the old story fall into the contradiction of maintaining, alternately, that he was free to do as he liked (when the play works satisfactorily), and that he was bound to follow his sources (when it doesn't). Once again, then, the explanation itself needs explaining.

1 We still hear a good deal about 'The Revenge Play' and the 'Revenge Convention'. The book that gave academic respectability to the notion of a distinct genre was Fredson Bowers's *Elizabethan Revenge Tragedy* (1940). The trouble is that an important part of his evidence is drawn from his own purely speculative reconstruction of the *Ur-Hamlet*, which (he assumes) 'did not differ materially from the main outline of the story as represented in the German play and in the first quarto of Shakespeare' (p. 86). It is hard to imagine a more circular proceeding than this – establishing as a corner-stone of the convention a play which you assume is similar to a later example of the convention whose existence is established by the existence of the earlier play. Bowers, however, honestly admits that the Elizabethans gave revenge-tragedy 'no critical recognition' as a genre (p. 259). It is time that some intrepid critic re-examined the evidence – and indeed the whole concept of 'genre'.

So the 'answers' that we get from outside *Hamlet*, or
from its 'background', are only answers in the sense that
they pose a different set of questions from the ones we are
trying to answer: they certainly don't settle any of the
problems finally. And, as I have been implying all along, I
very much doubt whether these problems can be settled.
Indeed, I would be inclined to point to the simple fact that
different critics – different in make-up but not necessarily
in insight – give such fantastically different accounts of
Hamlet, and argue that this in itself shows the play must
be deeply ambiguous. (I don't intend 'ambiguous' as a
term of praise – quite the reverse.) Of course, there are
degrees of ambiguity; it is not a matter of a given work
either being, or not being, ambiguous. Though (as we shall
see) *Othello* is not at all a straightforward play, no-one
offers us Iago as the 'typical kindly ancient'; and though
King Lear contains massive obscurities, nobody suggests
that Cordelia is corrupted by evil in the very act of trying
to destroy it. But in *Hamlet* everything is so blurred that
what a critic makes of the play depends, to an alarming
(and surely improper) extent, on what kind of man he is.
Shakespeare may have been experimenting with relati-
vistic ideas about perception – that what you see depends
on who you are and where you are standing; unfortunately,
that proposition is no less true of what we make of *Hamlet*
than of what the characters within the play think about
one another. In the case of Claudius, for instance, it is
undoubtedly subtle of the playwright to make us suspend
our judgment of him until half-way through the piece;
yet if we have spent half the play wondering (to put it
crudely) whose side we are on, the revelation in III.iii
that he is in fact a murderer leaves us wondering why
Shakespeare has hitherto thrown us off the scent by making
him considerate and affable, whereas the ostensible hero has
been presented as a moral and emotional chameleon.
Shakespeare, in other words, plants a series of clues which
can only be seen for what they are in retrospect. He juggles
our feelings and our sympathies. No doubt this is why

people feel there is something peculiarly lifelike about *Hamlet*: the characters are mysterious in a way analogous to the way in which people are mysterious in everyday life. We see a lot of them, but we know too little about them. In *Hamlet* we want to do what we can to some extent do in real life – take the characters aside and ask them what they really meant. We want to ask Claudius, for example, whether he was actually thinking of having Hamlet murdered as early as III.i, and whether it has dawned on him that he is living in sin with Gertrude. We want to ask Rosencrantz and Guildenstern whether they knew what was in Claudius' letters. And so one could go on.

Since the *Hamlet* we have is disorganised, one way of organising it is to be as starkly moralistic as some of the critics we have been looking at. I suspect they were worried by the artistic blurs – which are also, inseparably, moral blurs – that I have been discussing. They may have felt that the play needed tidying up; that altogether too many important issues were raised, flirted with, and pushed behind the arras. They wanted, perhaps, to vindicate Shakespeare. So they drastically simplified the piece by seeing inconvenient aspects of it from Hamlet's own point of view, with the result that they have produced a clear and coherent drama which bears only a tenuous relation to Shakespeare's. *Hamlet* is an astonishingly rich play ('we must allow to [it] the praise of variety', as Johnson said), but its richness is the result of its incoherence. The various points of view are never comprehended from one central, synoptic, point of view. *Hamlet* is

> that Ocean where each kind
> Does streight its own resemblance find.

Hence, no doubt, its popularity.

NOTE A
The 'Sealed Commission'

Bradley, writing of Claudius' prayer (*Hamlet*, III.iii), said: 'When he [Claudius] is praying for pardon, he is all the while perfectly determined to keep his crown; and he knows it. More – it is one of the grimmest things in Shakespeare, but he puts such things so quietly that we are apt to miss them – when the King is praying for pardon for his first murder he has just made his final arrangements for a second, the murder of Hamlet. But he does not allude to the fact in his prayer.'[1] The phrase 'he has *just* made' can only refer to Claudius' words at the opening of the scene, when he is speaking to Rosencrantz and Guildenstern:

> I like him not, nor stands it safe with us
> To let his madness range. Therefore prepare you,
> I your commission will forthwith dispatch,
> And he to England shall along with you.   (III.iii.1)

Claudius has already said he means to send Hamlet to England (III.i. 171f.) but decides, after Hamlet's fantastic behaviour in the play-scene, to hurry things up. Bradley's reading of this speech was perhaps unconsciously prompted by the Rev. C. E. Moberly's note on the lines, which is recorded in the Furness Variorum edition: 'Rosencrantz and Guildenstern are therefore privy to the traitorous scheme for killing Hamlet in England.'[2] There are two assumptions here: (*a*) that Claudius has in fact made such a plan, and (*b*) that Rosencrantz and Guildenstern are privy to it. Bradley takes over at any rate the first of these.

More recently, Bradley's interpretation of the lines has been adopted by Morris Weitz, in *Hamlet and the Philosophy of Literary Criticism*, and used as a stick to beat G. Wilson Knight with. Weitz says: 'Recollect. . . Wilson Knight's reading of Claudius in the prayer scene: Who, he asks, is closer to heaven in that scene, Claudius or Hamlet? But Bradley's report is a reminder that Claudius' prayer for pardon for his first murder, sincere or not, follows immediately upon his final arrangement for the second murder, that of Hamlet; hence his report is sufficient to blow Knight's question and implied answer to the moon.'[3] More recently still, W. W. Robson, in the course of his F. R. Leavis Lecture (read at Cambridge 5 March 1965), backed Weitz in

---

[1] Bradley, *Shakespearean Tragedy*, pp. 138–9.
[2] Furness Variorum edition of *Hamlet* (Philadelphia, 1877), I, 274.
[3] Morris Weitz, *Hamlet and the Philosophy of Literary Criticism* (Chicago and London, 1964), p. 231, cf. p. 31.

77

endorsing Bradley and rejecting Wilson Knight.[1] Robson quotes Weitz by way of making the point that 'the capacity to give correct descriptions of a work is important: descriptive judgments are not always trivial'. True enough: but the question is whether Bradley, Weitz and Robson *have* given a correct 'description' of what is said or implied by Claudius.

He refers to a 'commission'. Much later (in v.ii) we learn from Hamlet that when he unsealed the commission he found it contained instructions for his execution; but there is no hint, at any stage, that Rosencrantz and Guildenstern knew what was in it. They were, it seems, simply appointed as guards to escort Hamlet to England. We further notice that when Claudius speaks the lines quoted above from III.iii, he has apparently not yet written the commission out – why else should he use the future tense ('will dispatch')? And far from giving his courtiers any hint of what he means to do, Claudius gives *us* no hint either – not, at least, till much later. After Hamlet has killed Polonius (i.e. some 450 lines after the passage I have quoted), Claudius has a brief soliloquy which reveals that the 'letters' he has written command 'the present death of Hamlet' (IV.iii.57f.). If he had really made up his mind before this to have Hamlet executed, why wasn't he allowed to take us into his confidence? And if (as Bradley and others think) his words in III.iii do imply that he has so decided, why does he later tell us again? And why does Shakespeare baffle normal expectations by making Claudius beg forgiveness in his prayer not for his second murder (which, given the Bradleyan view, should be uppermost in our minds at this moment), but for his first (which, by the same token, should not)?

We are forced to one of two conclusions: either Shakespeare made a mess of things, or else the interpretation of Claudius' words in III.iii by Bradley, Weitz and Robson is dubious. An impartial look at the evidence suggests that Shakespeare knew what he was doing here and that Bradley misread him. One may guess that he noted the 'commission' in III.iii and identified it with the 'letters' at the end of IV.iii and with the 'commission' Hamlet mentions at v.ii.18. This hindsight enabled him to read back into III.iii a meaning for which there is no real evidence. I don't believe we know anything about the projected murder of Hamlet till the end of IV.iii; all we do know is that Claudius must hurry him out of the country as quickly as possible, in order to protect himself. If we take the King's words at the start of III.iii. in the way I have suggested, then the peculiarity conscientiously noted by Bradley – that Claudius' prayer makes no reference to the 'second' murder – disappears completely.

---

[1] W. W. Robson, *English as a University Subject* (Cambridge, 1965), pp. 28–9. Reprinted in *Critical Essays* (1966) – see pp. 36–7. Bradley's reading is also taken over by J. Q. Adams in his edition of *Hamlet*.

NOTE B
The Meaning of 'Nunnery'

'Get thee to a nunnery' is a famous phrase, but it isn't altogether clear what Hamlet means by it. Until about forty years ago people thought that by 'nunnery' Hamlet just meant 'a place of residence for a body or community of nuns' (*OED*, 1*a*), and that he was telling Ophelia to have nothing to do with the sordid business of love, marriage, and childbearing. But in J. Q. Adam's edition of *Hamlet* (1929)[1] the word was – for the first time, I think – interpreted as also meaning 'bawdy-house'; the editor having no doubt looked up the recently completed *OED* ('nunnery', 1*b*), which is presumably what gave him licence to describe the meaning as 'well-known'. Dover Wilson independently took the same line in his edition of the play (1934), saying that ' "Nunnery" was a cant word for a house of ill fame...'[2] The meaning has stuck firmly.

Shakespeare doesn't use the word anywhere else, so Dover Wilson, in order to illustrate its indecent meaning, followed *OED* in citing Fletcher's *The Mad Lover* (IV.ii), where the following snatch of dialogue takes place:

> *Chilax.* There's an old Nunnerie at hand.
> *Chloe.* What's that?
> *Chilax.* A bawdie house.[3]

The Mad Lover dates from 1616/17,[4] i.e. a dozen years after *Hamlet*. *OED* also gives an example from 1593 – from Nash's *Christs Teares over Ierusalem*. Nash is sermonising about the way bawds run their brothels: 'Some one Gentleman generally acquainted, they [bawds] giue his admission vnto sans fee, & free priuiledge thence-forward in theyr Nunnery, to procure them frequentance.'[5]

Hamlet's using 'nunnery' to mean 'brothel' has been challenged by Professor Kitto – not on the grounds that the word could not mean what Wilson says it means, but because such a meaning at this point in the play would be 'inept'. He says: 'In the soliloquy ["To be, or not to be..."] Hamlet showed how desperately he wishes he could get out

1 J. Q. Adams, *Hamlet* (Cambridge, Mass., 1929), 1957, p. 260.
2 Dover Wilson, *Hamlet*, p. 193. On page 301 Dover Wilson acknowledges Adams's prior ascription of a bawdy meaning to 'nunnery'.
3 Beaumont and Fletcher's *Complete Works*, ed. A. R. Waller (1906), III, 52.
4 See Alfred Harbage, *Annals of English Drama* (Philadelphia 1940), rev. S. Schoenbaum, London, 1964, p. 106.
5 Thomas Nash, *Works*, ed. R. B. McKerrow, rev. F. P. Wilson (1958), II, 152.

of this world... But Ophelia can escape from life; no need for her to continue the foul farce, to be a "breeder of sinners". "Get thee to a nunnery": a refuge from evil, not a flight into evil. Nothing else makes sense of the passage.'[1]

One strong point in Kitto's favour is that 'nunnery' kept its 'good' meaning at the same time as the other: *OED* gives examples taken from throughout the sixteenth and seventeenth centuries. An example from 1634 is the first stanza of Habington's well-known poem 'To Roses in the bosome of CASTARA':

> Yee blushing Virgins happie are
> In the chaste Nunn'ry of her brests,
> For hee'd prophane so chaste a fair,
> Who ere should call them *Cupids* nests.

In the third stanza of the same poem, Castara's breasts are called 'white Cloysters'. And in Richard Lovelace's even better-known poem 'To Lucasta, Going to the Warres', published in 1649 (and not cited in *OED*), we find what is apparently a reminiscence of Habington's metaphor:

> Tell me not (Sweet) I am unkinde,
> That from the Nunnerie
> Of thy chaste breast, and quiet minde,
> To Warre and Armes I flie.

Since *OED* gives further examples, from a love-poem by Cleveland and an elegy by Crashaw, we may presume that 'nunnery' was a favourite conceit up to about the middle of the century.

The Dictionary gives no example from Donne, but he uses the word in *The First Anniversary* (1611), where he says of Elizabeth Drury:

> [She], though she could not transubstantiate
> All states to gold, yet guilded every state,
> So that some Princes have some temperance;
> Some Counsellers some purpose to advance
> The common profit; and some people have
> Some stay, no more then Kings should give, to crave;
> Some women have some taciturnity,
> Some nunneries some graines of chastitie.   (417–24)

As often in Donne, it is hard here to disentangle the ironies. The 'positives' – princes, councillors, nunneries – are only invoked to suggest they are deficient in the very virtues they ought to have; and such virtues as they do have are entirely the result of Elizabeth Drury's ministrations. But the implication seems to be that, after all, one

1 Kitto, *Form and Meaning in Drama*, p. 280.

Note: The meaning of 'nunnery'

might hope to find chastity in a nunnery; otherwise, there would be
no point in saying that there is actually less than there should be.
Certainly, if we take 'nunneries' to mean 'bawdy-houses', the line
becomes pretty meaningless. My argument will perhaps become
clearer if we try substituting 'robbers' for 'Counsellers' or 'gourmands'
for 'Princes'.

Donne also uses the word in his Elegy 'The Anagram', an ironical
eulogy of Flavia,

> Who, mightier then the sea, makes Moores seem white,
> Who, though seaven yeares, she in the Stews had laid,
> A Nunnery durst receive, and thinke a maid,
> And though in childbeds labour she did lie,
> Midwifes would sweare, 'twere but a tympanie... (46–50)

The point seems to be the readiness with which all sorts of people –
mainly, of course, Flavia's lover – disbelieve the evidence of their
own senses: the credulousness of the midwives, who would ignore what
their medical expertise told them, is paralleled by the refusal of the
nuns to entertain impure thoughts about an obvious prostitute. Again,
unless 'nunnery' has an unequivocally 'good' meaning, the irony
falls flat. Moreover, we notice that Donne also uses the word in a
religious poem, where any *double-entendre* would be unthinkable.
In *The Litanie*, the poet addresses Christ and uses 'nunnery' in its
slightly different sense of 'a company of nuns':

> The cold white snowie Nunnery,
> Which, as thy mother, their high Abbesse, sent
> Their bodies backe againe to thee,
> As thou hadst lent them, cleane and innocent,
> Though they have not obtain'd of thee,
> That or thy Church, or I,
> Shoud keep, as they, our first integrity;
> Divorce thou sinne in us, or bid it die,
> And call chast widowhead Virginitie. (100–8)

The instances we have glanced at so far seem to me to suggest that
in the seventeenth century 'nunnery' didn't *necessarily* provoke a
snigger: while the fact that both Habington and Lovelace used the
word in a love-poem means that it was probably not difficult to
exclude the bawdy sense. The bawdy sense, that is, didn't leap to
mind without strong prompting on the writer's part; so that 'nunnery'
was very far indeed from being a stock equivocation like 'die'. Perhaps 'nunnery' was more like the modern 'come', which is only
bawdy if one provides a particular context.

And the more I ponder the Nash and Fletcher instances, the more
dubious I become about just what they establish. Nash's use of the

81

word could be glossed as a jocular nonce-use: much as today one might jokingly refer to a brothel as a 'girls' school' (I have just made this up). As to the instance from Fletcher, it seems very odd that as late as 1616 Chilax – an 'old merry Souldier' according to the Dramatis Personae – should have to *explain* what he means to Chloe, who is a 'camp baggage'! I don't think these instances establish more than that 'nunnery' was a piece of cant or jargon which may occasionally have got into ordinary idiom.[1] The obscure example of an apparently bawdy use of the word recently found by D. S. Bland,[2] and dating from 1594, is also questionable, because it occurs as part of a long train of normally innocent words which are used to stand for bawdy things and activities. While in the context he mentions 'nunnery' certainly means 'brothel', it's also true that 'abbess' and 'gennet' mean 'whore', 'grange' means 'brothel', and 'pikes, bills and halberds' stand for penises. Yet no-one argues that 'abbess', for instance, *normally* meant 'whore' in Elizabethan English; while if 'grange' meant 'bawdy-house', a flood of new light would be thrown on poor Mariana in *Measure for Measure*.

There is, however, another possibility. In early seventeenth-century England there was a great deal of anti-Catholic feeling, which found expression both in polemics and in art. The condemnation of religious houses goes back well into the sixteenth century and the break with Rome. In *The Anatomy of Melancholy* (1621), Burton twice refers to the sordid goings-on which he thinks characterised nunneries. Talking of 'enforced temperance' and the maladies it brings, he says: 'It troubles me to think of, much more to relate, those frequent aborts & murdering of infants in their Nunneries,...their notorious fornications, those *Spintrias*, *Tribadas*, *Ambubaias*, &c....'[3] And much later in the book he quotes Ulricius to the effect that 'Pope Gregory... saw 6,000 skulls and bones of infants taken out of a fishpond near a Nunnery...'[4] Burton thus raises the possibility that at this time one could refer to a 'nunnery' and mean *both* a religious house *and* a house, ostensibly religious, where fornication habitually took place. It may be that in *The First Anniversary* Donne had in mind not so much the slang meaning of 'nunnery' as the bad reputation possessed by

---

1 The Nash and Fletcher examples are the only ones given in Eric Partridge's *Dictionary of Slang and Unconventional English* and in his revision of Francis Grose's *A Classical Dictionary of the Vulgar Tongue*. In both cases he appears to be simply following *OED*. In *A Dictionary of the Underworld*, 3rd edn, 1968, he claims that 'nunnery' meaning 'brothel' is Standard English!

2 D. S. Bland, " 'Get Thee to a Nunnery' – A Comment," in *Notes & Queries*, September 1965, p. 332. Bland's reference is to the *Gesta Grayorum*, ed. W. W. Greg for The Malone Society (1914), p. 12.

3 Part I, sec. 3, Mem. 2, subs. 4: see *The Anatomy of Melancholy*, ed. A. R. Shilleto (1893), I, 481.

4 Part III, sec. 2, Mem. 5, subs. 5: edn cit., III, 280.

Note: The meaning of 'nunnery'

nunneries proper (and the poem is contemporary with the violently anti-Catholic *Ignatius his Conclave*). But we can only say that Donne could have had this meaning in mind because his poem itself provides a context which insistently sets us thinking about 'chastity' as being something you might hope to find in nunneries but all too often don't. In other words, we come back to the importance of context in deciding, in any given case, how the word shades.

Now in *Hamlet*, everyone will agree that the Prince's mind is full of sexuality when he is haranguing Ophelia. But *how* does he use 'nunnery' – what does he identify it with and oppose it to? Let us look at his five uses of the word (*Hamlet*, III.i.121–52):

(1) Get thee to a nunnery, why wouldst thou be a breeder of sinners?

(2) we are arrant knaves all, believe none of us – go thy ways to a nunnery.

(3) If thou dost marry, I'll give thee this plague for thy dowry – be thou as chaste as ice, as pure as snow, thou shalt not escape calumny; get thee to a nunnery, go, farewell.

(4) Or if thou wilt needs marry, marry a fool, for wise men know well enough what monsters you make of them: to a nunnery, go, and quickly too, farewell.

(5) we will have no mo marriage – those that are married already, all but one, shall live, the rest shall keep as they are: to a nunnery, go.

In case (1) Hamlet is putting forward going to a nunnery as an *alternative* to being a 'breeder of sinners' (in Elizabethan times a loose woman was presumably as likely to 'breed' as a wife, there being no contraceptives). In the second example, too, Hamlet offers the nunnery as an *escape* from the 'arrant knaves' (sc. men in general); neither a brothel nor a corrupt nunnery would be that. Again, in instance (3) Hamlet is *contrasting* what happens to even the purest married woman – who has necessarily involved herself in the squalid business of sex – with the spotless life of a nun; 'if you marry', he says, 'you can't escape nastiness: so avoid marriage by taking vows of chastity'. In example (4) he offers three possibilities: marry a wise man who will know when you make a 'monster' (sc. cuckold) of him – this is bad; marry a fool, who won't know – this is not much better, because you will still be doing it; don't marry anyone – that's the only way to avoid all sex both licit and illicit. And finally, in (5) he tells Ophelia to 'keep as she is', i.e. unmarried: the surest way of keeping single is to go to a nunnery. Now in each of these cases, it seems to me (unless I have completely misread the text), Hamlet is making an antithesis – an antithesis which would be ruined if we allowed the bawdy meaning of 'nunnery' to creep in for an instant. But not only would the antithesis be destroyed: Hamlet's remarks would be reduced to gibberish. He *cannot* be saying 'avoid sex by going to a brothel'!

We must conclude that 'nunnery' here means 'a place of residence for a body or community of nuns', and that this is all it means. 'Nothing else', as Kitto says, 'makes sense of the passage'.

3. Othello

ACCOUNTS OF *OTHELLO* usually start from a consideration of Othello's lapse into suspicion of his wife. Bradley said that the lapse wasn't very quick and that Iago had to work very hard indeed to make Othello suspicious, so that we can't call him 'jealous' in the true sense of the word until he has been told enough to make any man jealous. Leavis, on the other hand, claims that Othello responds to Iago's insinuations only too readily; and this, says Leavis, is precisely Shakespeare's point. Othello's readiness to respond shows that, whatever he felt for Desdemona, it wasn't a properly trusting love but one in which egotism played a major part. Thus, according to Bradley, Othello's fall is explicable in terms of Iago's diabolical ingenuity, and Iago is therefore worth a large amount of attention; while according to Leavis, Iago is only a piece of dramatic machinery: the play centres on Othello, and it is his internal weakness that causes his downfall. Obviously, both of these interpretations cannot be right.

I myself have no doubt that Shakespeare's interest, in writing this play, was in 'character'; but there are distinctions to be made. For example, I think it a waste of time to try and turn Iago into a full-length character-study, by conflating the (very different) things he says at various times and expecting something coherent to emerge. His grudge against Othello at being passed over for promotion is an adequate dramatic reason for his behaviour, and it isn't implausible to see it as leading to or touching off a whole collection of grievances, the reality of which is unimportant. At the same time, though, we are entitled to wonder whether Iago, if his state of mind isn't a major concern, should reveal that state of mind at such length and with such apparent conviction. By the end of Act II we have heard some 80 lines of his soliloquising, not to mention a good deal of his talk to Roderigo; so by that stage we might well be expecting him to take as much of the play's stress as Othello, and more than Desdemona. But the promised development doesn't happen; the play's emphasis shifts, permanently, in the next Act.

This would be an exceedingly trivial point if there were no more to it. But it goes some way towards explaining why critics still hold such very different views of Iago's importance. I imagine this was what Leavis meant when he said:

> ...in order to perform his function as dramatic machinery [Iago] has to put on such an appearance of invincibly cunning devilry as to provide Coleridge and the rest with some excuse for their awe, and to leave others wondering, in critical reflection, whether he isn't a rather clumsy mechanism. Perhaps the most serious point to be pondered is that, if Othello is to retain our sympathy sufficiently, Iago must, as devil, claim for himself an implicit weight of emotional regard that critical reflection finds him unfit to carry.[1]

Leavis doesn't explain just what he means by the last sentence, but it is interesting that his doubt was strong enough to need explicit mention. Did he perhaps feel dissatisfied with describing as a mere 'mechanism' a figure to whom a fair amount of attention is devoted and without whom the tragedy, so far as we can tell, wouldn't have happened at all? At all events, we are certainly justified in questioning the propriety of Othello's downfall being, at least in part, due to so enigmatic a figure – a figure about whom we know at once too much and too little. The problem becomes really acute in the temptation scene (III.iii), where our sense of what is going on in Othello's mind, and of why – or if – he cracks quickly, depends partly on our sense of how powerful his tempter is. If, like Leavis, we think of Iago as a mere mechanism, it is only logical to conclude that Othello needed very little pushing; if we think of him as a potent figure, it follows that Othello can scarcely be blamed for falling under his spell.

[1] Leavis, *The Common Pursuit*, pp. 154–5.

I don't think, as I have said, that these questions can be answered by treating Iago's soliloquies as 'clues' and trying to put together a coherent pattern from them. If the main action of the play – that which is concerned with the lovers – seems successful, then we can afford to ignore the soliloquies as being, at worst, the trifling lapses of a Shakespeare who hadn't yet made up his mind.

II   THE VENETIAN BACKGROUND AND THE LOVE
RELATIONSHIP

The play begins by giving us an image of a particular society, that of Venice, in which Othello is (nominally, at least) an outsider. And it is often thought that a main explanation of his downfall is that he either doesn't know, or is suspicious of, the *mores* which have conditioned his wife. It is thought too that the Venetians themselves regard Othello as something of an interloper – a man who doesn't belong and has only been called in to do a particular job – so that Othello has some reason to feel insecure. We could, for example, construct an argument to show that his colour is the main thing that makes him different from the Venetians, that it is frequently referred to, that the marriage between him and Desdemona is thought of as improper or even unnatural because he is black, and that he himself is uneasily conscious of the racial barrier. H. A. Mason, who is usually rather good at resisting *idées reçues*, falls for this one pretty thoroughly when he says:

Othello was in Venetian eyes as ugly as sin but as noble inside as degraded outside. The point is put beyond all discussion: Othello is not merely black – there is no trace of racial feeling – but *frighteningly* ugly.[1]

The logic here is a little tangled: *if* the Venetians think Othello is as ugly as all that, it seems improbable that his being black has nothing to do with the fact; and the contexts in which his ugliness is suggested are usually places

---

[1] H. A. Mason, *Shakespeare's Tragedies of Love* (1970), p. 78 (Mason's italics).

where his colour is also mentioned. But such remarks are, almost without exception, made by people who have a grudge of some kind against him – Iago, Roderigo and Brabantio – and who are trying to stir up trouble. Even Brabantio, significantly, when he is attacking Othello before the senators, can't quite bring himself to make racialism an issue, and confines himself to lame charges about sorcery. The senators don't seem to be conscious of any monstrousness in the racial disparity, and about the only suggestion we get that anyone thinks of Othello as 'ugly' occurs in the Duke's words as he leaves after the council of state: speaking to Brabantio he says

> noble signior,
> If virtue no delighted beauty lack,
> Your son-in-law is far more fair than black.   (1.iii.288)

I fancy that at this point the Duke is trying to see things through the old man's eyes, and to cheer him up by saying that the marriage is not as bad as it may seem at the moment: Othello, after all, is a good man (possessing 'virtue'), and that in itself should be enough to overcome Brabantio's feeling about his being 'black' by overwhelming it with moral 'beauty'. No-one, of course, suggests that Othello is not a formidable and awe-inspiring man both in countenance and in presence, or that Brabantio was telling a simple untruth when he said his daughter 'feared to look on' him (1.iii.98); but she would have been just as shrinking in the presence of Coriolanus or Henry V. Othello is by profession a man who has habitually had to 'imitate the action of the tiger' and 'lend the eye a terrible aspect'.

Again, if Othello's colour is an issue of importance, we might expect to find Cassio, after his humiliation, saying something like 'bloody black!' But he doesn't. Neither do Emilia or Lodovico, even after Othello has struck his wife in public. Othello himself, indeed, doesn't refer to his colour till after he has capitulated to Iago's insinuations. It could still be argued that he nevertheless feels socially awkward and inexperienced among these supersubtle Italians, with their complex codes of behaviour and exquisite turns of speech. And it is true that, when he is defending himself before the Senate, he says:

> Rude am I in my speech,
> And little blest with the set phrase of peace,
> For since these arms of mine had seven years' pith,
> Till now some nine moons wasted, they have used
> Their dearest action in the tented field,
> And little of this great world can I speak,
> More than pertains to feats of broil, and battle,
> And therefore little shall I grace my cause,
> In speaking for myself: yet, (by your gracious patience)
> I will a round unvarnished tale deliver... (I.iii.81)

Yet the story he actually proceeds to deliver is not 'unvarnished' at all, but a highly polished piece of oratory which is so effective that the Duke remarks at the end of it 'I think this tale would win my daughter too'. (One is reminded of Mark Antony, who in *Julius Caesar* breaks off in the middle of his funeral oration to say he is a 'plain blunt man' and 'no orator'.) A man capable of so exquisitely calculated a piece of persuasion is hardly to be suspected of feeling socially inexperienced and therefore inferior to his accomplished wife.

What we are apparently meant to assume, then, in the first couple of Acts, is that Othello and Desdemona, having fallen passionately in love, have made a match which, though it looks odd to the wounded father, the rejected suitor, and Othello's humiliated and cynical 'ancient', isn't specially unlikely to succeed. But – and this is the first point at which an awkward question poses itself – is 'passionately' quite the right word for the way in which they have fallen in love? What sort of love does the play in fact give us?

The first thing that strikes us is how little we see of the couple together. Before Act III, they only appear together a couple of times, and we don't see them alone together for long until the last scene, in which Desdemona is murdered. And what little we do see of them is puzzling – puzzling, that is, if we bring to the play certain expectations about 'love'.

When Othello steps ashore in Cyprus, he greets his wife like this:

> It gives me wonder great as my content
> To see you here before me: O my soul's joy,
> If after every tempest come such calmness,
> May the winds blow, till they have wakened death,
> And let the labouring bark climb hills of seas,
> Olympus-high, and duck again as low
> As hell's from heaven. If it were now to die,
> 'Twere now to be most happy, for I fear
> My soul hath her content so absolute,
> That not another comfort like to this
> Succeeds in unknown fate...
> I cannot speak enough of this content,
> It stops me here, it is too much of joy:
> And this, and this, the greatest discord be
> That e'er our hearts shall make! (II.i.183)

This is the only intimate speech we hear Othello make to his wife before the catastrophe strikes (the account of his love in Act I being a public defence of it to the Senate). But clearly, 'intimate' isn't at all the word for the lines just quoted: considering the occasion and the presumed feelings of the General, his terms are disconcertingly public and rhetorical. It is as if his feelings were on display – as though he were offering them for inspection as to their genuineness; and something tends to go wrong with feelings offered like that. We may be reminded of this:

> And if thou prate of mountains, let them throw
> Millions of acres on us, till our ground,
> Singeing his pate against the burning zone,
> Make Ossa like a wart! (*Hamlet*, v.i.274)

Hamlet, we would agree, deserves to have turned back upon him his own question,

> What is he whose grief
> Bears such an emphasis?

Similarly, Othello sounds more concerned with constructing an impressive mode of uttering than with what is uttered

or whom it is uttered to. As a contrast we may think of
Posthumus when he puts the ring onto Imogen's finger:

> Remain, remain thou here
> While sense can keep it on. And, sweetest, fairest,
> As I my poor self did exchange for you,
> To your so infinite loss, so in our trifles
> I still win of you.   *(Cymbeline*, I.i.117)

That, if you like, is commitment; something that can also
be found in *Romeo and Juliet*, in its slighter but still
touching way. The puzzle about *Othello*, which comes to a
head in the hero's speech of welcome to his wife, is precisely
that it is *not* touching: impressive, no doubt, noble, sonorous, even in a sense passionate, yet not touching – without
the power to enlist and engage us as though our personal
affections were in question. It is equally puzzling that
Desdemona sounds no more convincing than her husband:

> The heavens forbid
> But that our loves and comforts should increase,
> Even as our days do grow.   (193)

It could be argued that the couple feel embarrassed at
talking about something so private in such a public situation; but I don't see how we can (or should) infer the
intensity of love from the characters' inability to convey it.
The argument might stand if there were something else
in the play that gave us the love beyond any doubt; but, as I
have said before, Othello and Desdemona are usually
(except at the end) made to talk in a more or less public
way. In fact, considering how easy it would have been for
Shakespeare to write a love-scene, we can only conclude that
he had some reason for avoiding it.

From this point onwards I am going to make passing
reference to the opera by Verdi, set to a libretto by Boito
which is closely, but not slavishly, based on Shakespeare's
play. The differences between the opera and the play, it
seems to me, are radical and important enough to be highly
suggestive. Of course, that is true of any adaptation of a
good original – even of Nahum Tate's *King Lear*, as Dr
Johnson saw – but what distinguishes *Otello* is that it is not

only negatively but also positively a work of literary criticism. It drives us back to the original especially in connection with Desdemona and her relationship with her husband.

Now, in this opera there is, after the cashiering of Cassio, an extended love-duet, which ends as follows:

> *Otello.* Ah! la gioia m'innonda
> Sì fieramente...che ansante mi giacio...
> Un bacio...
> *Desd.*   Otello!
> *Otello.*   Un bacio...ancora un bacio.
> Già la pleiade ardente in mar discende.
> *Desd.* Tarda è la notte.
> *Otello.*   Vien...Venere splende.

There is an openness of feeling here which, I suppose, is very Latin; but then there is a good deal of openness too in *Romeo and Juliet* or *Antony and Cleopatra*, so it's not as if Shakespeare were a frozen Anglo-Saxon. All the stranger, then, that in *Othello* there is nothing of the eroticism of the burning Pleiad sinking into the sea under the light of Venus – and, come to that, nothing of the insistent 'a kiss...another kiss' (words that Otello repeats, set to the same motif, right at the end). It is noticeable, too, when we think of Othello's greeting as he comes ashore, that *his* syntax isn't broken by the stress of feeling – he doesn't speak in disconnected phrases, although the sense of what he says is close to the sense of what Verdi's hero says here ('la gioia m'innonda', for example, obviously derives from 'it is too much of joy').

The difference, then, is that Verdi and Boito seem to feel there is something lacking in Shakespeare's text – that the 'love', if conceived as a passionate romantic commitment, is insufficiently *done*. They therefore set to work to remedy the defect. From another point of view, though, it could be claimed (and I do claim) that the 'defect' in Shakespeare is wholly intentional and that it is the play's strength to be without the sort of love imported into it by the Italians. If you approach Shakespeare's play expecting it to be like *Romeo and Juliet* you will be puzzled and frustrated; and you will turn back with gratitude and relief to the world of the opera – in which (among other things) the villain is so firmly and unequivocally the villain that he is actually given an impressive aria proclaiming his perverted creed ('Credo in un Dio crudel').

III   THE CENTRAL ACTION

A major point of difficulty, and hence of disagreement among the commentators, is the brawl scene (II.iii); and since the immediate aftermath of the scene is Desdemona's plea for Cassio, which leads straight into the temptation and the crisis of the whole play, it is as well to be sure what we are meant to think here. People disagree about whether Cassio is supposed to be seen as seriously derelict in his duty; and this is the issue I shall look at first.

Othello's marriage hasn't yet been consummated, so the night is to see his celebration of his nuptials as well as a general celebration of the bloodless victory over the Turks. The Herald (II.ii) tells us exactly this. The brawl scene begins with Othello giving strict orders to Cassio:

> Good Michael, look you to the guard to-night:
> Let's teach ourselves the honourable stop,
> Not to outsport discretion.   (II.iii.1)

That is, he leaves Cassio temporarily in command while he goes off with Desdemona, and tells him not to let things get out of hand. Cassio, as befits a loyal second-in-command, doesn't demur:

> Iago hath directed what to do:
> But notwithstanding with my personal eye
> Will I look to it.

Shakespeare could hardly be making the point more clearly: the C-in-C has given his lieutenant an order and the latter has undertaken to carry it out punctiliously and be personally responsible. When Othello comes back, 150 lines (or some ten minutes) later, he finds Cassio incapably drunk, Montano the ex-Governor seriously wounded, and a general alarm being sounded –

> Silence that dreadful bell, it frights the isle
> From her propriety. (166)

It seems to me that Cassio's dereliction of duty is about as gross as could be imagined, and in most armies in wartime he would be lucky not to be court-martialled and shot the following morning. Othello indignantly exclaims:

> what, in a town of war,
> Yet wild, the people's hearts brim full of fear,
> To manage private and domestic quarrels,
> In night, and on the court and guard of safety?
> 'Tis monstrous. (204)

And quite apart from this public outrage, Cassio has, as everyone knows, committed the private crime of disturbing Othello's wedding night. Nevertheless, the Moor gives him a chance to defend himself –

> How came it, Michael, you were thus forgot?

and the answer is 'I pray you pardon me, I cannot speak' (179) – that is, he is too confused and/or drunk to make coherent excuses. Perhaps it is significant that neither now nor later does he try to exculpate himself by saying 'Well, it was all Iago's fault – he persuaded me to drink more than I can carry'; the fact that we aren't encouraged to think along these lines suggests that we mustn't see Cassio as just a passive victim (any more than Othello later turns out to be merely that).

Some critics stress Othello's loss of self-control, as shown in

> Now by heaven
> My blood begins my safer guides to rule,
> And passion having my best judgment collied
> Assays to lead the way. (195)

But his 'passion', we should notice, doesn't lead him to do anything that he ought to repent of in cooler blood; in fact Cassio, under the circumstances, gets off pretty lightly, and he never implies that he has been vindictively or unfairly treated; his reproaches after Othello has gone out are all directed at himself, not at Othello – nor, significantly, at Iago.

If, as I think, this episode stresses both the seriousness of Cassio's offence and Othello's striking self-control in dealing with it, then some points have been established which are going to prove important later on. For, in pleading that Cassio should be reinstated, Desdemona is asking for a great deal; and, in succumbing to Iago so quickly, Othello must, if we are going to argue for a coherent play, be shown to have received a violent and utterly disorientating shock. It won't do, *pace* H. A. Mason, to argue that Cassio's offence was venial, that Desdemona's plea should have been granted at once and that Othello, in granting it so unwillingly, is at best grotesquely ungracious and at worst already showing signs of suspicion before Iago begins his main attack.[1] Admittedly, it may look as though Othello, while offstage between the brawl scene and the start of III.iii, has expressed greater willingness to reinstate Cassio than he then proceeds actually to show; but it only looks like this because Emilia tells Cassio that

> all will soon be well,
> The general and his wife are talking of it,
> And she speaks for you stoutly: the Moor replies,
> That he you hurt is of great fame in Cyprus,
> And great affinity, and that in wholesome wisdom
> He might not but refuse you; but he protests he loves you,
> And needs no other suitor but his likings
> To take the safest occasion by the front,
> To bring you in again.   (III.i.43)

But we have only Emilia's word that Cassio's forgiveness has already been a subject of discussion between Othello and Desdemona and that Cassio is already half-way to being reinstated. Desdemona herself, when talking to Cassio a moment or two later, starts by saying:

> Be thou assured, good Cassio, I will do
> All my abilities in thy behalf.   (III.iii.1)

She adds, 'I will have my lord and you again / As friendly as you were.' Now, if she had already raised the matter with

---

1 Mason, op. cit., p. 101f.

her husband, and had extracted from him a promise to 'bring' Cassio 'in' again (as Emilia alleges), why would she use the future tense, as she does again when she tries to allay Cassio's fears? –

> before Emilia here
> I give thee warrant of thy place; assure thee
> If I do vow a friendship, I'll perform it
> To the last article; my lord shall never rest,
> I'll watch him tame, and talk him out of patience;
> His bed shall seem a school, his board a shrift,
> I'll intermingle every thing he does
> With Cassio's suit; therefore be merry, Cassio,
> For thy solicitor shall rather die
> Than give thy cause away. (19)

That she refers to all these helpful actions as things she is going to do, not things that she has already started to do, suggests that Emilia, in telling Cassio that Othello has already promised to 'bring [him] in again', is telling a white lie in order to cheer him up. The clinching point is surely that Othello, when we next see him (a moment after the lines I have just quoted), gives absolutely no sign of having thought about, much less discussed, his lieutenant's re-instatement: Desdemona's broaching of the subject appears to come as an unpleasant surprise. If they had already discussed it, Desdemona would hardly introduce it as if it were a new topic –

> I have been talking with a suitor here,
> A man that languishes in your displeasure

– and then, in reply to Othello's 'Who is't you mean?' proceed to *identify* the suitor and give him his former rank by saying 'Why, your lieutenant, Cassio...' Unlike Mr Mason, therefore, I can only take it that Cassio hasn't come up between the two before this point and that the situation is a quite new one for Othello. But if this is true, we can't accuse him of backing down from a promise he has previously given; and we have to ponder the likely effect on him of having such a painful matter brought up suddenly and in the presence of Iago and Emilia. This last point is important: we have to remember that, when Desdemona pleads, she has an audience.

This, indeed, may account for her tone – this, together with her inexperience, and her confidence in her hold over Othello. For after all, she knows nothing of military matters; and while it is natural enough for Cassio (who has lost his job) to try every possible means of getting it back, it is odd that Desdemona should feel equipped to tackle her husband on a professional matter in the expectation that it can be settled merely by a change of *heart* on his part.

> If I have any grace or power to move you,
> His present reconciliation take:
> For if he be not one that truly loves you,
> That errs in ignorance, and not in cunning,
> I have no judgment in an honest face,
> I prithee call him back.   (47)

She is suggesting, it seems, that her 'judgment' is superior to Othello's, in that she knows Cassio better and thinks he 'erred' out of 'ignorance' rather than 'cunning' – meaning, I take it, that his actions weren't voluntary and in that sense he didn't know what he was doing. But as the opening conditional clause shows, Desdemona is making her argument turn, not on the rights and wrongs of the case, but on Othello's devotion to her as his wife. This is the sort of personal appeal which it isn't easy for a new husband to resist. That is exactly my point (and, I judge Shakespeare's): Othello has been put in the impossible position either of sticking to his verdict and thereby implying he doesn't love his wife, or of reversing it and thereby conceding, in the presence of Iago and Emilia, that his wife's judgment is better than his own and that military discipline takes second place to her feelings.

The noble Othello of some critics – the man who is, besides being a soldier, a thoroughly nice chap – would presumably have given in straight away, love being so much more important than duty. Shakespeare's Othello, on the contrary, very obviously feels his divided allegiance and understandably – I am tempted to say 'humanly' –

tries to temporise with remarks like 'Not now, sweet Desdemona, some other time' (56). But Desdemona is determined to force him to make up his mind:

> I prithee name the time, but let it not
> Exceed three days: i'faith, he's penitent,
> And yet his trespass, in our common reason,
> (Save that, they say, the wars must make examples
> Out of their best) is not almost a fault
> To incur a private check: when shall he come? (63)

She has now added a time-limit and in addition claims that, after all, Cassio's offence was venial – scarcely a 'fault' worth even a 'private' telling-off, let alone public disgrace. She concedes she has heard that in military matters things are tougher ('they say'), but admits it only to dismiss it, though the difference between thoughtless private behaviour and grossly offensive public behaviour which cannot be ignored is precisely the point at issue. The tone, already impatient, rises nearly to exasperation as she carries on:

> Tell me, Othello: I wonder in my soul,
> What you could ask me, that I should deny?
> Or stand so mammering on? What? Michael Cassio,
> That came a-wooing with you, and so many a time
> When I have spoke of you dispraisingly,
> Hath ta'en your part, to have so much to do
> To bring him in? Byrlady, I could do much –

The first question is a pure debating-point: Desdemona is signing a blank cheque drawn on the future so as to get a present advantage. And she observes, without in the least understanding, Othello's 'mammering' (shilly-shallying). Another note of credit – this time signed by Cassio – is presented: Othello is given to understand that he owes his very marriage to him, for having convinced the sceptical Desdemona that the Moor was a fit husband. It doesn't greatly matter whether this last suggestion is 'true' or not (though there is nothing else in the play to support it); what matters is that, even if it is true, Desdemona should feel morally able to use it. I am not of course implying that she is diabolical or even bad; merely that, in this particular affair, her tactics are pretty questionable, and that she has made Othello's position even more impossible by implying the following parallel:

(1) Desdemona critical of Othello who was defended by Cassio;

(2) Othello critical of Cassio who is defended by Desdemona.

She means, 'If Cassio was successful in defending you when I criticised you (unfairly, as I now see), why shouldn't I be successful in defending Cassio when you (unfairly, as I've said) criticise *him*?' That is, if her defence fails, perhaps Cassio's defence of Othello ought to have failed, since he is obviously showing himself unworthy of such devotion by dismissing the man who felt it. Anyone who was inclined to call Desdemona naive would by this point have to change his mind: inexperienced she may be, but quick and resourceful. She strikes me as being more like Beatrice than Ophelia.

I don't know whether Desdemona's last words here, 'Byrlady, I could do much', imply a threat that if she doesn't get her way she will go on to claim that she was quite right to speak of Othello dispraisingly. At all events, Othello cannot bear insinuations (a point that Iago no doubt registers), and he gives in at once:

> Prithee no more, let him come when he will,
> I will deny thee nothing. (76)

Not that, because of the way Desdemona has put it, he has any choice; but it would be a pretty humiliating surrender even if he were alone with his wife when he had made it. But he isn't, and in Desdemona's ensuing speech we more than ever need to bear Iago and Emilia's presence in mind:

> Why, this is not a boon,
> 'Tis as I should entreat you wear your gloves;
> Or feed on nourishing dishes, or keep you warm,
> Or sue to you, to do a peculiar profit
> To your own person: nay, when I have a suit

> Wherein I mean to touch your love indeed,
> It shall be full of poise and difficulty,
> And fearful to be granted.

She has got her husband to agree to see Cassio at Cassio's convenience, which is presumably tantamount to saying he will be reinstated after a tactful interval; and her response to Othello's giving in is to say, in effect, 'Well, that wasn't much of a concession, really; I've only got you to agree to something that benefits yourself, not me; you wait until I have something really difficult to ask you – *then* we'll see if you love me or not!' If she is conscious of Iago and Emilia standing by (and even, to a lesser extent, if she isn't), she sounds as though she is deliberately flaunting her power over her husband and, as far as he is concerned, rubbing salt in the wound by suggesting that what for him has been an enormous concession is, if the truth were told, only a matter of doing himself a trivial favour ('keep you warm'). Again, I'm not accusing her of active malevolence; but the very fact that she doesn't know what she is doing to a man who follows a profession that has its own code makes her attitude, if possible, more humiliating still. Critics are fond of talking about Othello and his ignorance of women; we hear little of Desdemona and her ignorance of men – perhaps because most critics are men and therefore naturally chivalrous.

Iago could hardly have counted on Othello's being so usefully upset; nor that Desdemona, as she leaves, takes up Othello's reiterated 'I will deny thee nothing' with

> Shall I deny you? no, farewell, my lord...
> Emilia, come; be it as your fancies teach you,
> Whate'er you be, I am obedient.

The wit in her taking up Othello's very turns of speech comes perilously near mocking him – to his face and almost in public. So that, without Iago's lifting a finger, the way is now clear for him to mount his attack.

But of course he has started already, before Desdemona's plea. As he and Othello see Cassio leaving her, Iago says 'Ha, I like not that' (35), and there is a brief exchange until

Desdemona comes up to them. In themselves harmless enough, Iago's brief and cryptic words assume a quite new significance when Othello thinks about them retrospectively, in the light of Desdemona's insistent pleading. She doesn't try to disguise the fact that she has been talking to Cassio; but then neither does she conceal the rather less creditable fact that she is taking his side – implying, therefore, that Othello was wrong (or at the very least, hasty) in dismissing him. From Othello's point of view Cassio has acquired an ally in Othello's camp – an ally who uses her feminine power over him to make him change his mind. In retrospect, then, 'Ha, I like not that' can seem perfectly justified to Othello as a comment on Cassio's (apparently successful) attempt at subornation. Logically, of course, it is nothing of the sort, but then Othello is not likely to be thinking altogether logically by the time Desdemona goes out. True, he utters the famous lines,

> Excellent wretch, perdition catch my soul,
> But I do love thee, and when I love thee not,
> Chaos is come again. (91)

No doubt, as editors tell us, 'when' means 'if'; but that doesn't answer the question of how Othello comes to be thinking any such thought at all, whatever time it refers to. Is he perhaps responding to a situation that Desdemona's behaviour has forced him to figure to himself? I can't decide with any certainty; but to say, as Othello does, that he is thinking about even the *possibility* of not loving Desdemona, suggests at the very least that he is profoundly disturbed by something, and I don't know where we should look for this something if not in the episode I have just been discussing. If no explanation is there, the remark is pointless.

It is therefore a troubled man whom Iago now attacks. His question,

> Did Michael Cassio, when you wooed my lady,
> Know of your love?

takes up and deliberately echoes what Desdemona has just said: that

> Michael Cassio,
> That came a-wooing with you, and so many a time
> When I have spoke of you dispraisingly,
> Hath ta'en your part...

And when Othello adds that Cassio 'went between us very often' (101), we mentally supply the thought – as Othello himself may – that Cassio 'took' Othello's 'part', an expression that comes, again retrospectively, to have a dubious ring. Cassio *stuck up for* Othello, but did he also *act his role* of wooer? (We recall from *Much Ado* the hazards of wooing by proxy.) Desdemona's using her husband's affection for moral suasion (innocent though it is as she intends it) is going to have unfortunate consequences. For one thing, it means that Othello is now potentially interested in the Desdemona/Cassio relationship, in a way that he wasn't before she spoke; Iago's picking on this as his point of lodgement is as natural as Othello's curiosity about what more Iago knows than Desdemona has seen fit to divulge. So that the Moor's refusing to be satisfied with Iago's half-hints is not a crude 'device' of the playwright but, given the characters, in the nature of things.

Nevertheless, I don't think Iago makes any direct insinuations about Desdemona for some time – not till mention of 'jealousy' at line 169 and 'cuckold' a moment later. Of course, he is continually making points that are going to be useful in retrospect; but what he is now talking about, from *Othello's* point of view, is not (or not definably) Desdemona, but Cassio. Working with the materials at hand, Iago is suggesting that Cassio (as Othello knows) is untrustworthy, so that there may – may there not? – be some other instance of untrustworthiness hitherto unrevealed, which might somehow involve others (or another) besides Cassio. Some critics see Othello as here being already very eager to respond to Iago's hints, and H. A. Mason even goes so far as to say that Iago isn't leading Othello, but Othello Iago.[1] This notion, it seems to me, depends on our

[1] Mason, op. cit., p. 107.

ignoring the meaning to Othello of Desdemona's plea and
on assuming that Othello is telling a *visible* lie when he
says to Iago

> And when I told thee he was of my counsel,
> In my whole course of wooing, thou criedst "Indeed?"
> And didst contract and purse thy brow together,
> As if thou then hadst shut up in thy brain
> Some horrible conceit. (115)

To claim that Othello already wants to be led, or is really
doing the leading, is to discount both his understandable
curiosity and also Iago's significant facial expressions,
given to us with great vividness in the lines I have just
quoted, lines which are reminiscent of Hamlet's wish that
Horatio and Marcellus

> never shall
> With arms encumbered thus, or this head-shake,
> Or by pronouncing of some doubtful phrase,
> As, 'Well, well, we know,' or 'We could an if we would,'
> Or 'If we list to speak,' or 'There be an if they might,'
> Or such ambiguous giving out, to note
> That you know aught of me. (*Hamlet*, I.v.173)

A good way of getting a man's undivided attention is to tell
him that you mustn't go on with a story you have started –
it is really too scandalous. And the implied scandal in Iago's
mouth attaches to Cassio, the point at issue being whether
he is 'honest': a word picked by Othello (line 104) presumably because it is vague enough to cover all kinds of virtues,
to one of which – speaking one's mind – Othello is trying
to persuade Iago. Iago is on firm ground, because Cassio
has emphatically *not* shown one kind of honesty (doing
what he promised to do) in the brawl scene, and from one
sort of dishonesty it is – semantically and therefore perhaps
morally – but a step to any other. So that if, in view of what
happened the previous night, Iago can say of Cassio 'I
think that he is honest' (129), then honesty turns out to be
an unfortunate quality to have; and when Othello replies
'I think so too' he is talking nonsense if you apply his
remark to recent events, but not necessarily if you apply it

to the period of his courtship. Well, but suppose Cassio's honesty has all been only *seeming* honesty? –

> Men should be that they seem,
> Or those that be not, would they might seem none!

Here, 'be not' slyly insinuates 'dishonesty', appearing to concede that some people, as everyone knows, are dishonest, but actually implying that *no* man is what he seems ('There's no art', as Duncan says, 'To find the mind's construction in the face'). Othello seizes the one clear point in Iago's perplexing verbiage: 'Certain, men should be what they seem'; and Iago at once confronts him with the falseness of the logic:

> Why then I think Cassio's an honest man.

It is by these means that Othello, who is already angry with Cassio, comes to wonder whether his drunkenness wasn't a mere symptom of a general weakness or viciousness of character; by line 147 he is talking about himself as possibly having been 'wronged', so it is easy for Iago to go on and talk about 'abuses' (151) which, he implies, have been a matter of his 'scattering and unsure observance' – a phrase that admits the questionableness of the observation while still insisting it *is* observation, and not merely the 'uncleanly apprehensions' of a moment before. Iago can continue to build up what sounds to Othello like a case against Cassio by talking generally of reputation:

> Good name in man and woman's dear, my lord;
> Is the immediate jewel of our souls... (159)

– Cassio has only a few hours before lost his good name, as he told Iago at the time and as Othello knows perfectly well; while of course honesty, seeming honesty and a reputation for honesty are by now all confused with one another in Othello's mind. Iago has already talked about his own 'jealousy' –

> (As I confess it is my nature's plague
> To spy into abuses, and oft my jealousy
> Shapes faults that are not) (150)

– so that when he says 'O, beware jealousy' it sounds as

though he could mean 'try to avoid being as suspicious of other people as I am'; then, as an example of a specific kind of suspicion, he cites sexual jealousy:

> That cuckold lives in bliss,
> Who, certain of his fate, loves not his wronger:
> But O, what damnéd minutes tells he o'er
> Who dotes, yet doubts, suspects, yet strongly loves! (171)

Othello's only remark before his next long speech is 'O misery!' and, as that speech refers specifically to 'my wife', he must by now be realising – possibly in the very words 'O misery!' – that Iago's hints have all along been tending in this direction. What is significant about Othello's long speech, and what Bradley for one never faces, is that the Moor's even entertaining nasty hints about his wife is, though his energy goes ostensibly into rebutting them, already conceding their *possible* genuineness:

> 'tis not to make me jealous,
> To say my wife is fair, feeds well, loves company,
> Is free of speech, sings, plays, and dances well;
> Where virtue is, these are more virtuous:
> Nor from mine own weak merits will I draw
> The smallest fear, or doubt of her revolt,
> For she had eyes, and chose me. No, Iago,
> I'll see before I doubt, when I doubt, prove,
> And on the proof, there is no more but this:
> Away at once with love or jealousy! (187)

This, to me, is a startling speech, and I shall spend some time considering it. First, it is odd that Othello, far from telling Iago to mind his own business, starts by *defending* his wife. And what is more, he defends her against charges Iago hasn't made – the latter has *not* been saying that she is fair, feeds well, loves company, is free of speech, and so on; he has said nothing of the kind about her and indeed, at this stage, hasn't explicitly mentioned her. He has been talking about Cassio, jealousy, and cuckolds; it is rather as though Hamlet, when the Ghost says it was murdered, had jumped straight to 'mine uncle' without its having identified the murderer. Presumably, then, Desdemona's plea for Cassio has by itself been enough to antagonise Othello to the point where he will write his wife's name in the space Iago leaves – so much so that Iago, who is nothing if not canny, doesn't hesitate in his next speech to say 'Look to your wife, observe her well with Cassio' (201). I take it that Iago's saying this, and getting away with it (it draws no immediate word of protest from Othello), indicates that the Moor has finally fallen. Henceforward he will need little pushing.

Yet, as we have seen, there was no sign earlier in the play that he felt any social inferiority, or racial difference, and little sign that anybody else did, apart from those with an axe to grind. Either, then, we have to accuse Shakespeare of asking us at this point hastily to reinterpret the first two Acts, and supply something that he hasn't supplied (or only very ambiguously), or else Othello's invocation of Desdemona's social accomplishments is an evasion on his part – an evasion of the point he now sees Iago is driving at. For it is easy to guess that, if Iago is going to talk seriously (or at all) about a 'cuckold', he won't be leading up to it by vague hints about how the lady in question likes food and company; though what, half-consciously, may be in Othello's mind when he chooses these examples is another sort of appetite and another kind of 'company'. At all events, the plain sense of the speech shows that Othello now sees Iago has been talking about Desdemona and that he is denying the charges (or rather charges Iago hasn't made), without any obvious *indignation* on his wife's behalf. True, he has some provocation to feel cross with her, as we have seen; but to feel cross is one thing, while to perceive – and half-create – a fantasy-situation is quite another.

We note too how at the end of the speech his General's acuteness deserts him and he blunders into a confusion that makes the rest of Iago's task only too easy:

> I'll see before I doubt, when I doubt, prove,
> And on the proof, there is no more but this:
> Away at once with love or jealousy!

There are two possibilities: Desdemona either has, or hasn't, committed adultery. But Othello treats the matter as

if proof of innocence were as easy to produce, and as convincing when produced, as evidence of guilt. Proof which
will make him do 'away at once with love' is, of its nature,
easy to produce (or manufacture); but proof of innocence is
by the same token impossible to produce, since you can't
have positive evidence of something which only exists in
the sense that it hasn't happened. So that, by making
this confusion between what is verifiable and what isn't,
Othello has ensured that henceforward any allegation by
Iago will be 'proof', and any denial by Desdemona equally
proof, of her guilt.

Now Bradley saw the beginning of Othello's mental daze
on his reappearance in iv.i. I want to argue that already at
this point in iii.iii he is dazed, bewildered, and incipiently
irrational. As I am going to take that word 'irrational' much
further, I had better produce some more evidence that from
here on Othello is not thinking and feeling like a reasonable
man. When, for example, Iago alludes to Venetian customs
and says:

> In Venice they do let God see the pranks
> They dare not show their husbands: their best conscience
> Is not to leave undone, but keep unknown,   (206)

all Othello can find to answer is 'Dost thou say so?' It is an
odd question to come from a man who has spent long enough
in Venice to be a frequent guest of Brabantio (i.iii.128)
and who in any case must in the course of his travels have
heard mention of a great many kinds of social behaviour.
In order to exculpate Othello here from jumping at the
proffered thought, wouldn't we have to make him not
merely improbably innocent but downright simple-minded?
Again, when Othello starts reflecting 'how nature erring
from itself – ' (231), Iago takes him up with these words:

> Ay, there's the point: as, to be bold with you,
> Not to affect many proposéd matches,
> Of her own clime, complexion, and degree,
> Whereto we see in all things nature tends;
> Fie, we may smell in such a will most rank,
> Foul disproportion; thoughts unnatural.

When we unwrap Iago's thought it seems to mean that there *must* be something odd and perverse (to say the least of it) about Desdemona, for her to ignore suitors from her own country and rank, and of her own colour, and choose instead someone exotic like the Moor. It would be much more 'natural', Iago concludes, for her to choose Cassio, and perhaps this is what she is now doing. Othello doesn't protest; yet only a little while before he was himself saying 'she had eyes, and chose me' (193); so we have, as Leavis remarks of another speech in this scene, the extraordinary spectacle of Othello accepting as evidence against his wife the fact that she married him in the first place. It is plain that by this stage Othello will accept any nonsense from Iago as long as it can somehow be made to sound as though it supports the charge of adultery, which Othello has already made up his mind about. Only a few moments later we see him listening without protest to Iago coming full circle in the web of irrelevancies and non-sequiturs, when he claims that if Desdemona persists in her plea for Cassio, 'Much will be seen in that' (256).

It is worth breaking off briefly to examine what happens in other Shakespeare plays when someone makes an allegation which causes someone else to become suspicious without just cause. When we think of *King Lear* and remember Gloucester becoming suspicious of Edgar on Edmund's accusation, for example, two things become clear: first, that Gloucester is gullible and is patently meant to be seen as such (a 'credulous father', Edmund accurately calls him); but secondly, that he has, in the shape of the forged letter, much better evidence for believing in Edgar's disloyalty than Othello ever has for believing in Desdemona's infidelity. (Anyone who thinks the forged letter a clumsy contrivance should remember the part that Esterhazy's *bordereau* played in the Dreyfus case.) Again, think of *Hamlet*. The Ghost's allegations about Claudius, though they can't be accepted as simply true without further investigation, have more weight than if they came from a merely human character; and what is more, they justify the dislike of Claudius which Hamlet already feels on other grounds. Nevertheless, he spends all of Act II and half of Act III trying to test the allegations.

We have a closer parallel to *Othello* in *Cymbeline*, where the Posthumus/Imogen part of the story turns on Posthumus' accepting Iachimo's claim that he has slept with Imogen. In the relevant scene (II.iv) Iachimo starts with a description of Imogen's bedroom and then, when that is not enough, produces a bracelet which Posthumus knows is hers and says she gave it to him. Finally, as a clinching point, he talks about the mole under her left breast. *We* happen to know how Iachimo came to be able to say and show all this, because we have witnessed the second scene of Act II; but it is quite understandable that Posthumus shouldn't be able to imagine how Iachimo got his information, and the bracelet, unless he had actually (as he claims) slept with the woman.[1]

The point of these parallels is that, in every other case I can think of, Shakespeare goes to some trouble to make slander reasonably credible. Gloucester has a letter, Posthumus a bracelet and an intimate detail; Hamlet baits his mouse-trap. But Othello has nothing – nothing but words like 'honest', 'observance', 'good name', 'cuckold', and so on; and from these he himself constructs an adulterous affair which has not happened and which could not possibly have happened. Even the mere 'machinery' of this play is so constructed as to stress Othello's self-deception. Shakespeare, for example, makes it plain that the supposed adultery couldn't have happened on the voyage, owing to the sailing arrangements; and he goes out of his way (at I.iii.285 and the start of II.i) to emphasise the point when he could equally well have left it open. Or again, the 'short-time' element of the Double Time scheme stresses how fantastic is the situation that Othello has imagined. And over the handkerchief – a thing by which the Moor himself, it must be remembered, sets great store – we confront

---

1 The case of Leontes is too complex to be dealt with here. See Note A at the end of this chapter.

the spectacle of his not remembering at line 441 that he has
seen precisely this handkerchief in his wife's hands when
she offered to bind his brow at line 291 (and he has forgotten the whole matter, it appears, by IV.i.19). Emilia is
made to emphasise the gross impossibility of Desdemona's
being a whore when she says

> who keeps her company?
> What place, what time, what form, what likelihood?
>
> (IV.ii.139)

I am sometimes tempted to feel that Shakespeare allows
altogether too many points to pile up against Othello (it is a
related worry that he rings the changes on 'honest' to the
point of exhaustion). One explanation may be that he
wanted to inhibit the easy self-identification which, nevertheless, so many readers have felt with the hero. Another
explanation may be that, as I hinted a few pages ago, we
are being asked to see Othello as behaving, after some point
in III.iii, in a totally irrational way. I now want to take this
question further, and ask: once Othello has yielded to his
thoughts, is he sane? Could it be reasonably argued, I
wonder, that Othello in fact goes mad, in the sense that he is
living with and in a delusional system which requires no
evidence to sustain it?

If this idea seems absurd, I can at once point to critics
who, without actually bringing out the word 'mad', go a
long way towards it. Leavis talks about Othello's 'self-pride'
and says that by the end of III.iii it has become 'stupidity,
ferocious stupidity, an insane and self-deceiving passion'.
Rossiter talks about how Othello's self-pity changes to an
'insane self-love'; and talking of Coleridge's jealousy so as to
explain why he saw Othello's as he did, he refers to Coleridge's as at one point touching 'the "insane" or "delusional" kind'. And Mr Mason remarks that 'somewhere
along the line Othello did go to the devil in the sense that
his moral coherence disintegrated beyond the possibility
of restoration'.[1] Some critics, then, using words like 'insane'

---

[1] Leavis, *The Common Pursuit*, pp. 146–7; Rossiter, *Angel with Horns*, pp. 196,
199; Mason, *Shakespeare's Tragedies of Love*, p. 130.

for at any rate an *aspect* of Othello's behaviour, come close to talking about him in terms that wouldn't be inappropriate if used, *mutatis mutandis*, of Lear. Even Bradley, who is committed to Othello's nobility, says that at the end of III.iii 'the "madness of revenge" is in his blood', and talks about the Othello of Act IV as showing 'the madness of rage' and as being 'lost to all sense of reality';[1] though of course Bradley saves the situation by finding the Othello of Act V noble again, if still (in his innocent way) mistaken.

If then even Bradley conceded something like madness in the Othello of Act IV, I need only show that it begins earlier and finishes later – or not at all: I shall then have set up a strong presumption that Iago knew what he was about when he said that he would

> Make the Moor thank me, love me, and reward me,
> For making him egregiously an ass,
> And practising upon his peace and quiet,
> Even to madness... (II.i.303)

and that Lodovico is pointing to the *climax* of a clearly realised process when he asks Iago

> Are his wits safe? is he not light of brain? (IV.i.265)

And I take Iago's words after the first section of the temptation scene to be understating the case:

> The Moor already changes with my poison:
> Dangerous conceits are in their natures poisons,
> Which at the first are scarce found to distaste,
> But with a little act upon the blood
> Burn like the mines of sulphur... (III.iii.330)[2]

In fact Othello's lapse from jealousy and deep suspicion into a delusional state is given, it seems to me, in his soliloquy following Iago's exit at III.iii.261:

> This fellow's of exceeding honesty,
> And knows all qualities, with a learned spirit,
> Of human dealing: if I do prove her haggard,

---

1 Bradley, *Shakespearean Tragedy* (Papermac edn), pp. 159, 160.
2 It is worth mentioning that Shakespeare makes Claudius use the words 'conceit' and 'poison' in reference to Ophelia's madness: see *Hamlet*, IV.v.43, 74.

Though that her jesses were my dear heart-strings,
I'ld whistle her off, and let her down the wind,
To prey at fortune. Haply, for I am black,
And have not those soft parts of conversation
That chamberers have, or for I am declined
Into the vale of years, – yet that's not much –
She's gone, I am abused, and my relief
Must be to loathe her: O curse of marriage,
That we can call these delicate creatures ours,
And not their appetites! I had rather be a toad,
And live upon the vapour in a dungeon,
Than keep a corner in a thing I love,
For others' uses: yet 'tis the plague of great ones,
Prerogatived are they less than the base,
'Tis destiny, unshunnable, like death:
Even then this forkéd plague is fated to us,
When we do quicken...

First, for Othello to accept what Iago has been telling him as evidence of 'honesty' *tout court* is an abdication of moral responsibility as well as of thought; a plausible line of hinting patter never constituted honesty (in any of its various senses), any more than it revealed the wisdom – the 'learned spirit' – of the patterer. And it appears that the conditional clause, 'if I do prove her haggard', is offered as additional evidence of Iago's wisdom, in that proving her unfaithful is one of the 'qualities... / Of human dealing' which the wisdom exposes. But the conditional is really a bluff, and so is the ritual bow to 'proof': Othello is contemplating his wife's adultery, not on the supposition that it might have happened, but in the certainty that it has; and he is trying to adjust himself to coping with a fact for which he, at this stage, has nothing that even he could call proof (the handkerchief and Cassio's dream are yet to come). What is also interesting about his calling Desdemona a 'haggard' (badly trained hawk) is that he uses the subjunctive – 'though that her jesses *were* my dear heart-strings' – as if he is now unsure not merely about the future of their relationship but about the past too. The whole image of the hawk suggests in any case that he sees his wife as essentially predatory: even if she

isn't unfaithful, her function is still to prey. We recall
those curious words of Othello's in the second speech we
hear him make:

> know, Iago,
> But that I love the gentle Desdemona,
> I would not my unhousèd free condition
> Put into circumscription and confine
> For the sea's worth   (I.ii.24)

– odd words for a man to be speaking on what he thinks is
his wedding-night: odd because of the resentment they
suggest. That feeling, no doubt damped down before, but
rekindled by Desdemona's plea for Cassio, has now burst
out into seeing Desdemona both as a predator and as a
trained animal doing (or not doing) its master's bidding.
The implications of this last point for the relationship,
including its sexual side, are highly unpleasant.[1]

In what follows there is some ambiguity of sense, which I
judge intentional. The sentence in question is

> Haply, for I am black...
> She's gone, I am abused...

and the problem is to see what 'haply' applies to. Othello
could mean 'because I'm black, etc., it's possible that she's
gone'; or, 'it's possibly because I'm black, etc., that she's
gone'. It seems likely that what we have here is another
apparent doubleness of meaning, similar to that implied
by '*if* I do prove her haggard...': while appearing to leave
the possibilities open, and so give himself credit for putting
up the appropriate resistance, Othello doesn't dwell upon
the 'good' alternative at all. It is plain in the 'Haply, for I
am black' lines that his mind, for all the syntactical ambiguity, is dwelling on the possible reasons for something that
is assumed to have happened: he is coloured, he lacks social
graces ('Rude am I in my speech'), and he is substantially
older than his wife. When we reflect that 'conversation'
could mean 'sexual intimacy' (it is so used by Shakespeare
elsewhere[2]), and start to wonder about the implications of

---

1 Cf. Mason, op. cit., pp. 117–18.
2 *Richard III*, III.v.31.

'soft parts', we may feel that Othello is suffering from an intimate sense of sexual inadequacy. But, taking this with the hawk image, we want to ask, Who has been preying on whom? Mayn't the hawk business be a matter of Othello's projecting onto Desdemona an obscure guilt about his own lack of tenderness?

If so, then it's no accident that he goes on at once to talk about 'appetites'. The thought may derive from Iago's 'will most rank' (236), but there the insinuation was that Desdemona's appetite was perverse in that she'd married Othello: that thought has now been transformed into the suggestion that it's rank because she has slept with Cassio. It is striking, the way in which Othello takes obscene suggestions of Iago and gives them a further twist in the direction of delusion. But the 'toad', like the hawk, is of his own invention, and it is a curious one. Living upon 'vapour' seems to suggest the lack of 'appetite' that you might find in a truly 'delicate creature'; yet toads aren't delicate, quite the reverse: so we have Othello in one breath attributing physical desire to a creature who shouldn't feel any, and in the next denying that an animal – and a loathsome beast at that – has physical needs that must be satisfied. He is again unloading all his own guilt onto Desdemona in order that he may see his hatred for her as justified by the facts. This, I take it, was what Leavis was getting at when he talked about Othello's lack of self-knowledge; and the possessiveness that Leavis also diagnoses comes out with appalling clarity when Othello talks about keeping

> a corner in a thing I love
> For others' uses,

although 'corner', taken with 'uses' (cf. 'used thee' at V.ii.71), has also an obvious sexual connotation of the nastiest kind.

Now comes the first attempt on Othello's part to relate himself and his predicament to a wider context: ' 'tis the plague of great ones...' It is curious that editors usually say the line

> Prerogatived are they less than the base

is corrupt because what Othello must really mean is that 'great ones' are *no more* exempt from cuckoldry than any-one else. No doubt he must; but it is surely appropriate if, after all the emotional confusion we have been seeing, resulting from his being seized by his *idée fixe*, we should now find him falling into verbal confusion too. And it is peculiarly fitting that the verbal muddle should occur just as the sense forces itself upon him of how outrageous it is that this should happen to a man like Othello, a 'great one'. Again we recall his second speech in the play:

> 'tis yet to know —
> Which, when I know that boasting is an honour,
> I shall provulgate – I fetch my life and being
> From men of royal siege, and my demerits
> May speak unbonneted to as proud a fortune
> As this that I have reached... (I.ii.19)

And we recall too, when pondering 'prerogatived', the resentment about the loss of his 'unhoused free condition', noted earlier.

It is true that, at the end of the speech, when he sees Desdemona coming, Othello says

> If she be false, O, then heaven mocks itself,
> I'll not believe it

and that a moment later, half-aside, he adds 'I am to blame'. Yet to take these and similar remarks as indicating that his love and intelligence are still putting up a strong fight is to make the mistake of seeing the situation exclusively through Othello's eyes and allowing ourselves to think that he has a serious case for doubting his wife. A fully rational man would have no case, and even a jealous though still sane man should, I think, require something in the way of evidence before even entertaining the thought that she might be 'false'. How weak a fight he is in fact putting up is shown pretty finally by his at once going on to say 'I have a pain upon my forehead, here', of course an allusion to the 'forkéd plague' of line 280, and by his resentment at Desdemona's offer to bind his brow with the fatal handkerchief.

Othello is off the stage for forty-odd lines, while Iago persuades Emilia to give him the handkerchief. When he comes back ('Ha, ha, false to me, to me?') his monomania has grown to a point where – still without any evidence beyond Iago's allegation – he can talk about disgusting accomplished facts:

> What sense had I of her stol'n hours of lust?
> I saw't not, thought it not, it harmed not me,
> I slept the next night well, was free and merry;
> I found not Cassio's kisses on her lips...
> I had been happy if the general camp,
> Pioners, and all, had tasted her sweet body,
> So I had nothing known... (344)

I take it that Shakespeare deliberately makes Othello obtrude the impossible time-factor here ('stol'n hours', 'slept the next night well') so as to stress the fact that he has decided Desdemona was unfaithful not merely without but actually in the teeth of the evidence. And after the 'Farewell' speech (353–63), we have this:

> Villain, be sure thou prove my love a whore,
> Be sure of it, give me the ocular proof... (365)

Compare:

> I'll see before I doubt, when I doubt, prove,
> And on the proof, there is no more but this:
> Away at once with love or jealousy! (III.iii.194)

The point could hardly be made more sharply. Yet the later speech goes on

> give me the ocular proof,
> Or by the worth of man's eternal soul,
> Thou hadst been better have been born a dog,
> Than answer my waked wrath...
> Make me to see't, or at the least so prove it,
> That the probation bear no hinge, nor loop,
> To hang a doubt on: or woe upon thy life!

The entirely characteristic ambiguity here is whether woe will come to Iago if he fails to prove Desdemona guilty when she is, or whether it will befall him if he fails to prove her guilty because she isn't. The meaning is not really clarified by what follows –

> If thou dost slander her, and torture me,
> Never pray more, abandon all remorse.
> On horror's head horrors accumulate:
> Do deeds to make heaven weep, all earth amazed,
> For nothing canst thou to damnation add
> Greater than that. (374)

If Desdemona is being 'slandered', a sane man's first thought would be of her and the effect of such slander on her; but Othello goes off into a wild fantasy about Iago's committing further deeds of horror. 'If you've slandered her, you might as well let yourself go and commit all the horrors you can think of – you'd already be damned in any case.' It is astonishing that Othello should at this point be worrying (even if in a purely rhetorical way) about Iago's damnation, and not about the moral and physical results of the slander upon the slandered. I think it is reasonable to speak of a mind which behaves thus as being unhinged.

But it doesn't much matter exactly where the reader decides that he parts company with Othello as being insane; though I should imagine that most people, when they see him accepting Iago's preposterous dream (419f.) and his tale of the handkerchief (440f.) – the latter being a 'trifle' *literally* 'as light as air' – would agree that we feel more like alienists than like fallible fellow-creatures. And I'm confident that, by the time we reach Act IV, all readers (Bradley included) would think it fair to call Othello mad. It is one of the symptoms of madness, I take it, that the lunatic won't listen to, or take any notice of, evidence which seems to threaten his delusion; and Othello's questioning of Emilia at the start of IV.ii – undertaken in order to strengthen the delusion – shows exactly that: he dismisses her testimony that she has never seen or heard anything in the least improper between Desdemona and Cassio by saying

> she's a simple bawd
> That cannot say as much (IV.ii.20)

117

and going on at once to call his wife

> a subtle whore,
> A closet, lock and key, of villainous secrets,
> And yet she'll kneel and pray, I ha' seen her do't.

Counter-evidence has merely strengthened his belief in her infidelity; the delusional system accommodates it by extending itself to Emilia and making her a procuress. In the ensuing interview with Desdemona, Othello simply refuses to believe her solemn oath: 'Are you not a strumpet?' he asks, and she replies:

> No, as I am a Christian:
> If to preserve this vessel for my lord
> From any hated foul unlawful touch,
> Be not to be a strumpet, I am none. (84)

She repeats her denial, but Othello is deaf:

> I cry you mercy,
> I took you for that cunning whore of Venice,
> That married with Othello...

Again he isn't interested in getting evidence, but a confession; and Desdemona's very innocence and difficulty in understanding what he is driving at exacerbate his suspicion not merely of her unfaithfulness but also of her 'cunning'.

Othello is thus convinced from III.iii onwards till a certain point in v.ii that Desdemona is a strumpet. If any further evidence is needed of his total moral disintegration, I'd mention his question to Emilia as Desdemona dies: 'Why, how should she be murdered?' (v.ii.127), and his next speech, 'You heard her say, herself, it was not I.' But then, in order to make Emilia realise that his wife has damned herself, he vindictively confesses to the murder which a moment before he had denied:

> She's like a liar gone to burning hell,
> 'Twas I that killed her.

But what I find startling and really horrible about the Othello of these closing episodes is that he comes to a realisation of what we know to be the truth on grounds no

better than those on which his delusion was based. At line
211 he is still obstinately convinced:

> Iago knows
> That she with Cassio hath the act of shame
> A thousand times committed,

and he goes on to mention the handkerchief. This gives
Emilia her opportunity: she says she found the handkerchief 'by fortune' and gave it to Iago, who had often begged
her to steal it (226). She repeats herself (231) and adds

> O murderous coxcomb! what should such a fool
> Do with so good a woman?

Othello is at once persuaded he has been wrong, and tries to
kill Iago. But Emilia's testimony as to Desdemona's
innocence is quite as flimsy as Iago's about her guilt; for if
Emilia had (as Othello believed) been playing the bawd,
this is precisely the kind of story she would have invented
to clear her own name, since her reputation is very much
involved with her mistress's. And if Emilia is proclaiming a
foul lie, it involves Iago too: so he would have every reason
to draw his sword upon her, as he does at line 224. It is not
till *after* Othello has changed his mind that Iago actually
uses the weapon and kills his wife – and even that could
look like something done on the spur of the moment in a
rage at losing his 'reputation' for 'honesty'. It's not till
Iago's quasi-confession and the production of the incriminat-
ing letters (304f.) that anyone – least of all Othello – has
anything tangible to go on. But in a remarkable way, the
Moor can simultaneously admit he was wrong and at the
same time claim that he was (so to say) right to be wrong:

> An honourable murderer, if you will:
> For nought did I in hate, but all in honour.   (295)

I think Shakespeare meant us to feel the appalling falsity of
this claim, because we can hardly dismiss from our minds the
many words earlier in the play which have been endued
with the bitterest hatred – 'lewd minx', for instance, or
'impudent strumpet' or 'cunning whore'. And we recall his
words as he completed the stifling:

> I that am cruel, am yet merciful,
> I would not have thee linger in thy pain, –
> So, so.   (88)

No SS man can ever have made a ghastlier joke; except that, as his words later in the scene show, Othello is even worse in that he supposes himself to be telling the truth and is unconscious of any gallows-humour.

One may agree with Leavis that the end is a 'superb *coup de théâtre*', and yet feel dissatisfied, as Mr Mason does.[1] For it seems to me that, despite the patent self-deception of Othello's closing speech, there is a good deal in the last 130-odd lines that pushes us towards apportioning responsibility for the crime in the way that Othello would himself like to see it apportioned. To him, Iago is (understandably) a 'demi-devil' who has 'ensnared' his 'soul and body' (302); but we have already heard Montano call Iago a 'notorious villain' and a 'damnéd slave' – the latter phrase being later repeated by Lodovico when he asks

> O thou Othello, that wert once so good,
> Fall'n in the practice of a damnéd slave,
> What should be said to thee?   (240, 244; 293)

And while the only explicit epitaph on Othello is Cassio's

> For he was great of heart,   (362)

we find Lodovico saying to Iago, in the very last speech of the play:

> O Spartan dog,
> More fell than anguish, hunger, or the sea,
> Look on the tragic lodging of this bed:
> *This is thy work*...

so that Cassio, now Governor, must determine how to punish 'this hellish villain'. Responsibility is thus being shifted from Othello's shoulders onto Iago's. Shakespeare, it seems to me, is trying (rather as he does at the end of *Hamlet*) to return upon himself, to avoid drawing the conclusions he has been arriving at and, in general, to allow us to leave the theatre feeling that, after all, we know the

[1] Leavis, op. cit., p. 152; Mason, op. cit., pp. 131–5.

difference between a good man and a villain. Shakespeare's shrinking from his own discovery that the difference is sometimes not easy to make out gave Bradley a considerable provocation to read the whole play as he did: he was simply applying to the whole action the hints that, as we have seen, are scattered through the last 130 lines. The logic of what Shakespeare has been doing up to that point should have led him to have Othello's delusion firmly seen as such by the other characters on the stage; but I judge his problem to have been that for a nature like Othello's there is no real recovery from his delusion: if his idea of himself and of others is as finally shattered as it would be if he came to realise *what* he has done, he will become inarticulate – literally speechless – since his speech is dependent on there being a self for it to create; a self egotistical, deluded, and finally insane. So, at the end, if there is sanity, there is silence; only if there is delusion can there be articulateness.

Yet, if the reader accepts however tentatively my suggestion about Othello's madness, mayn't he want to ask whether the critical problem about our sympathy with Othello isn't thereby emphasised rather than solved? I think he may; but before considering that question I shall glance aside to Verdi's opera and see what it tells us about Shakespeare and more particularly about Desdemona and her role in the tragedy. Only in the last section shall I come back to the problem I've just raised about Othello.

IV   DESDEMONA IN THE PLAY AND THE OPERA

People have a tendency to regard Desdemona as a peculiarly conventional sort of girl. I hope that some of the things I have said may incidentally have shaken that idea, but I now want to look at it more closely, particularly since it is a point upon which both admirers and questioners of Othello's nobility seem to be substantially agreed. The note sounded by Bradley is characteristic, and not characteristic of him alone: Desdemona is the "eternal womanly" in its most lovely and adorable form, simple and innocent as a child, ardent with the courage and idealism of a saint, radiant with that heavenly purity of heart which men worship the more because nature so rarely permits it to themselves...

She appears passive and defenceless, and can oppose to wrong nothing but the infinite endurance and forgiveness of a love that knows not how to resist or resent.

One need only comment that Bradley is making a great many bricks with a very little straw. A little after this passage, however, he goes on to sound a warning note, although he doesn't follow it up; Desdemona, he says, has

a frank childlike boldness and persistency, which are full of charm but are unhappily united with a certain want of perception. And these graces and this deficiency appear to be inextricably intertwined.[1]

To have investigated that 'want of perception' would have been to ask some awkward questions about whether Shakespeare meant us to see it as an essential part of the marriage he is enquiring into. Whatever we make of Othello, and *Othello*, isn't something beyond a 'heavenly purity of heart' necessary to such a relationship – something that Desdemona apparently can't provide?

There is, however, a good deal more to Shakespeare's heroine than this, although it is amusing to notice that when commentators see it they are embarrassed and don't know what to do with it. No reading of the play should leave out of account the frivolous dialogue between Desdemona and Iago in II.i; but English critics wish it wasn't there, and Verdi and Boito simply omit it (as did Olivier in his film). The process by which a conventional 'purity' is assumed in Desdemona and is preserved by critics' embarrassment at her frivolity is highly visible in M. R. Ridley, the Arden editor. He says that it is, in II.i, 'unnatural' for Desdemona to send someone to the harbour rather than going herself, and then continues:

it is distasteful to watch her engaged in a long piece of cheap backchat with Iago, and so adept at it that one wonders how much time on the voyage was spent in the same way.

[1] Bradley, op. cit., pp. 164, 166, 167.

He quotes, rather dubiously, Granville-Barker's claim that the episode shows us her 'silent anxiety'; yet so little relevant to Shakespeare's Desdemona does Ridley consider all this that he makes no mention of it in his sketch of her character in his Arden introduction. Of course the notion of 'silent anxiety' comes from her own excuse –

> I am not merry, but I do beguile
> The thing I am, by seeming otherwise. (II.i.122)

If that is true, it's hard to see why she should seem so much more at home and relaxed here then she does a little later, after Othello's arrival, when (as we saw) she sounds oddly stilted. It's even harder to think how the episode could be fitted into the Bradleyan notion of her character, especially when we remember that phrase 'the innocence of a child'. Indeed, if this were all we had to go on, we should be justified in thinking she was not all that different from Cressida.

The opera leaves out the frivolous chatter. The effect of removing it is not merely to smoothe out what looks like a local inconsistency in Shakespeare; it is to make the whole drama (or that part of it which turns on Desdemona) altogether simpler. For while Verdi's heroine becomes more guileless, Shakespeare's remains an odd and interesting mixture, as we shall see.

The Italian heroine, however, is neither odd nor particularly interesting; and it is the differences of emphasis as between play and opera that suggest what Shakespeare was up to. In the opera, the temptation scene is divided into two by a long serenade sung to Desdemona by sailors, women and children. The first part runs from 'Ciò m'accora' ('Ha, I like not that', line 35) up to 'vigilate' ('look to your wife', line 201) but omitting the plea for Cassio (42–90); and it is then interrupted by a serenade in which the sailors give Desdemona coral and pearl necklaces and the women and children strew lilies and leaves before her, accompanying themselves on a sort of mandolin. The episode isn't merely operatic decoration, though certainly it is charming enough. The intention is clearly that it shall reflect on the girl it is addressed to. Take this, for instance:

T'offriamo il giglio
Soave stel
Che in man degl' angeli
Fu assunto in ciel
Che abbella il fulgido
Manto e la gonna
Della Madonna
E il santo vel.

One reflects that for Boito there was some advantage in being a Catholic or at any rate living in a Catholic country: no English writer in either the seventeenth or the nineteenth century could have risked juxtaposing Desdemona with the Madonna, far less done it so unselfconsciously. And the comparison works to make Desdemona carry hints of fertility, because 'il giglio' (the lily) is often seen in pictures of the Annunciation, and she has just had her wedding night. The serenade, that is, establishes a kind of natural piety about Desdemona which is missing from Shakespeare; and it is all in keeping that Verdi and Boito give her that touching prayer, the Ave Maria, in the last scene just after the willow song. Yet, beautiful as this all is, one might be pardoned for wondering whether it wasn't all a bit too beautiful to be true: whether inconvenient corners of Shakespeare's heroine hadn't been quietly chipped off.

The same thoughts recur when we hear Verdi's treatment of her plea for Cassio. It is here – *after* the serenade and after Iago has already dropped some hints – that Verdi/ Boito make Desdemona beg for Cassio's reinstatement. One effect of this transposition is that the Italian heroine doesn't have to be nearly so insistent as the English one: after Iago's insinuations about 'la gelosia', only one mention of Cassio is needed to make Otello start losing his balance; Desdemona doesn't have to nag and has no victory to flaunt. Her plea is over in a few bars because Otello's immediate response leads her to ask why he is talking so oddly (cf. Shakespeare's III.iii.287). No doubt Verdi and Boito felt that a romantic heroine shouldn't be shown embarrassing her husband by making tactless requests in the presence of other people; but half the interest of the character is gone if that aspect of it is omitted. What is more, Othello's jealousy (which in Shakespeare follows or possibly begins during Desdemona's plea) is completely altered in the opera, and made causeless in the sense of being totally without provocation, since the Otello who listens to Iago's first hints has not yet been irritated by his wife's intervening in military affairs.

One's impression that the operatic heroine is absurdly faultless is confirmed by her reaction to Otello's first show of temper, which occurs just afterwards when Otello throws her handkerchief down and says 'Mi lascia!' ('leave me alone!'). The Italian girl, ever sensitive to her lord's moods, grasps at once that something is seriously amiss: 'If I have sinned accidentally against you, O husband, pardon me . . . ' Shakespeare's heroine, on the other hand, seems singularly slow to realise that anything has gone wrong; I suppose

> I am very sorry that you are not well   (III.iii.293)

could be a dignified reproach to Othello for his mentioning something so ugly and irrelevant as the cuckold's horns, but to me it sounds more as though she has simply not gathered what he is getting at. Similarly, when Othello later says

> A liberal hand; the hearts of old gave hands,
> But our new heraldry is hands, not hearts,   (III.iv.42)

she brushes aside the implications, which she can't or won't see, and gets back to her plea for Cassio:

> I cannot speak of this; come, come, your promise.

If the Verdi/Boito heroine is too aware of her husband's moods to be altogether convincing outside the operatic convention of the sweet wife, Shakespeare's girl is entirely convincing as a person who, partly perhaps because she is newly married but also partly because she is not particularly perceptive, cannot see what is happening to her husband. I suggest Shakespeare was not only saying something about Othello's incomprehension of his wife, but also hers of him. And it is this *mutual* incomprehension that may have led

Wilson Knight and others to talk about the play's atmosphere of 'separateness'.[1]

The Verdi/Boito Act III includes Shakespeare's III.iv and most of his Act IV. When Othello tries to get his wife to produce the handkerchief he gave her, there is a marked difference of treatment between the play and the opera. The interview starts about III.iv.30, and in both texts Desdemona starts by thinking that her husband's insistence on the handkerchief is just a way of putting her off her plea for Cassio; in both, too, she ignores for a while the obvious fact that the handkerchief means something important to Othello. But while in Shakespeare her manner is a kind of prattling nagging –

> A man that all his time
> Hath founded his good fortunes on your love,
> Shared dangers with you   (III.iv.91)

– in Boito she wheedles rather like David Copperfield's Dora. More importantly, Shakespeare's heroine doesn't grasp that anything is wrong until after Othello has stormed off with a furious 'Zounds!' when she says, with a naivety that is perhaps rueful but affects one as being almost comic:

> I ne'er saw this before:
> Sure there's some wonder in this handkerchief,
> I am most unhappy in the loss of it.   (97)

But Boito's heroine's response is quite different: again she grasps much more quickly than the English girl that something is seriously amiss. In Shakespeare, however, this episode leads on to a further exchange between Desdemona and Cassio (III.iv.103f.) in which, trying to convince Iago that Othello can indeed be 'angry', Desdemona tries to explain away her husband's disturbance:

> something sure of state,
> Either from Venice, or some unhatched practice,
> Made demonstrable here in Cyprus to him,
> Hath puddled his clear spirit, and in such cases
> Men's natures wrangle with inferior things,
> Though great ones are the object.   (137)

---

[1] Wilson Knight, *Wheel of Fire*, pp. 130–1.

Perhaps I am merely being unsympathetic in finding this a pathetically inadequate response to what has happened. No doubt she is trying to cover up for Othello, but she doesn't begin to see how *deeply* he is disturbed – though Emilia, on Othello's exit, at once asks 'Is not this man jealous?' Apart from anything else, Desdemona's first suggestion – that there has been bad news from Venice – is obviously impossible because no news of any kind arrives at Cyprus until well into IV.i. (208). In any case, she herself has a little earlier, in lines I've already quoted, realised that whatever is the matter is closely connected with the handkerchief, not with something else; so that what she is now doing is rationalising away this not very profound insight. And what is curious about the last couple of lines is that Desdemona herself evidently accepts the masculine view of marriage, or at least Othello's soldierly view, that wives are 'inferior things' and matters of state are 'great' things. No doubt Bradley would have taken this as a further indication of Desdemona's modesty; but mightn't one wonder whether self-respect wasn't involved too? Interestingly enough, the rest of the speech shows a kind of ambivalence about the male view which suggests that Desdemona's self-respect is in fact putting up a fight:

> 'Tis even so; for let our finger ache,
> And it indues our other healthful members
> Even to that sense of pain; nay, we must think
> Men are not gods;
> Nor of them look for such observances
> As fits the bridal: beshrew me much, Emilia,
> I was (unhandsome warrior as I am)
> Arraigning his unkindness with my soul;
> But now I find I have suborned the witness,
> And he's indicted falsely.

Whatever is wrong with Othello, it isn't conceivably the equivalent of a finger-ache; but perhaps this is a way of implicitly slighting the 'unhatched practice' etc., so that the meaning is 'there's not much wrong with him really, trust a man make a fuss and have a row with his new wife over a flea-bite – women have a much better sense of proportion'.

That kind of reading would certainly make sense of the apparently sharp change at 'nay, ... men are not gods' and of the quasi-Emilian sentiment that follows, which reminds us strongly of

> 'Tis not a year or two shows us a man:
> They are all but stomachs, and we all but food;
> They eat us hungerly, and when they are full,
> They belch us.   (III.iv.100)

In other words, Desdemona, starting out with the intention of clearing Othello, is now condemning him; the phrase

> Nor of them look for such observances
> As fits the bridal

perhaps suggests that she is feeling her way towards some of the realities of marriage and seeing the glamorous captain whose marvellous tales made him almost mythical as being, in fact, a limited and fallible person – just a man. Yet is he *just* a man if his latest marvellous tale is the sinister and suggestive one about the handkerchief? The 'Egyptian' who gave it to Othello's mother

> told her, while she kept it
> 'Twould make her amiable, and subdue my father
> Entirely to her love: but if she lost it,
> Or made a gift of it, my father's eye
> Should hold her loathly, and his spirits should hunt
> After new fancies...   (56)

The clear threat that, if she doesn't find the handkerchief, Othello will fall out of love with her and into love with another or others, scarcely seems to me to be what a bride might expect to be told immediately after her wedding-night. So that even the concession

> Nor of them look for such observances
> As fits the bridal

shows Desdemona making a very large excuse for her husband, especially in view of the really nasty turn at the end of his tale:

> And it was dyed in mummy, which the skilful
> Conserve of maidens' hearts.   (72)

Yet no sooner does Desdemona make the criticism, the concession, and the excuse, than she begins to exculpate
Othello entirely, saying that she has accused him 'falsely'.
But she has no 'witness', after all, beyond the evidence of
her own senses; and whatever the excuse, he has been
startlingly 'unkind'.

Desdemona, then, is being shown as a woman who,
despite some stirrings of natural self-assertion, slips into
accepting a conventional feminine role rather easily. And
this characteristic becomes more marked as Othello's
behaviour grows more inexplicable.

What, for example, are we to make of her conduct in
IV.1, where Othello publicly strikes her? When she says to
Lodovico, of Cassio,

> Cousin, there's fallen between him and my lord
> An unkind breach, but you shall make all well,
>
> (IV.i.220)

it's not just our own knowledge of what is in Othello's
mind that makes us wonder why she hasn't noticed that
any mention of Cassio produces immediate fury. When
Othello strikes her, she says

> I have not deserved this, (236)

and, when she is first dismissed,

> I will not stay to offend you. (242)

The rebukes are dignified and even courteous. But I wonder
if I am alone in feeling that there is something missing?
Hasn't Desdemona, at this point, become a bit too much
like Verdi's heroine? It is hard to credit that a woman who
stood up to her husband over such a matter as Cassio's
reinstatement should, now that it is a matter of her being
cast off herself, have so little to say for herself and should
become – and remain for the rest of the play – so passive.
Her stirrings of self-assertion have disappeared for good.
After the end of the third Act her function as a champion of
a woman's independence within marriage is wholly taken
over by Emilia; the result is to throw that sort of thinking
rather out of focus, since Emilia is a subordinate character

and we don't look to her for any fineness of response. But what she says carries at least some weight, and it is not surprising that Verdi and Boito omit it. The opera runs IV.iii (the willow-song scene) and v.ii (the last scene) together, so that Desdemona's 'good night' to Emilia runs into the (inserted) prayer, and that in turn into the last exchanges between her and her husband before the murder. But from Shakespeare's IV.iii there is, in the opera, a significant omission. When Emilia says 'I would you had never seen him!' Shakespeare's heroine replies:

> So would not I, my love doth so approve him,
> That even his stubbornness, his checks and frowns, –
> Prithee unpin me, – have grace and favour in them.
>
> (IV.iii.18)

The last time we saw her and Othello together he was calling her an 'impudent strumpet'; so what are we supposed to make of the lines I have just quoted? One would think 'stubbornness' (viz. roughness) was a pretty feeble noun to describe Othello's recent behaviour; and to say that it has 'grace and favour' in it is surely to carry charity to the point of suspending moral judgment altogether – or of annihilating the self that has felt the 'stubbornness'. This, no doubt, is what social custom requires Desdemona to do; but in case we think the play is endorsing that kind of custom, Shakespeare gives Emilia a long and very pointed speech about masculine and feminine roles. It looks as though it's only about the wickedness of men but, studied more carefully, reveals an implicit criticism of what women do in the parts men cast them for (it was also omitted in the Olivier film):

> But I do think it is their husbands' faults
> If wives do fall: say, that they slack their duties,
> And pour our treasures into foreign laps;
> Or else break out in peevish jealousies,
> Throwing restraint upon us: or say they strike us,
> Or scant our former having in despite,
> Why, we have galls: and though we have some grace,
> Yet have we some revenge. Let husbands know,
> Their wives have sense like them: they see, and smell,

And have their palates both for sweet, and sour,
As husbands have. What is it that they do,
When they change us for others? Is it sport?
I think it is: and doth affection breed it?
I think it doth. Is't fraility that thus errs?
It is so too. And have not we affections?
Desires for sport? and frailty, as men have?
Then let them use us well: else let them know,
The ills we do, their ills instruct us so.   (IV.iii.86)

The charges of masculine selfishness and stupidity don't
need comment. What does call for remark is that Emilia,
given the context, can only be implying 'well, even if you
weren't unfaithful before, you have every provocation to be
so now; why not go ahead and get your revenge on your
brute of a husband by giving him a pair of horns?' That is,
Emilia is standing up for the rights of women as well as
condemning the wrongs of men; and she is implying a
criticism of Desdemona, who has very strikingly *not*
stood up for herself. Of course, Emilia's sensibility is
crude; yet when fully experiencing what Shakespeare wrote
we are, I think, brought face to face with the question:
What, in human terms, is the value of Desdemona's kind of
behaviour? In what way, things being as they are, does her
continual acquiescence improve matters, for her or for her
husband? Ought there to be a sticking-point beyond which
no woman, however much in love, will let herself be pushed?
Is there a point at which self-sacrifice makes a person less
than fully human? And doesn't her acquiescence make
things easy not only for Othello's delusion but also for
Shakespeare the playwright? Mightn't the given case have
been more complex and explored more of human nature if
Desdemona had had a smack of Cordelia? As the play stands,
she seems for the last two Acts to be playing the 'game'
which Eric Berne calls 'Kick Me', but without realising –
and without Shakespeare's realising – that this is what she's
doing.

V

Perhaps the reader will grant that the worry I have just

expressed about Desdemona and her role in the play is intensified when we reflect on the consequences of taking Othello as becoming, in III.iii, so deluded as to be insane. Madness is always a problem for the artist, as we shall again see when we come to look at *Lear*: the main problem is to make the madman still human enough to command some sort of sympathy. A madman is a person who is suffering from a delusion so gross that, while I can feel pity for him, I can't in the strict sense of the word feel sympathy: his state of mind is too unlike anything I know for me to be able to put myself in his place. (The difference between the neurotic and the psychotic is, I take it, precisely this: the neurotic's mind can be understood easily enough by the 'normal' person.) Well, if Othello goes mad during the action of the play, we find ourselves in the awkward predicament that he has shut himself off from us, so that we can't *feel with* him; we may still pity him, but then the pity may be qualified (as it is, I confess, in my case) by the sense that his delusion is a silly delusion. We pity Lear, but much more intimately, because what drives him mad is after all an event that really happens in the real world. What drives Othello mad is a non-event which not only didn't happen but couldn't have happened, a

> monster,
> Begot upon itself, born on itself,   (III.iv.159)

as Emilia puts it; and, unless the reader happens to be peculiarly sensitive about the matter for some private reason, the delusion becomes not just horrid but ridiculous too. Lear likewise becomes ridiculous ('Come, an you get it you shall get it by running. Sa, sa, sa, sa'), but for him a recovery – however partial – is in store; in *Lear* there is 'something understood' – not much, not enough, but at least something. In *Othello* nothing is understood, either by Othello or, except dimly, by anyone else.

One sometimes scoffs at students who demand that they should be able to 'identify with' the characters in plays; but it is the expression, not the instinct, which is crude. Characters in whom we can't see something of ourselves

must remain mere 'cases', almost specimens; and it is
worth remembering, in order to point up what an odd play
Othello is, that in most Shakespeare tragedies we can and
do see ourselves in the personae on the stage. In *Hamlet* or
Lear, we keep on meeting ourselves all over the place: in
the former, we see ourselves in Polonius and Claudius as
well as in Hamlet and Horatio; in the latter, the play's
singularly painful effect depends, I think, on our being (for
the first half, anyway) on all sides at once – both with parent
against children and with children against the parent.
'Painful' is a weak word: 'lacerating' is more like it.

Now, many people have found *Othello* painful too, but I
suggest that it is a different kind of pain. It arises, I think,
from frustration; from our not being able to let our sympathies flow, because the play is so framed as to dam and
inhibit and baffle them. This is a further reason, perhaps,
why some people sentimentalise the play in the teeth of the
facts: sentimentalising it is the only way of making it
emotionally viable, felt along the blood. People who don't
sentimentalise it, like Dr Leavis, tend – for very good
reasons – to be slightly uncertain about the value of what
they have found. When we look into 'Tragedy and the
"Medium"' we read that

the attitude represented by Othello's last speech is radically untragic.
This is so obvious as to seem, perhaps, not worth saying: Othello, for
those who don't join in the traditional sentimentalization of the play,
is a very obvious case. The essential point that has to be made is that
his valedictory *coup de théâtre* represents a rhetorical inflation, a
headily emotional glorification, of an incapacity for tragic experience
that marks the ordinary moments of us all.[1]

True enough; but in that case I wonder if we emerge from
the theatre having experienced the

profound impersonality in which experience matters, not because it is
mine – because it is to me it belongs or happens, or because it subserves or issues in purpose or will, but because it is what it is, the
"mine" mattering only in so far as the individual sentience is the
indispensable focus of experience.[2]

[1] Leavis, 'Tragedy and the "Medium"', in *The Common Pursuit*, p. 128.
[2] ibid., p. 130.

If that were true of *Othello*, we should hardly feel, or be encouraged by Shakespeare to feel, so distanced from the hero. If the play is a tragedy, it is an odd one; and nothing in Leavis's penetrating essay on it (or in the remarks quoted above) makes me feel that it is any the less odd.

There is indeed a cold, inapprehensible quality about *Othello*: the critical irony in the valuing of the hero's nobility is so reductive as to be annihilating. Nowadays we have abandoned the romantic view of Tragedy, as represented and summed up by Bradley; we see adverse criticism of the tragic hero as being an essential part of the tragic effect – as witness Leavis's essay on *Othello* and Knights's on *Hamlet*. But in the case of *Othello*, once we open the way to such criticism there is no stopping it; and we end up with a hero, and a play, which are dismayingly rebarbative. To note that a certain way of reading makes a piece of literature repugnant is not to imply that the way stands self-condemned: we have to try and see things as they are, however unpleasant. If our reading of *Othello* suggests that Shakespeare himself found it hard, at the end, to face the consequences of what he had seen, that is no reason for us to take the way out which he spasmodically offers us in the last 130-odd lines, particularly since in *Othello*, unlike *Hamlet*, it is offered without much conviction or solidity.

Yet if we grant that *Othello*, properly read, is a bleak play, mayn't we still be entitled to wonder whether it isn't too bleak – whether, that is, it doesn't achieve its peculiar tone by shutting its eyes to certain human possibilities, rather as *Troilus and Cressida* does? After all, *King Lear*, if we set aside the Christian sentimentalisation of it, is a bleak enough play, in all conscience; but isn't its bleakness richer and more valuable by virtue of its taking on so much more of life than *Othello* cares to tackle?

NOTE A
Leontes' Jealousy

The first two scenes of *The Winter's Tale* have come in for a good deal of critical comment, most of it concerned with the sudden eruption of Leontes' jealousy at I.ii.108 ('Too hot, too hot.'). The problem, of course, is whether this jealousy is adequately motivated, or whether Shakespeare simply imposed it on Leontes as a matter of dramatic convenience at the cost of sacrificing plausibility.

First of all, I don't think we can understand what is going on in I.ii without glancing at I.i – a scene which, at least on a hasty reading, seems to be doing no more than giving us some basic *données* about Leontes, Polixenes and Mamillius. The information is there, of course, and it is important. But no less important is the tone of the exchange between the two courtiers Camillo and Archidamus. Is it accidental, for instance, that Archidamus' remark, 'Believe me, I speak as my understanding instructs me, and as mine honesty puts it to utterance' (19) immediately recalls the highflown Euphuism of Osric? Again, what is the point of the combat of courtesy a moment before? –

> *Cam.* I think, this coming summer, the King of Sicilia means
> to pay Bohemia the visitation which he justly owes him.
> *Arch.* Wherein our entertainment shall shame us: we will be
> justified in our loves: for indeed –
> *Cam.* Beseech you –
> *Arch.* Verily I speak it in the freedom of my knowledge: we can-
> not with such magnificence – in so rare – I know not what
> to say – We will give you sleepy drinks, that your senses
> (unintelligent of our insufficience) may, though they
> cannot praise us, as little accuse us.

Again, the interruptive courtesies remind us of that highly suspect brand of politeness we find in King Claudius, except that here the two men seem more than half-aware of the absurdity of the convention and are themselves burlesquing it. I am not suggesting there is anything exactly sinister in their doing this; but the scene is, I think, asking implicit questions about what words the voice of true feeling could ever find in this court. To burlesque a convention of speech is all very well, but if the convention embodies genuine habits of feeling you may find yourself burlesquing not merely the fake but also the genuine article. If, in this court, politeness – courtliness, courtesy – have reduced themselves to a superior game, it will not be possible to

express deeply felt respect or affection except in terms which con-
taminate the very qualities they are supposed to mediate; and the
only way out is to find oneself in the grip of an emotion so powerful
(and probably so violent) that it shatters the conventions for good and
all since it cannot find satisfaction within them. It is true that in the
second portion of 1.i (from line 21 to the end) there is apparently a
change of tone and style going with the change in subject-matter;
from 'Sicilia cannot show himself over-kind to Bohemia' the accents
deepen, the badinage disappears. Yet while the second part of the
scene deals with 'Sicilia' and 'Bohemia', so does the first; so that the
change in matter is purely nominal. And though the tone may seem
to become more serious in the latter part, it may very well be that it
is the characters who have dropped their banter, but not Shakespeare.
Thus, for example, Camillo says that Leontes and Polixenes 'have
seemed to be together, though absent; shook hands, as over a vast;
and embraced, as it were, from the ends of opposed winds'. We need
to know nothing of the two kings to detect here a note of rhetorical
exaggeration corresponding, perhaps, to a false inflation of the feelings
involved; courtesy may no longer be a game, but it is something that
enables people to strike attitudes, to see themselves (and make others
see them) as acting a part– sincerely and convincingly, no doubt, but
still with a certain ostentation. To Camillo's last phrase, 'The heavens
continue their loves.' Archidamus replies: 'I think there is not in
the world either malice or matter to alter it.' In a way, he isn't
playing the game, because Camillo's remark was presumably meant
as a mere verbal gesture, but Archidamus' reply takes it literally
(perhaps the 'heavens' won't continue their 'loves') and solemnly
counters it. By doing so he reminds us that *no* human affections are as
firmly based as that: which in turn suggests that the serious-courtly
mode is one in which people's expectations of one another tend to be
set impossibly high.

Armed with these hints, we are listening, at the start of 1.ii, for
the kind of *speech* – tone, diction, movement, feeling – that the two
kings and Hermione will feel appropriate. And we register it as being
peculiarly appropriate that Polixenes should start off like this:

> Nine changes of the watery star hath been
> The shepherd's note since we have left our throne
> Without a burden. Time as long again
> Would be filled up, my brother, with our thanks;
> And yet we should, for perpetuity,
> Go hence in debt: and therefore, like a cipher
> (Yet standing in rich place) I multiply
> With one "We thank you" many thousands moe
> That go before it.   (1.ii.1)

Note: Leontes' jealousy

The suave, fluent rhetoric may momentarily blind us to the fantastic nature of what Polixenes is saying – the exaggeration of his claim that nine months of saying 'thank you' would be insufficient, that he owes Polixenes 'thousands' of thanks. A man who talks like this either means less than he says (in effect, nothing at all), or else a good deal more. Leontes' reply – 'Stay your thanks a while,/And pay them when you part' – tells us at once that it is the latter: that Polixenes is trying, with the utmost politeness, to wriggle out of an awkward situation. And what is paradoxical about the situation is that it is precisely the language of courtesy that is inadequate for courtesy; it is inadequate because, however much genuine gratitude there may be in Polixenes' mind, the dominant impulse is not courteous at all. But the idiom of this court is such that he cannot come right out with his (perfectly understandable) reasons for wanting to go home. His second speech is obscure for just this reason – Polixenes is trying to say something blunt and simple in an idiom which has no place for bluntnesses and simplicities:

> I am questioned by my fears, of what may chance
> Or breed upon our absence; that may blow
> No sneaping winds at home, to make us say
> "This is put forth too truly." Besides, I have stayed
> To tire your royalty.

Polixenes is reduced at the end to accusing himself of having outstayed his welcome: a polite gesture which enables Leontes to expose the falsity of the self-accusation, in a tone which sounds sardonic – 'We are tougher, brother,/Than you can put us to't.' What he is doing, essentially, is to try and force Polixenes to be discourteously blunt; to match his own forthrightness; to put him on the spot by forcing him to abandon his circumlocutory good manners.

To take the analysis of this opening of I.ii further would be to make the same kinds of points again: there is a real contest of real feelings going on, and there are signs of a jarring antagonism between the two kings, which comes out more obviously in the very nearly rude refusal Polixenes is making by line 23:

> My affairs
> Do even drag me homeward: which to hinder
> Were (in your love) a whip to me; my stay,
> To you a charge and trouble: to save both,
> Farewell, our brother.

What is significant is that it is here, when Polixenes is clearly having some difficulty in maintaining his *politesse* and in the 'whip' image almost isn't, that Leontes turns for the first time to Hermione:

'Tongue-tied our queen? speak you.' What note does Hermione
procede to strike? –

> I had thought, sir, to have held my peace until
> You had drawn oaths from him not to stay. You, sir,
> Charge him too coldly. (28)

Given an occasion when (one might have thought) she would take
care to present a united front with Leontes, her very first words in
fact dissociate herself from him, with an undertone of something like
contempt, 'The way *you're* going about it, Polixenes will soon be
swearing an *oath* not to stay!' is roughly what she means; the implication being, 'why didn't you get me to speak [stop holding my
peace] earlier?' She criticises her husband for arguing 'too coldly' and
then goes on:

> Tell him, you are sure
> All in Bohemia's well: this satisfaction
> The by-gone day proclaimed: say this to him,
> He's beat from his best ward.

She refuses to address Polixenes directly, contenting herself with
(rather rudely) supplying Leontes with a cogent argument that he can
use on his friend. It is striking that this is the first attempt made to
counter any of Polixenes' reasons for wanting to go home – to counter
them, that is, in a rational way rather than by mere assertion of will
and desire; so that there is an implicit contempt in Hermione's claim
that Leontes is talking 'too coldly' and in her then handing him not a
warm plea but a false premise.

I'm not suggesting that the three are at one another's throats;
what I am trying to do is to undermine the usual assumption that
they are fond of one another in a simple, uncomplicated way and that
there are no strains or tensions. When, for example, Hermione goes
on to say this –

> To tell, he longs to see his son, were strong:
> But let him say so then, and let him go;
> But let him swear so, and he shall not stay,
> We'll thwack him hence with distaffs

– it should be obvious that what she is doing is to implicitly accuse
Polixenes of putting up fake reasons when he was in fact able
to put up reasons that couldn't be questioned; the suggestion being,
therefore, that he hasn't any real reasons and is being hypocritical in
pretending he has. And to reduce a man to the indignity of swearing
an oath that the motive he gives is his real motive must itself question
that reality; so my remark – that 'I want to see my son' is a reason
which can't be questioned – is one I must immediately qualify.
Addressing Polixenes, she goes on to say:

Note: Leontes' jealousy

> When at Bohemia
> You take my lord, I'll give him my commission
> To let him there a month behind the gest
> Prefixed for's parting: yet, good deed, Leontes
> I love thee not a jar o'th' clock behind
> What lady she her lord.

The change at 'yet, Leontes...' is puzzling at first glance: why does she need to reassure her husband? Presumably because she means that Leontes shouldn't take her permission to stay a month extra when he goes to Bohemia as meaning that she doesn't love him; she is again bringing up the family reasons for going home which Polixenes, curiously enough, has never given: 'When Leontes goes to Bohemia *I* shan't mind if he stays a month longer than he said he would; why should your wife mind if you do?' If Hermione had left it there, she would have been doing nothing worse than implying Polixenes was disingenuous; but she has to turn to Leontes and, by denying that she doesn't love him, raise the question of whether she does. I am not saying she doesn't, of course: what I mean is that emotions have become so tangled after the first forty-odd lines of this scene that henceforward anything that anybody says, no matter how innocent, will sound double-edged to someone else.

It is debatable, in the exchange between Hermione and Polixenes that follows (lines 44 to 86), whether Leontes is supposed to overhear what is said; the first Folio – the only substantive text – doesn't indicate that he moves away, but on the other hand he says nothing at all and is not addressed. Nor do his wife and Polixenes seem conscious in any way of his presence. Whether he overhears their conversation has been thought important, because there is a good deal in it which could easily be misinterpreted. I think that the *fact* of whether or not he overhears is unimportant, since I believe we are meant to feel the whole conversation as *happening to* Leontes. What then becomes remarkable about it is, first, that it takes Hermione only a dozen lines (less than a minute of playing-time) to persuade Polixenes to stay, and, secondly, that the rest of the conversation has nothing at all to do with the subject under discussion.

Hermione gets Polixenes to stay by the simple method of refusing to allow him to leave: she threatens him with becoming her 'prisoner', says she will ignore any oaths he may swear, and in general expresses herself so forcefully that Polixenes, if he wanted to persist in his refusal, would quite clearly be losing her friendship. Yet Leontes' importunities have been pretty well as insistent, so what Hermione says cannot, in itself, be the reason why Polixenes changes his mind. Not what she says, but what she is, and Polixenes' feeling for what she is – those must be the decisive factors. She is a woman, and in her words to Polixenes she is very obviously using her sex. Her sex allows her to take towards Polixenes a tone that would be impossible for another man:

> Verily,
> You shall not go: a lady's Verily's
> As potent as a lord's. Will you go yet?
> Force me to keep you as a prisoner,
> Not like a guest: so you shall pay your fees
> When you depart, and save your thanks? How say you?
> My prisoner? or my guest? By your dread "Verily,"
> One of them you shall be.

No man could have achieved just this combination of playfulness, vivacity, and aggressiveness, of warmth and power. We are reminded of Desdemona interceding for Cassio to her husband – a memory which prompts us to say that the exercise of cajoling charm is also, in any relationship but particularly where the parties are of opposite sexes, the exercise of power. (It would be all in keeping – though this is a thought for the producer – if Hermione emphasised 'prisoner' by holding onto Polixenes' wrists, an action that could very easily be misinterpreted by Leontes.)

The significance of the rest of the conversation (lines 60 to 86) is less easy to determine. Hermione says:

> Come, I'll question you
> Of my lord's tricks, and yours, when you were boys.
> You were pretty lordings then? (60)

Is this a digression? If so, it would be curious for Shakespeare to have diverted the course of a scene which has hitherto been so full of meaning. One may, then, reasonably look for some connection – it will probably not be an obvious one – between what has been going on up to this point and what is now happening. In the lines I have quoted above, 'tricks' sounds a harmless enough word; but when we remember the atmosphere of hostility that has earlier surrounded Hermione and Leontes, we may wonder whether her enquiry about the boys' 'tricks' isn't intended – or at least has the same effect on us as if it *were* intended – to find out something discreditable. Perhaps, too, we are to think her inquisitive about the origins of a relationship which has just shown how strongly it persists. Polixenes, who fences with great skill throughout the exchange, says nothing about the tricks but instead takes up the 'pretty lording':

> We were, fair queen,
> Two lads that thought there was no more behind,
> But such a day to-morrow as to-day,
> And to be boy eternal.

Note: Leontes' jealousy

Not 'lordings' but 'lads': Polixenes is denying that there was anything special about them, and by doing so is escaping neatly from the contemptuous inflection of the diminutive. 'Was not my lord' continues Hermione, 'The verier wag o'th' two?': she tries to bring him back to the 'tricks'. Polixenes, in reply, rebuts the suggestion that there was any difference; but his speech also develops in a new and surprising direction:

> We were as twinned lambs that did frisk i'th' sun,
> And bleat the one at th' other: what we changed
> Was innocence for innocence: we knew not
> The doctrine of ill-doing, nor dreamed
> That any did. Had we pursued that life,
> And our weak spirits ne'er been higher reared
> With stronger blood, we should have answered heaven
> Boldly "not guilty", the imposition cleared
> Hereditary ours.

I take it that Polixenes has recognised the unspoken drive behind Hermione's questions and is saying that, far from there having been any 'tricks', the boys exchanged 'innocence for innocence'. But if Hermione's probing has a (possibly) nasty edge to it, Polixenes' idyllic vision of youth is unreal in a way that is close to being sentimental. Yet, even if unconsciously, Polixenes has grasped some of the (possible) implications of 'tricks': his speech brings in a range of terms from orthodox Christian morality, only, of course, in order to deny that any of them applied to Leontes and himself. The conditional sentence 'Had we...' and the obviously sexual connotations of 'spirits' and 'higher reared' shift the notion of sin from childhood to adulthood and connect it with sex. The note seems almost one of regret at having to grow up: the last phrase, 'the imposition cleared/ Hereditary ours', suggests that, as boys, they were literally unfallen – a strange and pretty self-indulgent piece of theology. Hermione, in her reply, gives up the attempt to get Polixenes to reveal something discreditable about Leontes' childhood and switches the attack to his later life: 'By this we gather/You have tripped since.' She turns Polixenes' assertion of childhood innocence into an admission of adult guilt. But most skilfully, he turns the 'tripping' into a matter of his and Leontes' relations to their wives, not to woman in general. His apparently playful reply has some startling consequences:

> O my most sacred lady,
> Temptations have since then been born to's: for
> In those unfledged days was my wife a girl;
> Your precious self had then not crossed the eyes
> Of my young play-fellow.

Hermione is quick to perceive these consequences:

> Grace to boot!
> Of this make no conclusion, lest you say
> Your queen and I are devils...

What is being raised here, in a passage of seeming badinage, is the whole issue of sin, sexuality, and marriage. Polixenes' refutation of Hermione's insinuations has led him inexorably to saying that love, sexual and married love, is itself a temptation – and, being something that he and Leontes have given in to, is itself sinful. This, as Hermione perceives, casts her and Mrs Polixenes as devils of temptation; but it also throws doubt upon the nature of matrimony. If marriage is but legalised 'ill-doing', then there is no question of 'tripping'. Hermione seems partly aware of this implication as she goes on:

> Th'offences we have made you do, we'll answer,
> If you first sinned with us, and that with us
> You did continue fault, and that you slipped not
> With any but with us.

Again, the tone is light but the implications grave: if sexuality is sinful it doesn't matter whether it takes place within or outside marriage, and there is no distinction therefore between the marital act and adultery – no distinction, that is, except personal preference, taste, pride.

It is at this point that Leontes rejoins the dialogue, with 'Is he won yet?' If he has overheard the conversation (or if, as I suggested earlier, we in any case sense it as happening to him), he cannot be feeling very reassured about the way in which his wife regards her commitment to him: a commitment that (in his eyes) could amount only to taking responsibility for the sin she makes him commit when he makes love to her. Nor, as a matter of simple pride, can he have been pleased to hear her efforts to find out about his 'tricks'. Pride, too, is involved by the speed with which Hermione has got Polixenes to agree to stay – 'At my request he would not', says Leontes, sourly. He adds that she only once spoke to better purpose, and Hermione says:

> What! Have I twice said well? when was't before?
> I prithee tell me; cram's with praise, and make's
> As fat as tame things: one good deed, dying tongueless,
> Slaughters a thousand, waiting upon that.

The sarcasm is pertly triumphant; and the sexual overtones of 'cram' and 'fat' – Hermione presumably being visibly pregnant – must jangle in the ears of a man already thinking about married sexuality. The Queen goes on:

Note: Leontes' jealousy

> Our praises are our wages. You may ride's
> With one soft kiss a thousand furlongs ere
> With spur we heat an acre. But to th' goal:
> My last good deed was to entreat his stay:
> What was my first? It has an elder sister,
> Or I mistake you...

More sexual sarcasm; Hermione is turning the knife in the wound. The other occasion when she 'said well' was, it turns out, when she finally gave in and said 'yes' to Leontes' proposal of marriage; and this leads her to conclude with what is from her husband's point of view the disastrously sinister juxtaposition:

> Why, lo you now; I have spoke to th' purpose twice:
> The one, for ever earned a royal husband;
> Th' other, for some while a friend.

Shakespeare's art is consummate in bringing the superficially innocent conversation to a close on the ambiguous word 'friend'.

It is straight after this that Leontes falls into the jealous fit signalised by 'Too hot, too hot!' If we have been responding closely and appropriately to the first hundred-odd lines of the scene, his jealousy cannot possibly seem 'unmotivated' in the sense that from his own point of view he has no provocation (*we* know he is wrong, but that is another matter). Not even Shakespeare has elsewhere succeeded better in creating the conflicts of affection and antagonism that are inherent in close human relationships.

4. King Lear

I INTRODUCTORY

I CAN CONFIDENTLY SAY that there is a received reading of *Lear* – 'received' in the sense that pretty well everyone seems to accept it. It is a reading that reached full explicitness in Bradley, although he refers us back to Edward Dowden for an adumbration of it. Bradley proposed that we should change the title to 'The Redemption of King Lear', because the intention of the gods was 'neither to torment him, nor to teach him a "noble anger," but to lead him to attain through apparently hopeless failure the very end and aim of life'.[1] In the Bradleyan context 'redemption', and the term he borrowed from Dowden, 'purification', don't have any specifically theological overtones; but in his successors such overtones become deafening and are generally associated with a sort of unctuous religiosity which I, for one, find most distasteful in itself as well as absurdly inappropriate to the spirit of Shakespeare's play.

I have in mind critics such as Traversi, Danby, Heilman, L. C. Knights, G. I. Duthie and Kenneth Muir (the last two being the play's most recent scholarly editors).[2] All of these take a more or less redemptive view of Lear's fate and all of them use words like 'purification', 'purgation', etc. According to Duthie, for example, Lear dies 'in a state of spiritual health'; Lear's and Gloucester's 'sufferings are

---

[1] Bradley, *Shakespearean Tragedy*, Papermac edn, p. 235.
[2] A. Traversi, *An Approach to Shakespeare* (3rd edn, 1969), II, 146f.; J. F. Danby, *Shakespeare's Doctrine of Nature* (1949), 1961, passim; R. B. Heilman, *This Great Stage* (1948), 1963, passim; L. C. Knights, *Some Shakespearean Themes and An Approach to "Hamlet"* (1959 and 1960), Peregrine edn, 1966, ch. on *Lear*; G. I. Duthie (ed.) *King Lear* in the New Cambridge series (1960), 1968, Introd.; Kenneth Muir (ed.) *King Lear* in the New Arden series (1952), 1964, Introd. Cf. also Martin Lings, *Shakespeare in the Light of Sacred Art* (1966), pp. 64f.; and Paul A. Jorgensen, *Lear's Self-Discovery* (California U.P., 1967), passim. In *Shakespeare's Royal Self* (New York, 1966), James Kirsch succeeds in reconciling Jesus with Jung.

redemptive. There is no ultimate ground for pessimism here.'[1] Even the death of Cordelia isn't a matter for pessimism, because we all know that God moves in a mysterious way. The critic almost seems to be taking the curious position that the more unjust things look, the more that shows how little we can understand about God: so that the less apparent justice there is in the world, the more real justice there must be somewhere or other. The mercy and justice of God are, it appears, demonstrated by the lack of either. Some of the extremer developments of this view seem to me to show, in their eagerness to make Shakespeare an edifying writer, an incredible callousness about the torture, physical and mental, that characterises this play above any other of Shakespeare's. One standard ploy, for instance, is to inform us that Gloucester is wrong to complain about being blinded by Cornwall, because he had had a bastard son, and that is unspeakably wicked; in any case, the argument runs, he is much improved by being blinded.[2] The effect of this kind of claim is to make one wonder whether such critics don't conceive of God as being rather like the Duke of Cornwall. They may be right, of course.

The trouble with the redemptivist view of *King Lear*, as I have been implying, is that it ignores the play's power to unnerve – a power noted long ago by Dr Johnson:

I was many years ago so shocked by *Cordelia's* death, that I know not whether I ever endured to read again the last scenes of the play till I undertook to revise them as an editor.

Johnson has got hold of a crucial point here; the words that count are 'shocked' and 'endured', because we know the man who wrote *The Vanity of Human Wishes* wouldn't use them lightly; nor would so pious a man as Johnson have easily missed what modern critics see as an obvious opportunity for finding something improving in the piece. Another crucial comment comes from George Orwell:

Shut your eyes and think of *King Lear*, if possible without calling

1 Duthie, edn cit., p. l.
2 Paul N. Siegel, 'Adversity and the Miracle of Love in *King Lear*', *Shakespeare Quarterly*, 1955, pp. 327–9.

to mind any of the dialogue. What do you see? Here at any rate is what I see; a majestic old man in a long black robe, with flowing white hair and beard,... wandering through a storm and cursing the heavens, in company with a Fool and a lunatic. Presently the scene shifts and the old man, still cursing, still understanding nothing, is holding a dead girl in his arms while the Fool dangles on a gallows somewhere in the background.[1]

This (apart from the fanciful 'long black robe') has an admirable plainness and sobriety about it. And it contains one really startling phrase, when Orwell says that Lear dies 'still cursing, still understanding nothing'. If *that* or something like it is true, most of what has been written about the play since Dowden is nonsense; perhaps that is why no-one, except William Empson,[2] has bothered to take Orwell seriously. Nevertheless, if we take him literally, and agree that at the end Lear dies 'understanding' *nothing at all*, we'd be hard put to it to explain why the end of the play is so moving (a fact of experience which, I imagine, nobody would want to deny). The death of an egocentric old man, who is no less egocentric in Act v than he was in Act I, wouldn't be significant enough to leave us feeling that what we had been witnessing was a tragedy. Are the redemptivists right, then? Or can Orwell be? And what, in either case, are the critical consequences?

II   LEAR AND CORDELIA

Lear's relationship with his youngest daughter clearly dominates the play from first to last: the first major incident is his quarrel with her, the last his lament over her dead body. One of the main consequences of the redemptive reading has been to reduce Cordelia to a high-minded prig or a Christ-figure (the two being apparently synonymous). It is taken for granted that, throughout the first scene of the play, all that is wrong with Cordelia is inarticulateness – the very claim she herself makes when she says

---

[1] George Orwell, *Selected Essays* (Penguin edn, 1957), p. 108.
[2] William Empson, *The Structure of Complex Words* (1951).

> Unhappy that I am, I cannot heave
> My heart into my mouth.   (I.i.90)

But she at once goes on to say:

> I love your Majesty
> According to my bond, no more nor less.

'Bond' is a tricky word here; an obvious way of taking it is to think it means a 'natural tie', and to suppose that Cordelia is claiming that she loves Lear 'naturally', as any decent child loves its parent.[1] But then her addition, 'no more nor less', makes nonsense of its being simply a *natural* tie, because if you love someone there can be no question of more or less, you just love them. I think what Cordelia means is, sarcastically, that Lear wants her to think of love as being like a contract to pay the loved-one £2-10-0; very well then, she *will* think of it like that, and she'll pay him not a penny more than she owes. Lear has hitherto always spoken of 'love' as something that can be counted or measured; 'Which of you shall we say doth love us most?' he has asked (line 50); to Regan he has given a 'third' of 'our fair kingdom' (79) and has told Cordelia to try and get 'a third more opulent than your sisters' (85). At first she decided not to play, repudiating the numbers game with 'Nothing'; but now she has taken Lear's terminology and way of looking at things and turned them against him. The 'no more nor less' is taken up in her next speech:

> Good my lord,
> You have begot me, bred me, loved me. I
> Return those duties back as are right fit,
> Obey you, love you, and most honour you.
> Why have my sisters husbands, if they say
> They love you all? Haply, when I shall wed,
> That lord whose hand must take my plight shall carry
> Half my love with him, half my care and duty.
> Sure I shall never marry like my sisters,
> To love my father all.   (94)

Is it difficult to see that Cordelia is bitterly angry – absolutely furious at the way her father has put her in a false

---

[1] Cf. Danby, op. cit., p. 129.

position? She's getting her own back. 'Duties' become ambiguous because, while the surface meaning is 'I am punctilious in carrying out my obligations', the under-meaning is 'Oh well then, if you want to regard love as a *duty* – something I'm obliged to carry out whether I like it or not – I'll regard it that way too: see how you like that!' She is thinking of the fifth commandment, and saying that if her father wants to make natural affections a matter of legal obligations, two can play at the same game; and two can also play at the game of swapping fractions – Cordelia's reiterated 'half' takes up and parodies her father's repeated 'third'. The 'half' is sarcastically contrasted with the 'all' ('they love you all. . .'; 'to love my father all') that Goneril and Regan have professed: the repetition suggests a contempt which is both icy and furious. It is emphatically not the emotion of a saint, nor is it that of someone who just loses her voice at an important moment. If she is speaking sincerely in disparaging her sisters (and there is no reason to doubt that she means what she says), then she has managed to heave her heart into her mouth to devastating effect.

If we take the episode in the way I have proposed, it becomes clear that Cordelia is proud and quick-tempered – very much her father's daughter, in fact – so that at the very beginning of the play Shakespeare is refusing to make anyone's behaviour, even Cordelia's, inhumanly saint-like; that is, saintliness is simply not an issue here. This claim can be confirmed by looking at Cordelia's speeches towards the end of I.i (222f., 266f.) where her defence of herself and her attack on her sisters even have a kind of moral gusto which isn't in the least lamb-like. And I'd argue that saintliness, at least of that kind, never does become an issue in *King Lear*.

Something that does become an issue, however, is the extent to which Lear realises the wrong he has done his daughter. It is often said that a realisation of the wrong he has done her gradually thrusts its way into his mind during

Acts II and III. Here, for example, is Kenneth Muir:

When Cordelia refuses to barter her love for material profit, Lear
banishes both her and the one man who dares to take her part...
As the play progresses, Lear's subconscious realisation that he has
committed a sinful mistake gradually rises into his consciousness.[1]

This sounds very plausible away from the text; but look at
the text and what happens? The curious fact emerges that
Lear scarcely ever refers to Cordelia, and never mentions
Kent at all. The trouble is that we allow the reconciliation
scene (IV.vii) to colour our memory of what has gone before:
we assume that if Lear is finally brought to the point of
begging forgiveness, he must have been growing steadily
towards that point all along. I shall now try to show that,
while he hardly spares Cordelia a thought, his mind is in
fact occupied by quite different matters, and that it is only
by grasping what these matters are that we can read the
central sections of the play properly.

  Lear's mention of Cordelia during the quarrel with
Goneril looks, at first glance, as though it is genuinely
contrite:

> O most small fault,
> How ugly didst thou in Cordelia show,
> Which, like an engine, wrenched my frame of nature
> From the fixed place, drew from my heart all love,
> And added to the gall. O Lear, Lear, Lear!
> Beat at this gate that let thy folly in
> And thy dear judgment out!   (I.iv.267)

But what we need to remember is the context – how these
lines are led up to:

> Detested kite, thou liest!
> My train are men of choice and rarest parts,
> That all particulars of duty know,
> And in the most exact regard support
> The worships of their name. O most small fault...

Taking the context into account doesn't make us say that
Lear is being insincere in mentioning Cordelia; but it does
lead us to suspect that (as commonly happens in family

[1] Muir, edn cit., p. liii.

rows) he is using what may or may not be a genuine feeling in order to make a debating point – to be as hurtful as possible to Goneril. So, while not exactly insincere, Lear's words certainly aren't evidence of repentance, the beginning of spiritual re-education, or what not. The most they show is that he is *capable* of seeing earlier events in a new light; so it is important to see whether this incipient insight is maintained or not.

After the quarrel, when Lear is waiting for his horses to be saddled, he devotes four words to (presumably) Cordelia, 'I did her wrong' (I.v.25). But he is very easily distracted from this line of thought by the Fool, who is nagging away at Lear's folly, not in disowning Cordelia, but in giving away his kingdom to the other daughters: in half a minute Lear is saying 'I will forget my nature. So kind a father!' The distraction is effective, in that he doesn't mention Cordelia again till a whole Act later.

Not, in fact, till nearly the end of Act II does Lear's mind revert to her. Shortly after Goneril has arrived at Glouces-ter's castle, where he has been having an uneasy conversa-tion with Regan, the latter suggests that he should return to the former. Lear sees this advice as being impudent –

> Why, the hot-blooded France, that dowerless took
> Our youngest born, I could as well be brought
> To knee his throne and, squire-like, pension beg
> To keep base life afoot.   (II.iv.208)

If his 'subconscious realisation that he has committed a sinful mistake' is gradually rising into his consciousness, we can only wonder why this mention of Cordelia, coming so much later than 'I did her wrong', shows so little concern with *why* she was 'dowerless' and is in effect putting Cor-delia on a par with Goneril, it being equally insufferable to go to either of them. He goes on at once, pointing to Oswald, to make another comparison:

> Return with her?
> Persuade me rather to be slave and sumpter
> To this detested groom.

It is a curious sense of contrition that puts Cordelia into such company: and that is surely just the point Shakespeare is making about Lear.

And it is a curious sense of contrition that doesn't prompt Lear to say one word about her during the storm scenes or the last mad scene (IV.vi). Since there is literally no evidence, I can't very well quote it; so I shall pass on to what we hear of the King in Act IV.

I have great difficulty with IV.iii, the scene between Kent and the Gentleman. Partly the trouble is the unnecessary nature of the Gentleman's explanation of why the King of France has gone home:

> Something he left imperfect in the state, which since his coming forth is thought of, which imports to the kingdom so much fear and danger that his personal return was most required and necessary.

But no-one would notice the King's absence if our attention hadn't been drawn to it in this clumsy way. Also, the description of Cordelia's joy-and-grief on hearing about her father seems curiously strained:

> patience and sorrow strove
> Who should express her goodliest. You have seen
> Sunshine and rain at once; her smiles and tears
> Were like, a better way: those happy smilets
> That played on her ripe lip seemed not to know
> What guests were in her eyes, which parted thence
> As pearls from diamonds dropped. (IV.iii.17)

One sees where the redemptivist critics have got at least some of their provocation to unctuousness; but the Cordelia we have seen before and are soon to see again, in the very next scene, is a great deal tougher than this verse would suggest.

The main trouble I find with this scene is what it tells us about Lear himself. He is 'i'th'town' (Dover), and

> sometime, in his better tune, remembers
> What we are come about, and by no means
> Will yield to see his daughter...
> A sovereign shame so elbows him: his own unkindness,
> That stripped her from her benediction, turned her
> To foreign casualties, gave her dear rights

To his dog-hearted daughters – these things sting
His mind so venomously that burning shame
Detains him from Cordelia.   (IV.iii.39)

The problem here is that this Lear is a quite different man
from the one we saw last, in the mock trial scene (III.vi),
and from the one we are to see next, when he is fantastically dressed with wild flowers (IV.vi): in both cases he is a
raving lunatic. So I think it profoundly disturbing that
Shakespeare won't undertake to let us hear what the 'better
tune' sounds like, particularly when this is the only hint we
get between II.iv and IV.vii that Lear is even thinking about
Cordelia and what he has done to her. Perhaps he doesn't
show us Lear's 'sovereign shame' because, at this stage, he
can't – he would be too obviously anticipating the reconciliation. Yet the lucid interval is quite inconsistent with
the development of Lear between III.i and IV.vi, because
(with this one exception) he steadily becomes madder and
madder: that is, Shakespeare has constructed an otherwise
intelligible curve which, at this point, goes off the graph-
paper altogether. It's possible that Shakespeare himself was
here momentarily tempted by a quasi-redemptive view,
thus providing literary critics with some pretext for their
attempt to extend that view to the whole play.

If, then, Lear's mind is mostly not running on Cordelia at
all, what is it running on? To answer this question we first
have to go back and look rather carefully at what the
characters say about his going into the storm, and whether
what they say squares with what we actually see.

III   THE EXPULSION OF LEAR

The *Oxford Companion to English Literature*, summarising
some of the events of Acts I and II of *King Lear*, remarks:
'Goneril and Regan reveal their heartless character by
grudging their father the maintenance that he had
stipulated for, and finally turning him out of doors in a
storm.' What I want to do here is to ask whether that

account of what happens is in fact true and, if it isn't, why
it is an account that almost any reader of the play would give.

There is, of course, plenty of evidence to support such a
reading. In the first of the storm scenes (III.ii), Kent says he
will return

> to this hard house
> (More harder than the stones whereof 'tis raised,
> Which even but now, demanding after you,
> Denied me to come in)...   (III.ii.63)

The sisters, then, have apparently had the doors of
Gloucester's castle locked, and we learn a little later that
they have taken from Gloucester the use of his own house
(III.iii.3). Lear confirms the general impression by exclaim-
ing, in the second storm scene,

> In such a night
> To shut me out?   (III.iv.17)

Later, in the same scene we learn from Gloucester that the
daughters' 'injunction' is to 'bar [his] doors' (III.iv.150) and
that they even 'seek [Lear's] death' (163). The same implication is made by Gloucester when, cornered by Goneril and
Regan, he defends his helping the King:

> If wolves had at thy gate howled that dearn time,
> Thou should'st have said 'Good porter, turn the key'.
> All cruels else subscribe: but I shall see
> The wingéd Vengeance overtake such children.   (III.vii.62)

Cordelia, as reported by the Gentleman, is made to imply a
similar account of events, when he says she

> Cried 'Sisters, sisters! Shame of ladies! Sisters!
> Kent! father! sisters! What, i'th'storm? i'th'night?
> Let pity not believe it.'   (IV.iii.28)

Finally Cordelia, just before Lear awakes and they are
reconciled, gives by implication another account of what
she believes happened:

> Mine enemy's dog,
> Though he had bit me, should have stood that night
> Against my fire; and wast thou fain, poor father,
> To hovel thee with swine and rogues forlorn,
> In short and musty straw?   (IV.vii.36)

All these quotations – which should of course be referred back to their various contexts – make the same point, the very point, in fact, made by the *Oxford Companion*: that Lear has been turned out of doors by his wicked daughters. But before accepting this account as simply being true, we might enquire whether the characters who elaborate it have any axe to grind – whether they are disinterested or not. And when we realise that the above quotations are spoken by Kent, Gloucester, Lear, and Cordelia, we should pause to wonder whether it is quite proper to accept these passionate partisans as necessarily telling the literal truth. Then we remember that there is at least one piece of evidence which points in the opposite direction. When Lear meets Regan at Gloucester's castle, he complains bitterly of his ill-treatment at the hands of his other daughter and compares Regan favourably to her:

> 'Tis not in thee
> To grudge my pleasures, to cut off my train,
> To bandy hasty words, to scant my sizes,
> And in conclusion to oppose the bolt
> Against my coming in.   (II.iv.169)

The last accusation – that Goneril locked him out – is supported by absolutely nothing in the text of I.iv or I.v. The King, therefore, is – quite understandably – telling a fib in order to gain Regan's sympathy. But then, how true is the rest of what he says? Is it the fact that Goneril 'grudged' his 'pleasures' and 'scanted' his 'sizes' (cut down his allowance)? However we feel about this, it seems to me that the only clearly true thing Lear says is that she cut off his train – though even here 'cut down' would be more accurate. Of course a great deal depends, as always in Shakespeare, upon one's point of view, and it is critically dubious to assume that the point of view held by the hero and his partisans is identical with the play's.

What do we see if we turn back to I.iii and iv and ask how our sympathies are meant to be divided between Lear and Goneril? I.iii begins with the interview between her and Oswald: 'Did my father strike my gentleman for chiding of

his fool?' How are we meant to take this? Admittedly
Goneril isn't speaking in soliloquy, where by convention
she would have to be telling the truth as she sees it; but we
arguably have what amounts to a straightforward revelation
of the truth, because she can have no conceivable motive for
deceiving Oswald, who must know at least as much about
what is going on as she does herself. And if we don't read
back into this scene what we later learn about Goneril,
don't we at once detect in her speeches a note of angry
sincerity, a note that can't simply be put on? –

> By day and night he wrongs me. Every hour
> He flashes into one gross crime or other
> That sets us all at odds. I'll not endure it.
> His knights grow riotous, and himself upbraids us
> On every trifle. (I.iii.4)

Now, it is possible that Goneril is sincere but wrong; yet
doesn't the kind of behaviour she attributes to Lear here
sound, in the light of what we have witnessed in the first
scene, horribly plausible? It is true that she *wants* to have a
quarrel –

> I would breed from hence occasions, and I shall,
> That I may speak (I.iii.25)

– but clearly something has to give; the present situation
cannot possibly last. A sinister meaning might no doubt be
read into what she then adds –

> I'll write straight to my sister
> To hold my very course

– but only, again, if you assume she has some motive other
than bringing Lear to a sense of the realities of the position
he has himself created.

When Lear comes in (I.iv.8) he has just been hunting,
not crawling towards death; and we notice that he starts by
saying to an attendant: 'Let me not stay a jot for dinner;
go get it ready'; so presumably there are two different sets of
servants in Goneril's household, hers and her father's. No
wonder there is strife. We notice too, when Lear meets the
disguised Kent, that whatever agreements he may have

made about the size of his establishment, he is hiring and firing people at will – I could say 'at whim' in view of his words to Kent, 'If I like thee no worse after dinner I will not part from thee yet' (I.iv.41).

The deliberate provocation by Oswald (acting on Goneril's instructions) leads eventually to her entrance and confrontation with her father. I don't see any reason why we need look at what is happening through Lear's eyes alone, although a lot of critics are content to. If for a change we try looking at events through Goneril's eyes, what does she see when she comes into this room in her own house? A surly retainer (Kent) who has just given her steward a drubbing; an elderly father who at once attacks her for not smiling ('How now, daughter? What makes that frontlet on?'); and a Fool capering around and saying exactly what he likes. Is it any wonder she thinks her palace has been turned into a bear-garden? 'Rank and not-to-be-enduréd riots' is, if we take the first hundred lines of the scene as shorthand for what has been going on, a not unfair description of what we have been seeing; and once again Goneril's voice has the ring of angry sincerity. At the very least we can't say her tone is that of *conscious* hypocrisy:

> Not only, sir, this your all-licensed fool,
> But other of your insolent retinue
> Do hourly carp and quarrel, breaking forth
> In rank and not-to-be-enduréd riots.
> I had thought, by making this well known unto you,
> To have found a safe redress; but now grow fearful,
> By what yourself too late have spoke and done,
> That you protect this course, and put it on
> By your allowance; which if you should, the fault
> Would not scape censure, nor the redresses sleep
> Which, in the tender of a wholesome weal,
> Might in their working do you that offence,
> Which else were shame, that then necessity
> Will call discreet proceeding.   (I.iv.201)

This seems to me totally unlike the kind of thing we hear when a character is pretending to an emotion he doesn't feel – quite unlike for example Claudius' scrupulously

rehearsed sixteen lines of double-talk on his first appearance in *Hamlet*. Goneril is so genuinely angry that she
almost loses her syntactical way amid the proliferating
relative clauses (which ... which ... which ... that). And
we notice that, while she is certainly complaining, she isn't
threatening, unless 'redresses' (210) is an oblique hint that
if Lear won't right things, she will have to.

The King's response to all this is to start playing an
elaborate game the point of which is that he pretends not to
know who Goneril is, or who he is – 'Are you our daughter?'
'Who is it that can tell me who I am?' He makes no attempt
to answer what his daughter has been saying; he is trying
to deny her right to say anything of the kind. He utters a
clear threat in

> by the marks
> Of sovereignty, knowledge, and reason,
> I should be false persuaded I had daughters.   (232)

This is tantamount to saying that if Goneril goes on in the
same way he will disown her as he disowned Cordelia.
Goneril refuses to play this game –

> This admiration, sir, is much o' th' savour
> Of other your new pranks   (237)

– thus neatly reversing what she did in I.i: with frigid
sarcasm she accuses Lear of merely faking surprise; and
then she goes on to push the charges much further,
mentioning gluttony and lust. Of these we have no evidence;
yet it has always seemed to me incredible that Goneril, who
wants the whole business to be properly sorted out, would
have needed to overplay what is evidently a strong hand by
making complaints that were plainly trumped-up and would
be easy to rebut. In the end she does make a definite
threat:

> Be then desired,
> By her that else will take the thing she begs,
> A little to disquantity your train...   (247)

To remonstrate was one thing, but to threaten is quite
another: Lear stops playing games and calls her a 'degenerate

bastard' and a 'destested kite'; he then simply denies her charges by claiming

> My train are men of choice and rarest parts,
> That all particulars of duty know,
> And in the most exact regard support
> The worships of their name.   (264)

We reflect here, perhaps, that if his train take their lead from him, *duty* is the last thing they'd know. There follows Lear's curse (276f.) – the plea to Nature to make Goneril sterile. Redemptivist critics are not fond of quoting this passage, and one can see why: after such a curse, what forgiveness? What can we think of a man who, asked to cut down the number of his retainers, begs Nature to 'dry up' his daughter's 'organs of increase'? The egotism that speaks here is so insanely malevolent that I can only suppose we are being prepared for Lear's total moral collapse later. After further furious curses, all embodying the idea of vicious revenge, Lear storms out.

From my reading of I.iv it seems, then, that the account Lear later gives of it to Regan is biased to the point of being wildly distorted. If we look at II.iv with I.iv in mind, this becomes plain. And if we look at II.iv in the light of accounts given of it later in the play by Lear and others, it becomes patent that those accounts too are inaccurate. When Regan suggests to her father that he should go back to Goneril after dismissing half his train, he responds violently and decisively:

> Return to her? and fifty men dismissed?
> No, rather I abjure all roofs, and choose
> To wage against the enmity o'th'air,
> To be a comrade with the wolf and owl –
> Necessity's sharp pinch! Return with her?
> Why, the hot-blooded France, that dowerless took
> Our youngest born, I could as well be brought
> To knee his throne and, squire-like, pension beg
> To keep base life afoot. Return with her?
> Persuade me rather to be slave and sumpter
> To this detested groom [Oswald].   (II.iv.203)

Lear is quite unequivocally saying that the reason he won't go back to Goneril is not that she won't have him but that he refuses to return on any terms but his own – which are the restoration of the fifty knights whom he learnt Goneril had dismissed at I.iv.295. Lear actually says in so many words that, rather than compromise in any way at all over what he sees as a matter of principle, he would go out into the open air. And note that it isn't merely Goneril's house he rejects; he abjures '*all* roofs'. Of course, we can't say that he left of his own free will; but it seems equally questionable whether it is strictly true to say he was *forced* to leave. The savagery of his tone now, in II.iv, can only be meant by Shakespeare to underline that his decisions (past and future) are conscious and deliberate – a matter of choice, as Goneril's reply to the above speech shows: 'At your choice, sir.' After the squalid game of inverted bidding, in which Lear tries to find out which of his children will take the larger retinue and the children progressively cut it down, Regan asks why he needs even one servant of his own when theirs are at his disposal, and Lear, after the long speech beginning 'O reason not the need!' (260), rushes out into the night. What follows – the last twenty lines of the scene – is intensely interesting. For a moment Regan, Cornwall and Goneril are left alone on the stage (Gloucester having followed Lear off), and so whatever they now say it will have to reveal what they are really thinking and feeling, because they have no motive to conceal it from one another or from us. 'Let us withdraw; 'twill be a storm,' says Cornwall (283), thus verbalising the stage direction 'Storme and Tempest' which the Folio prints at line 280; 'withdraw' because they are outside Gloucester's castle. But perhaps it is not a castle – certainly Regan implies it is something smaller:

> This house is little: the old man and's people
> Cannot be well bestowed.

If some partisan of Lear's were on stage, this would sound like a feeble attempt at self-justification, but as things are Regan can have no motive to try and justify what her husband and sister presumably approve anyway, so that we must take the statement as having some truth. Goneril then repeats the charge that what has happened is Lear's own choice:

> 'Tis his own blame; hath put himself from rest,
> And must needs taste his folly.

Shakespeare would hardly have put this charge in such a salient position if he'd wanted us to think that the boot was wholly on the other foot. Regan goes on to make a claim on whose accuracy hangs a great deal:

> For his particular, I'll receive him gladly,
> But not one follower.

'So am I purposed,' adds Goneril. Now, is it true or not that the sisters would have been prepared to 'receive' their father (even if not 'gladly')? If not, then the accounts I've already quoted, about Lear's being personally turned out into the storm, are quite true, and in no way reflect the bias of their speakers; if so, then those accounts are but partially true, or largely untrue. If the accounts are dubious, then the development of Goneril, Regan and Cornwall in Act III becomes very surprising indeed, in the sense that it couldn't have been fully foreseen from their earlier behaviour (up to the end of Act II).

Gloucester returns, saying 'The king is in high rage' (292) and that he doesn't know where he is going –

> He calls to horse, but will I know not whither.

Cornwall answers,

> 'Tis best to give him way; he leads himself.

We could take this advice as being intended to stop Gloucester from even trying to 'lead' the king; but since Gloucester has already admitted that Lear won't speak to him, it seems more plausible to assume that Cornwall is trying to soothe the old man's feelings: 'Never mind his not listening to you, he won't listen to anybody – he's so headstrong that he'll do what he wants to anyway.' Goneril adds (anxiously?),

My lord, entreat him by no means to stay.

A good deal hangs on our reading of this line, too. If we take it to mean, 'For God's sake don't try to persuade him to stay, I can't stand him at any price, and what I just said about being happy to receive him was pure nonsense,' then Goneril's character becomes blacker at this point (although she has, after all, had plenty of provocation to feel like this about her father, back in Act I). If, on the other hand, we think the line means, 'Please don't persuade him to stay – in his present mood of "high rage" he'd be utterly impossible,' then she is merely pronouncing an obvious truth. Now Gloucester indirectly points out that Lear is going to brave the elements:

> Alack, the night comes on, and the bleak winds
> Do sorely ruffle. For many miles about
> There's scarce a bush. (296)

Is this meant as a timidly oblique reproach to the daughters? Or is it tantamount to saying, 'What a pity Lear is so unreasonable – it's night, stormy, inhospitable countryside, and yet he *will* insist on rushing out into it'? I don't know, but perhaps the issue is decided when we remember that Gloucester, by his own account, has just been snubbed by the king. The safest thing to say is that the key-word is 'Alack' – that the whole speech is a matter of Gloucester's wringing his hands. Regan, in reply, reiterates the standard claim – it's all Lear's fault:

> O sir, to wilful men
> The injuries that they themselves procure
> Must be their schoolmasters. Shut up your doors;
> He is attended with a desperate train,
> And what they may incense him to, being apt
> To have his ear abused, wisdom bids fear.

It's true that she tells Gloucester to shut his doors, but notice the reason she gives – Lear is attended with a 'desperate train'. Again we have to ask if this is true or not. And the answer is not easy to give. We know that Lear had some attendant knights when he was staying with Goneril, and that some of them followed him to Regan's place and thence to Gloucester's; at the beginning of this scene Kent asks

> How chance the king comes with so small a number?
> (II.iv.61)

and the Fools' reply suggests that some of the knights have deserted their lord. Much later, Oswald remarks of Lear that

> Some five or six and thirty of his knights,
> Hot questrists after him, met him at gate,
> Who, with some other of the lord's dependants,
> Are gone with him toward Dover... (III.vii.16)

Apparently, then, Kent's account of a 'small train' tallies more or less with Regan's and Oswald's; all three characters can't be making it up. Whether the 'train' was 'desperate' (reckless) or not is another question, which throws us right back to Goneril's charge that her palace has been turned into a bear-garden; surely Kent's behaviour to Oswald has not suggested that the rest of Lear's followers were outstandingly well-behaved. It is, then, reasonable to assume that Lear's 'train' at the end of Act II are 'desperate', at least in the sense in which Regan uses the word; and if they are desperate there is every reason why Gloucester should shut his doors against them. Lear, after all, has just a few moments before been threatening –

> I will have such revenges on you both
> That all the world shall – I will do such things –
> What they are yet I know not, but they shall be
> The terrors of the earth! (II.iv.275)

What more appropriate 'revenge' than a night attack by a desperate band of soldiers? In any case, the advice that Gloucester should shut his doors (advice repeated immediately by Cornwall) turns out to be quite superfluous: Lear, as he openly said, would rather die than go back.

In view of all this, I think the interpretation of the daughters' actions given by Lear and his followers is very partial – a series of statements by interested parties who can't escape blame. Goneril and Regan have plenty of

provocation, which is such that we can't avoid asking ourselves the hurtful question, 'All right then, what would *you*
have done with Lear?' He is their father; he behaves impossibly; so apparently do his knights; when remonstrated
with he loses his temper, will not discuss the conduct of his
followers or any change in the domestic arrangements,
resists Albany's attempts to mediate (I.iv.262, 274) – just as
he resisted all attempts to mediate in I.i when he was casting
off Cordelia – will not be taken in save on his own con-
ditions, and flings out into the storm for no reason other
than that, like a child, he can't get his own way. It is in
this frame of mind, this towering rage, that he says he was
'shut out' (III.iv.18); and it was as a follower of his, possibly
desperate, that Kent (III.ii.63) was denied entrance.

I think this is a fair account of the text up to early in Act
III, though by now I shall have provoked, no doubt, a lot of
disagreement. The trouble is, however, that when we look
back at the first half of the play from the second half, the
above account looks all wrong. What has happened, I think,
is that Shakespeare (as so often) isn't too concerned to
preserve consistency, and he wanted to use Goneril and
Regan to carry out two quite different functions, which don't
coincide completely (whether or not this is a fault I shall
consider later). So they have to change as the play goes on.

   The change I have in mind starts in III.iii, is further
developed in III.iv and emerges into unequivocal explicitness in III.iv. It paves the way for the blinding of Gloucester
in III.vii and indeed for the whole action of the last couple of
Acts. The first hint of any radical change in the presentation
of Goneril and Regan occurs, as I said, in III.iii, where
Gloucester tells Edmund that they are acting differently
from before:

> When I desired their leave that I might pity him [Lear], they
> took from me the use of mine own house, charged me on pain of
> perpetual displeasure neither to speak of him, entreat for him,
> or any way sustain him.   (III.iii.2)

The tone implied by 'charged me on pain of perpetual displeasure' is quite different from Cornwall's tone to Gloucester at the very end of Act II:

> Shut up your doors, my lord; 'tis a wild night:
> My Regan counsels well. Come out o' th' storm.
>
> (II.iv.304)

Cornwall there was addressing the Earl pretty much as an equal; but the reported words in III.iii suggest that he has now asserted himself in a quasi-regal way (as a sort of Joint Prince Consort, one supposes), aided and abetted by his wife and Goneril. The royal plural is clearly discernible behind that 'perpetual displeasure', although, as we shall see, the displeasure itself is going to turn into something much more sinister within a surprisingly short time (in fact all the events from II.iv to III.vii inclusive apparently take place on the same night). Indeed, within a few lines in the same scene we get a different notion of what 'displeasure' might imply:

> If I die for it (as no less is threatened me), the King, my old
> master, must be relieved.   (III.iii.17)

It's a long step indeed from displeasure to death, all in a dozen lines, but this is not the most surprising of the developments in these scenes. Shakespeare's method is, as we have just seen, to give first a small extension of what we have already heard and then to follow it up within a short time by a larger extension, so that we are made to think we are registering a steadily logical process of development. For example, in the next scene we first have the small extension:

> my duty cannot suffer
> T'obey in all your daughters' hard commands.
> Though their injunction be to bar my doors
> And let this tyrannous night take hold upon you,
> Yet have I ventured to come seek you out
> And bring you where both fire and food is ready.
>
> (III.iv.148)

We already know about barring the doors, but the next line, which insinuates an *active* desire on the daughters' part that Lear should suffer, pushes their malice a little further. The real surprise comes a dozen lines later when, in reply to

Kent's comment that Lear's 'wits begin t' unsettle', Gloucester says

> Canst thou blame him?
> His daughters seek his death. (162)

This is the first we have heard about any plan to kill Lear; but it is a trifle ambiguous, because it could mean either 'his daughters want to kill him' or 'they have left him to his fate (and you know what *that's* likely to be at his age and in this weather)'. I think the ambiguity is deliberately insinuated and paves the way for the entirely explicit reference to a plan to kill Lear – nearly at the end of the mock trial scene, when Gloucester says to Kent,

> Good friend, I prithee take him in thy arms.
> I have o'erheard a plot of death upon him...
> If thou should'st dally half an hour, his life,
> With thine, and all that offer to defend him,
> Stand in assuréd loss. (III.vi.87)

This explicates the first of the two alternative meanings of 'his daughters seek his death'; and it is only when we wrest these pronouncements from their contexts and consider them together that we can see how far we have come in such a short space – less than one Act, to be precise. And we can also see how misleading it is to look back from Act III to the earlier Acts and to read into them intentions and meanings which don't actually develop till halfway through the play. Indeed, in the light of Acts III and IV it would be perfectly possible to construct a plausible argument to the effect that Goneril and Regan had always intended something like this to happen. After all, there is the (on this reading) sinister conversation they have at the end of I.i, when Goneril says,

> Pray you let us hit together. If our father carry authority with such disposition as he bears, this last surrender of his will but offend us. (I.i.300)

Much depends on how we take this – which in turn depends on what we think the words mean, for anyone can elaborate a range of meanings from mere discontent right up to explicit plotting. For example, 'hit together' no doubt means 'agree together'; but agree *to what*? To trying to get rid of their father, or to bringing him to his senses? There is no way of telling, here, so we have to look at later scenes with much care. However, we can more confidently gloss the rest of the speech as meaning roughly, 'if our father goes on acting with such authoritativeness as we've just seen [in the disowning of Cordelia and Kent], despite the fact that officially he's abdicated, then his abdication will cause us more annoyance than if he'd remained king' (I have adapted this from Muir and Duthie). I can think of interpretations of the phrase 'will but offend us' that would give it a nastier ring (e.g. 'will be so offensive that we'll have to take steps ... '), but such readings would, I think, merely be prejudging the issue. My commentary on this speech may sound evasive, but I want the reader to keep an open mind.

All this of course raises the question of whether the inconsistency between the girls of Acts I and II and the girls of Acts III to V is not too gross to be acceptable. I'd be inclined to answer this query by saying simply: Shakespeare succeeds. But I would have to add that he succeeds so well in deluding us into believing in the daughters' consistency that we tend, as I said, to read back into their earlier behaviour hints of their later. Of course, it would be a matter for critical condemnation if the later daughters *couldn't* have developed out of the earlier ones: it would be absurd, for instance, if we were asked to think of Cordelia as blinding Gloucester, or Regan being imprisoned with her father in 'joyful renunciation'; but if that kind of thing happened we would merely say Shakespeare was incompetent and cease to read him.

Nevertheless, there is a critical problem, which is sufficiently exposed by the (as I see it) wildly inaccurate account of what 'happens' in Act II given by the *Oxford Companion* – and innumerable critics. If a well-known Shakespeare play can suffer so much misrepresentation at the hands of intelligent readers (and even H. A. Mason is not sure whether to talk about Lear's being 'locked out' or

'let loose into' the storm[1]), is that Shakespeare's fault or
ours? How should we read him? How much consistency
should we expect or demand? Obviously such questions
can't be answered in the general way in which I've put
them. But if it is true that, at one point in a play, some
propositions are true of certain characters, and at another
point, later on, other but not contradictory propositions are
true of the same characters, then we are obviously confronted
with a difficult task in distinguishing between surprising
development and flat incredibility. The trouble is that
critics are so eager to give Shakespeare credit for the uni-
form and steady development of character within each play
that they don't allow him to proceed, when he wants to,
by fits and starts; and the upshot is that not merely does
King Lear get itself misread in some important respects, but
also Shakespeare is deprived of any recognition for his
dramatic tact in keeping Goneril and Regan offstage for
nearly a whole Act (II.iv to III.vii) so that their surprising
evolution can proceed by hearsay, in terms of 'hints
followed by guesses', and so that it never occurs to us to
question whether they could have changed so much in so
short a time.

IV   THE NAKED TRUTH

It is natural enough that Lear and his partisans should give
a somewhat biased account of what happened about his
'expulsion'; it is natural enough too that the expulsion
should be something his mind runs on obsessively during
Acts III and IV. And in answer to the question I raised in
section II – if Lear isn't worried about his treatment of
Cordelia, what *is* he worried about? – we need only look at
the things that keep rising to the surface of his mind. I
would maintain that there is a definite thread connecting
pretty well all he says, that it mostly refers to his 'expulsion',
and that its nature is such that we can't help asking in what
sense a man in whose mind *this* is uppermost is on the path

1 Mason, *Shakespeare's Tragedies of Love*, pp. 195, 196.

to spiritual health. Nor, I shall maintain, can we avoid wondering in what sense such a man can be credited with discovering as much of The Truth as (going with his en- lightenment of spirit) he is often believed to have found.

The note Lear continually strikes is heard first, as a matter of fact, in the scene where he quarrels with Goneril:

> Ingratitude, thou marble-hearted fiend,
> More hideous when thou showest thee in a child
> Than the sea-monster!   (I.iv.260)

A little later, at the end of his dreadful curse on Goneril, he asks that Nature should

> Turn all her mother's pains and benefits
> To laughter and contempt, that she may feel
> How sharper than a serpent's tooth it is
> To have a thankless child!   (287)

'Ingratitude' and 'thankless' are the words that strike the keynote: the sentiment echoes endlessly through what is to come. We need only recall a few phrases: 'Monster Ingratitude!'; 'Sharp-toothed unkindness ... '; 'Dues of gratitude – thy half o'th'kingdom'; 'I gave you all ... '; 'Ingrateful man ... '; 'Filial ingratitude ... '; one could go on indefinitely. The point I'm allowing these quotations to make for me is that what Lear continually comes back to is the (to him) incredible fact that Goneril and Regan, to whom he gave away his kingdom, are not grateful enough and even suppose that they have rights over him and that he has duties towards them. This is the thing his mind can't cope with, this is what drives him to his most gigantic out- bursts of rage. And for him to say that his elder daughters are ungrateful means, obviously, that he is saying 'it's all their fault'; it never occurs to him to wonder whether what has happened mayn't have been his fault, even partly. If that is the case, how can we say (for example) that 'through suffering, Lear learns wisdom and attains salvation'?[1] At all events, it is worth looking at the storm and mad scenes with that redemptive proposition in mind.

[1] Duthie, edn cit., p. xxxiii.

What strikes me about the first of them (III.ii) is that Lear is very much aware of the figure he's cutting; but now, instead of only having a domestic scene to act in, he has the universe; and he would be happy if it were overwhelmed by some cosmic deluge so long as what happened was in harmony with his feelings. But those feelings change so swiftly that his psychological relation to the storm keeps changing *pari passu.*

> Blow, winds, and crack your cheeks! rage! blow!
> You cataracts and hurricanoes, spout
> Till you have drenched our steeples, drowned the cocks!

He begins by speaking as one who is the equal of the elements, or even their superior: he can command them to do his bidding. What follows seems to continue the same note but actually there is now a difference:

> You sulphurous and thought-executing fires,
> Vaunt-couriers of oak-cleaving thunderbolts,
> Singe my white head!

Starting as being apparently another command to destroy others, this switches at the end to being a plea to destroy him: he is now seeing the elements as allies of Goneril and Regan, and the fact that his head is 'white' makes him, or should make him, an object of pity.

> And thou, all-shaking thunder,
> Strike flat the thick rotundity o'th'world,
> Crack Nature's moulds, all germens spill at once
> That make ingrateful man!

This is a return to the anarchic desire to bring everything down with him ('Weltmacht oder Niedergang!'); but the feelings become more complex the moment we interrogate them. What, for instance, is Lear identifying himself with, the annihilating thunder or the annihilated world? But then, *can* the world be annihilated? isn't its 'thick rotundity' something that is clearly going to resist the thunder? In fact Lear is torn between the desire for self-destruction and the desire for revenge; but the self-hatred is only a means to self-pity, and while he calls 'man' in general 'ingrateful' he

has no sense that he might be so accused himself. Earlier
on, Lear has called Goneril

> a disease that's in my flesh,
> Which I must needs call mine. Thou art a boil,
> A plague-sore, or embosséd carbuncle
> In my corrupted blood. (II.iv.218)

But he only means this in the sense that she has, as it were
from the outside, infected him; he doesn't mean that it is
his 'corrupted blood' which has produced this plague-sore of
a daughter. Not till very much later does the possibility
dawn on him that he might himself be involved in the
disastrous human condition; and (as I shall argue later) it is,
even then, doubtful how far he really wants to implicate
himself.

When Lear resumes after the Fool's interjections, his
mind has drifted back to the quarrel-scenes:

> I tax not you, you elements, with unkindness:
> I never gave you kingdom, called you children;
> You owe me no subscription. (III.ii.16)

He is still thinking of gratitude as something that can be
calculated, and being consciously generous in not arraign-
ing the storm; then he rapidly changes from nobility to
pathos:

> Then let fall
> Your horrible pleasure. Here I stand your slave,
> A poor, infirm, weak, and despised old man...

But if he is their slave, whose slave are they? –

> But yet I call you servile ministers,
> That will with two pernicious daughters join
> Your high-engendered battles 'gainst a head
> So old and white as this. O, ho! 'tis foul!

It seems to me that the only constant element in this
kaleidoscope of shifting relationships is Lear's sense of
grievance. Even when he steps briefly into the role of the
stoic –

> No, I will be the pattern of all patience;
> I will say nothing (37)

– he clearly thinks that he has a good deal to be patient about and is demonstrating his forbearance in not specifying what. But a different preoccupation rises into consciousness a little later:

> Let the great gods,
> That keep this dreadful pudder o'er our heads,
> Find out their enemies now. Tremble, thou wretch
> That hast within thee undivulgéd crimes
> Unwhipped of justice. Hide thee, thou bloody hand,
> Thou perjured, and thou simular of virtue
> That art incestuous. Caitiff, to pieces shake,
> That under covert and convenient seeming
> Has practised on man's life. Close pent-up guilts,
> Rive your concealing continents, and cry
> These dreadful summoners grace. I am a man
> More sinned against than sinning.   (49)

Apostrophising the gods, Lear talks like a god himself, and what's more a pretty vindictive one: his notion of divine justice is that it is supernaturally-sanctioned revenge, in which Lear takes part, in imagination, with a scarcely concealed gusto. It is easy to identify ourselves with his feeling of moral superiority, but I take it that the sheer wrongness of

> I am a man
> More sinned against than sinning,

with its deliberate repudiation of responsibility for Cordelia's fate, is meant by Shakespeare as a sharp reminder to us not to confuse destructive fury with disinterested justice.

When he first becomes conscious of the onset of madness ('My wits begin to turn', line 67) he at once speaks to the Fool with the first kind words we have heard during the play:

> Come on, my boy. How dost, my boy? Art cold?
> I am cold myself. Where is this straw, my fellow?
> The art of our necessities is strange,
> And can make vile things precious. Come, your hovel.
> Poor fool and knave, I have one part in my heart
> That's sorry yet for thee.

Critics usually date the beginning of Lear's salvation from

this point; I suppose no-one would question that it represents a new development of feeling on his part, and on the play's. But what we need to be careful about is reading this play in an evolutionary fashion, so that each sentiment Lear expresses is seen not merely as a passing feeling but as a conquered position. If we do that, and tactfully throw out of focus the many places where he could be said to lapse back into egotism or rage, we shall obviously emerge with a coherent line of development from lesser awareness to greater awareness; we shall also have failed to read what Shakespeare wrote because we shan't have grasped the essentially fitful and sporadic way in which Lear's insights arise and are then forgotten in the increasingly disordered whirl of his moral imagination. In the lines I have just quoted we can reasonably say that he is, for the first time, aware of somebody outside himself not as a means to self-gratification but as a separate suffering thing; we can also ask whether this concern for the Fool's welfare is maintained. At this point we tend to think ahead to the prayer for poor people in III.iv and see it as arising from this sympathy with the Fool. When we turn up the text, however, we notice first of all that Lear arrives at the prayer only after re-capitulating many of the obsessions we have heard previously:

> this tempest in my mind
> Doth from my senses take all feeling else
> Save what beats there – filial ingratitude!
> Is it not as this mouth should tear this hand
> For lifting food to 't? But I will punish home!
> No, I will weep no more. In such a night
> To shut me out? Pour on; I will endure.
> In such a night as this? O Regan, Goneril!
> Your old kind father whose frank heart gave all!
> O, that way madness lies; let me shun that!
> No more of that. (III.iv.12)

The difference between this and what we heard at the beginning of III.ii is that the phrases here are shorter, more ejaculatory: the mind is going its round of emotions faster and faster, from resentment to outrage to vengefulness to

stoicism again to outrage again to self-pity again. I presume
that the fantastic touch in 'your old kind father' is meant to
remind us anew just how far Lear is from grasping what he
was – and is.

Now we come to the prayer:

> Poor naked wretches, whereso'er you are,
> That bide the pelting of this pitiless storm,
> How shall your houseless heads and unfed sides,
> Your looped and windowed raggedness, defend you
> From seasons such as these? O, I have ta'en
> Too little care of this! Take physic, pomp;
> Expose thyself to feel what wretches feel,
> That thou mayst shake the superflux to them
> And show the heavens more just. (28)

A good deal is made of this by critics. Bradley said it is 'one
of those passages which make one worship Shakespeare';
Muir, that Lear 'becomes aware of the common humanity
he shares with the poor naked wretches'; and Duthie
concurs.[1] I can see that this is roughly what Lear is *saying*,
but in what spirit is he saying it? 'There! I've learnt my
lesson, haven't I?' seems to me to get near it; in other
words it is far less disinterested than it looks, because there
is a suggestion of bargaining with the gods – 'if I got my
throne back I would be certain to look after the poor better
in future; I admit I made a bad job of it in the past'. There
is, I think, a certain selfconsciousness about the nobility at
the end ('Take physic, pomp ... '): the cadences indicate a
kind of sombre satisfaction. And we note that he wants to
show the heavens more just', although he knows very well,
and has often said, that they are far from it; the implication seems to be of some artificial contrivance for making it
appear that things are nicer than in fact they are. Another
pointer to the entirely theoretical nature of Lear's feelings
for the poor is given by his reaction to Tom o' Bedlam, who
runs out of the hovel just after this speech. If they had been
genuine, you would have expected him to say 'this is
exactly the sort of poor fellow I was just talking about'. He

---

[1] Bradley, op. cit., p. 237; Muir, edn cit., p. liii; Duthie, edn cit., pp. xxxiii, xxxvii.

says nothing of the kind: 'Didst thou give all to thy
daughters? And art thou come to this?' (48) is what it
actually occurs to him to say – that is, he is making Tom into
a 'case', the case not of a man who was born poor (like the
'naked wretches') but that of a man who, like Lear, was
rejected by his daughters. In other words he is assimilating
Tom to himself, not going out to meet him as he momentarily did with the Fool. What finally makes the speech
indecisive in terms of Lear's regeneration, or rather
perhaps decisive as regards his lack of it, is the obvious
contrast with Gloucester's much later variation on the same
feeling (a standard critical comparison, of course):

> Let the superfluous and lust-dieted man,
> That slaves your ordinance, that will not see
> Because he does not feel, feel your power quickly;
> So distribution should undo excess,
> And each man have enough. (IV.i.66)

This seems to me the voice of real experience and real
feeling; where has Lear's speech anything to compare with
the colloquial bite and edge of Gloucester's 'that will not
see / Because he does not feel'? – words spoken, moreover,
by a man who has just had his eyes torn out.

Lear's reaction to Tom o' Bedlam indicates, as I implied,
not how aware of the poor he has become, but how totally
insulated he still is from them; indeed it is the irruption
into his morally cosy world of something he had never
apparently dreamed of that is mainly responsible for throwing his mind finally off balance. If that is what happens in
III.iv, we can't avoid the conclusion that Lear will henceforward talk about what is really on his mind, without any
social or moral restraints: so that as his madness grows upon
him we can take what he says as being a progressively truer
account of the contents of his mind.

Nevertheless, critics are fond of symbolical interpretations
of incidents in this scene, notably where Lear tears off his
clothes with the words:

> Is man no more than this? Consider him [Tom] well. Thou
> ow'st the worm no silk, the beast no hide, the sheep no wool, the

cat no perfume. Ha! Here's three on's are sophisticated: thou
art the thing itself. Unaccommodated man is no more but such
a poor, bare, forked animal as thou art. Off, off, you lendings!
Come, unbutton here!   (III.iv.103)

Kenneth Muir's comment runs as follows:

The Bedlam beggar provides [Lear] with a living example of the
poverty he has been pitying; and by tearing off his clothes he identifies himself with unaccommodated man...[1]

The trouble is that it is no solution to the problem of poverty
to make yourself poor; you don't accommodate people by
unaccommodating yourself, any more than you morally
become 'the thing itself' by contriving to look like it. What
Lear is really doing, I think, is seeing Tom as being *essentially* like himself, in that they have both been disowned
by their daughters: so he sets to work to make himself look
externally like Tom so that the outer man shall jump with
the inner. The logic is crazy, of course, but then so is Lear –
and that is the point. One may wonder why critics have been
so eager to find something enlightened and enlightening in
Lear's feelings here. An obvious answer is that they are
determined to make Shakespeare edifying, somehow; a
less obvious answer is that I think a good many of us are
conditioned to regard kicking the bottom out of things as
being in itself a sign of wisdom – to believe that the real
truth about things is invariably reductive and rather mean,
much as Svidrigailov does in *Crime and Punishment* when
he says:

Men always represent eternity as an incomprehensible idea, as a
something immense – immense! But why should this necessarily be
the case? Imagine, on the contrary, a small room – a bathroom, if you
will – blackened by smoke, with spiders in every corner. Supposing
that to be eternity!   (Part IV, chapter 1)

There is no need to suppose that Svidrigailov speaks for
Dostoevsky; nor that Lear necessarily speaks for Shakespeare: though clearly both characters are being made to
contemplate a possibility. I say a possibility, and not a fact;
Lear's question, 'Is man no more than this?' remains

[1] Muir, edn cit. p. liv.

strictly a question for the play and for us, if not (at this moment) for him. Even so he is deceived because Tom is not what he seems: the irony of his later calling Tom a 'noble philosopher' prevents us from taking it as a simple truth.

What are we to think of the point Lear's mind has reached in the mock trial scene? His mood has certainly changed since the end of III.iv, where he was calm: now the keynote is set by

> To have a thousand with red burning spits
> Come hizzing in upon 'em! (III.vi.15)

His thoughts, that is, have reverted to revenge, and it is to take this revenge that he ordains the trial. Whatever significance we think ought to be attached to his prayer for the poor, earlier, and his tearing off his clothes, it doesn't now seem that those incidents marked any permanent advance in insight; if anything he has lapsed back into the mood of

> I will have such revenges on you both
> That all the world shall – I will do such things –
> What they are yet I know not, but they shall be
> The terrors of the earth! (II.iv.275)

It is no accident that Tom o' Bedlam says, pointing to an imaginary devil, 'Look where he stands and glares!' and later, 'Croak not, black angel': we can scarcely avoid the thought that it is Lear's expression and tone that have put the words into his mouth, any more than we can avoid seeing that Lear is still acting as King and supreme justiciar, with a dissociation from the actual state of things which now seems absolute. He, though the plaintiff, has the arranging of the court: to Edgar he says 'Come sit thou here, most learned justicer,' and to the Fool, 'Thou sapient sir, sit here.' The actual crime he charges Goneril with is curious:

> I here take my oath before this honourable assembly, she kicked
> the poor king, her father. (III.vi.46)

176

He is too mad now even to remember what he thought her
real crime was; but, after the 'corruption in the place' has
let the daughters escape, he is very sure about the penalty:

> Then let them anatomize Regan; see what breeds about her heart.
> Is there any cause in nature that makes these hard hearts? (75)

Commentators are notably shy about glossing 'anatomize':
actually it means 'dissect, cut up', so that the suggestion
seems to be of vivisection. It's horrifying enough to make us
wonder whether we are supposed to think 'yes, that's the
just thing to do'. At all events, the next scene shows us
that kind of justice in action, with Cornwall tearing out
Gloucester's eyes, when Lear's 'red burning spits' become all
too real as bloodstained fingers. The analogy-by-juxtaposi-
tion leads to further disquieting thoughts about Lear's
notion of justice – not an eye for an eye, but a life for a
kick. This isn't to deny the King his power to move us, for
instance when he says

> The little dogs and all,
> Tray, Blanche, and Sweetheart; see, they bark at me. (61)

And for that matter 'let them anatomize Regan' moves us
too, but only because of its appalling witness to Lear's moral
breakdown – not because it is discovering what is true, or
proper, or right.

The final mad scene (IV.vi) is generally felt to embody Lear's
most searching insights into justice and authority; people
feel that there is something peculiarly, even fearfully,
significant about him here. And people believe that in this
scene the insights achieved earlier converge into a definitive
statement. Duthie says that some of Lear's words – the ones
about the 'rascal beadle' and the whore – recall the words of
Christ to the woman taken in adultery ('He that is without
sin among you, let him first cast a stone at her') and that
they show Lear to have acquired a 'sense of common
humanity'. D. A. Traversi speaks of Lear 'exposing instincts
which normally remain hidden under the "simperings" of
affected "virtue"'; by so doing he is revealing the 'true

state of man'.[1] I should quote at greater length from Kenneth Muir because he makes fully explicit the assumptions underlying the claims just mentioned:

> . . .in the fourth act, we see [Lear] in a new stage of self-knowledge. He realises that he has been flattered like a dog, and that a king is merely a man. He inveighs against sex, partly because, as the Elizabethans knew, certain kinds of madness are accompanied by such an obsession, and partly because sexual desire has led to the birth of unnatural children, if indeed their unnaturalness does not prove that their mother's tomb sepulchres an adulteress. Lear returns to the subject of justice and authority in his next long speech. "A dog's obeyed in office." All men are sinners, and successful men cloak their crimes and vices by the power of gold. Justice is merely an instrument of the rich and powerful to oppress the poor and weak. But since all are equally guilty, none does offend. Since all are miserable sinners, all have an equal right to be forgiven.[2]

What worries me about this comment is that the critic doesn't quite seem to realise what he is committing himself to. Let us look at Lear's main speeches to see if we can work out what our attitude ought to be:

> They flattered me like a dog, and told me I had the white hairs in my beard ere the black ones were there. To say 'ay' and 'no' to everything that I said! 'Ay', and 'no' too, was no good divinity. When the rain came to wet me once and the wind to make me chatter, when the thunder would not peace at my bidding, there I found 'em, there I smelt 'em out! Go to, they are not men o' their words: they told me I was everything; 'tis a lie – I am not ague-proof. (IV.vi.96)

One wonders how profound a sort of self-knowledge this is meant to be. Admittedly Lear sees he has been flattered (and not only by his daughters) and that, like any other man, he gets wet when it rains; but is there much more to it? I know you could say these are very considerable admissions for a man like Lear: but all that concedes is that, in absolute terms, he doesn't get very far. And what seems to me to underline the poverty of his self-knowledge is what he doesn't say; he sees he has been flattered but doesn't admit that, after all, *he* asked for flattery, he wanted people to

---

1 Traversi, op. cit., II, 166.
2 Muir, edn cit., pp. liv–lv.

agree with him, and now he is surprised that others 'are not men o' their words'. It is an odd sort of self-knowledge that attributes all faults to *les autres*; odd too that the admission 'I'm not a superman' should clearly be accompanied by the thought 'but I wish I were'. The references to flattery can only have been included by Shakespeare to make us realise sharply that to accuse other people of flattery without saying you invited it is to display the very reverse of self-knowledge.

The adultery speech lands us in yet deeper water:

> When I do stare, see how the subject quakes.
> I pardon that man's life. What was thy cause?
> Adultery?
> Thou shalt not die. Die for adultery? No!   (108)

We note that Lear is still behaving as king and justiciar, so that, arbitrarily enough, he can pardon the man's life before finding out what he has been condemned for. And would anyone maintain that he isn't enjoying his ability to make the subject quake?

> The wren goes to 't, and the small gilded fly
> Does lecher in my sight.
> Let copulation thrive: for Gloucester's bastard son
> Was kinder to his father than my daughters
> Got 'tween the lawful sheets.
> To 't, luxury, pell-mell! for I lack soldiers.

I take it that the mention of Edmund, with the blind Gloucester standing there (Lear doesn't yet recognise him), is supposed to make us compare and contrast the two fathers and their treatment by their children. If having one's eyes gouged out is not a 'kinder' fate than flinging out into a storm, we can't help asking what the extravagant wrongness is meant to say about Lear's moral priorities. Now comes the sickened revulsion from the orgy of copulation he has just been enjoining:

> Behold yond simp'ring dame
> Whose face between her forks presages snow,
> That minces virtue and does shake the head
> To hear of pleasure's name;

> The fitchew nor the soiléd horse goes to 't
> With a more riotous appetite.
> Down from the waist they are centaurs,
> Though women all above.
> But to the girdle do the gods inherit,
> Beneath is all the fiend's.
> There's hell, there's darkness, there is the sulphurous pit;
> Burning, scalding, stench, consumption: fie, fie, fie, pah, pah!

It seems to me inadequate to talk, in this context, about
'Christian dualism', as Heilman does.[1] The emphasis falls
too overwhelmingly on the soilure and the stench of the
female Yahoo for us to be able to think even notionally of
the other half of the alleged duality. I am in the habit of
startling my students by asking them, tactlessly no doubt,
whether they think that what Lear is saying about Woman
is *true*. They tend to answer that, while it certainly isn't the
whole truth, they can imagine moods in which it would
seem so. If anyone feels like this all the time, and says so,
we call him mad and give him psychiatric treatment – and
we know very well that Lear *is* mad. Perhaps comparison
will suggest what we are to think:

> I have heard of your paintings too, well enough. God hath given
> you one face and you make yourselves another, you jig, you
> amble, and you lisp, you nickname God's creatures, and make
> your wantonness your ignorance... (*Hamlet*, III.i.145)

or

> O thou public commoner!
> I should make very forges of my cheeks,
> That would to cinders burn up modesty,
> Did I but speak thy deeds. What committed!
> Heaven stops the nose at it, and the moon winks,
> The bawdy wind, that kisses all it meets,
> Is hushed within the hollow mine of earth,
> And will not hear 't: what committed, –
> Impudent strumpet! (*Othello*, IV.ii.75)

We don't say that Hamlet and Othello have discovered truth
when they express their nauseated loathing of woman as a
sexual being, we say their minds are unhinged – though

[1] Heilman, *This Great Stage*, p. 270.

both of them have some provocation, however illusory in fact. Lear hasn't any immediate provocation – the affair between Edmund and the sisters, even if he knew of it, hardly seems serious enough to provoke such an outburst. It is quite true, as Muir says, that he thinks of his own sexual desire as having led to the birth of unnatural children; but if that is true, he is surely making the most staggering generalisation from his own case. And that, I have been arguing, is what he does all along: he is not going out to meet reality, he is drawing it in and adapting it to his own needs – and, we notice, blaming women but not men for their pleasure in the sexual act. 'If my wife hadn't had such a riotous appetite, I'd never have had such daughters': but what about his appetite? What is he below the waist? If his discovery is that 'appetite is well nigh universal' (L. C. Knights[1]), how can he exclude himself? Yet in 'Let me wipe it first; it smells of mortality' (133) he identifies sex with death and thinks that a mere wipe will cleanse him from his – presumably quite nominal – involvement. We have no difficulty in recognising Lear as a great human force; whether we are supposed to accept that force at its own valuation is another matter entirely.

We come now to the final statement about Authority – 'a dog's obeyed in office':

> Thou rascal beadle, hold thy bloody hand!
> Why dost thou lash that whore? Strip thy own back;
> Thou hotly lusts to use her in that kind
> For which thou whipp'st her. The usurer hangs the cozener.
> Through tattered clothes great vices do appear;
> Robes and furred gowns hide all. Plate sin with gold,
> And the strong lance of justice hurtless breaks:
> Arm it in rags, a pigmy's straw does pierce it.
> None does offend, none, I say none. I'll able 'em;
> Take that of me, my friend, who have the power
> To seal th'accuser's lips. Get thee glass eyes
> And, like a scurvy politician, seem
> To see the things thou dost not. (159)

I find this disturbing; I also find disturbing the fact that

---

[1] Knights, *Some Shakespearean Themes and An Approach to "Hamlet"*, p. 91.

most other critics don't. Professor Muir, whom I quoted a
while ago, gives this as his summary of one tendency of the
speech: 'successful men cloak their crimes and vices by the
power of gold' – in other words he is not merely repeating
what Lear says but is endorsing it. Of course another way of
escaping from the disturbing power of the speech is to deny
that what Lear says is true at all; but this would clearly be
as dubious a proceeding as saying that it was quite true.
Lear's indictment of authority is doubtless true of his world,
the world of a mad and (as he feels) utterly rejected old
man; and it's true too of the regime he has left behind him
by his abdication that the dogs have come to power. On the
other hand, once we start trying to apply his indictment
more closely to the world of the play, we find that it doesn't
work specially well. It is only a short while since we saw how
little Cornwall's furred gown protected him from the fatal
attack of his own servant; while Gloucester's robes haven't
protected him at all. Indeed, one of the appalling things
about that scene (III.vii) is that the monster Cornwall gets
comfort and support from his wife when he is wounded (just
as Kent's fidelity is matched by Oswald's – to Dr Johnson's
disgust). It all depends, in IV.vi, how general you think
Lear (and Shakespeare) are trying to be. If the indictment
as it were takes off from the play and launches itself into a
general truth, we have no choice but to say that it is nothing
of the kind – that no society so profoundly corrupt could
last for six months; and that the appropriate word for that
kind of social thinking is 'cynical' or 'reductive'.

I have the same difficulty with this speech as with Lear's
others in this scene: how far is he applying his thoughts to
himself? Is he saying that *his* regime, before he abdicated,
was totally corrupt? If so, we are very much left to draw the
inference for ourselves – so much so that I doubt whether
Shakespeare, if he meant that to be the point, would have
left it so inexplicit. Perhaps he is including himself in the
'none' of 'None does offend, none, I say none'; but if he is
the manoeuvre is another piece of self-exculpation. In any
case, either from the Christian point of view or from any

other I can think of, it doesn't make much sense to think that there is absolutely no moral distinction between (say) Cornwall and Cordelia: are we to think the one's sadism no worse than the other's obstinacy? 'Since all are miserable sinners, all have an equal right to be forgiven,' says Muir, blandly; a Christian would I imagine retort that this is Pelagianism, if not worse; and even a non-Christian might be pardoned for being troubled about the practical effects of abandoning all discrimination.

What confirms me in believing that this scene has been freely misread is Lear's attitude to Gloucester. No doubt it is the fault of his madness that he doesn't at first recognise him and doesn't grasp what has been done to him or why; but I would expect a man who was on the highroad to re-generation to recognise that there was *someone there*, as he temporarily did with the Fool back in iii.ii. On the contrary Lear is living in a world with a population of one; that is his madness too, but I want to insist on how far it has gone. He sees Gloucester as a mere adjunct to the scene he is acting, a sort of stage 'prop' or 'feeder', mere grist to the incessant grinding of his mind; and while he is very con-cerned about the wickedness of beadles and the miseries of their victims, he doesn't seem in the least put out by Gloucester's blindness or by the fact that this victim is a former courtier ('I know thee well enough; thy name is Gloucester,' line 176). Lear, that is, responds to general ideas of suffering but not to the particular case – precisely as he did with Tom o' Bedlam in iii.iv. There, of course, Tom was gibbering madly; but here Gloucester speaks with quiet dignity, a dignity that has been very much earned, and the steady poise of a reply like 'I see it feelingly' makes Lear's outbursts sound bombastic. I am not saying that throughout this scene we respond to Lear with cold distaste, or anything like it: I am concerned that the poignant fullness of our response shouldn't make us suspend our thinking and feeling altogether.

It seems to me, then, that the 'truth' Lear sees in his madness, or the insight he has, is very partial and fitful. Of course, it can be argued that, although Lear himself understands little, we the spectators come, through witnessing his suffering, to understand very much more. This is a plausible-sounding argument, except that I'm not at all sure *what* it is that we come to understand. It can also be claimed that, while Lear doesn't grasp truths during his madness, he does after it – that, as a result of his reunion with Cordelia, he finds something more stable and disinterested; and that by the time she dies he has achieved a really significant relation with her and with the world. Is this true?

V REDEMPTION OR DISINTEGRATION?

The reunion of Lear and Cordelia (IV.vii) is poignant almost beyond anything else in Shakespeare: for the first time in the play, Lear is capable of reaching out to another human being as a person, admitting both his own humanity and the other's. When he met Tom o' Bedlam and the blinded Gloucester all he could do, as we have seen, was to draw them into his own derangement: the mad King, like the earlier sane one, could only see others as objects for the gratification of his feelings. The change is established so fully by the reunion scene, and is one which I imagine so many readers will agree about, that I gratefully take it as being something I don't have to argue.

Yet what for me takes the stress here is not only the change in Lear but also its extreme precariousness. Lear has come through to seeing a deep truth about the relation between the self and other people, or another person; but he is a ruin, and there is no real prospect that he will be able to make his insight a living one in the sense of its growing, embracing perhaps other people beyond Cordelia. And there is a disturbing sense too that, with the insight achieved, Lear's mind has lost something as well as having gained something: the terrible energy of his mania, his power to assemble and juxtapose strongly contrasting states of feeling, his drive towards generalising (however misguidedly) from experience. That makes me wonder about the accounts of him which see him to be 'resurrected as a fully human being' (Muir[1]); there is a sense in which, for his last three appearances, he's less than *fully* human – less *alive* than he was in his ravings. And it is this, quite as much as the external fact that war impends (we first hear a 'beaten drum' at the end of the previous scene), which makes me feel that the poignant precariousness of the reconciliation and what it tells us about Lear is given an almost unbearable edge, and makes me resist taking it as a kind of static moral position that Lear has finally conquered. It may all be snatched away by external events; or Lear's mind may simply crumble again.

His mood at the start of the last scene is very hard to make out; certainly all kinds of accounts of it are current, ranging from saying it is so detached from reality as to be quite unreal to saying that it represents 'the last stage of Lear's process of redemption, viz. a joyful and "serene renunciation of the world with its power and glory and resentments and revenges"' (Dover Wilson, quoting Bradley[2]). Bradley, elsewhere, seems to be making a rather different point, although (perhaps significantly) he doesn't follow it up:

> It is evident that Cordelia knows well what mercy her father is likely to receive from her sisters; that is the reason of her weeping. But he does not understand her tears; it never crosses his mind that they have anything more than imprisonment to fear. And what is that to them? They have made that sacrifice, and all is well. . .[3]

Bradley couldn't perhaps afford to press this any further, because if he had he would have found himself saying something that wouldn't have gone at all with his desire to retitle the play 'The Redemption of Lear'. He would have found himself saying that Lear is wholly out of touch with his surroundings and that the 'great enfeeblement' which he rightly notes as characterising Lear here isn't only

1 Muir, edn cit., p. lv.
2 In Duthie, edn cit., p. 263, referring to Bradley, p. 239.
3 Bradley, op. cit., p. 240.

physical. He may no longer be 'mad' in the sense of raving; but is he really aware of his surroundings? In reply to Cordelia's savage 'Shall we not see these daughters and these sisters?' Lear says:

> No, no, no, no! Come, let's away to prison:
> We two alone will sing like birds i'th'cage;
> When thou dost ask me blessing, I'll kneel down
> And ask of thee forgiveness. So we'll live,
> And pray, and sing, and tell old tales, and laugh
> At gilded butterflies, and hear poor rogues
> Talk of court news; and we'll talk with them too –
> Who loses and who wins, who's in, who's out –
> And take upon 's the mystery of things,
> As if we were God's spies; and we'll wear out,
> In a walled prison, packs and sects of great ones
> That ebb and flow by th'moon.   (v.iii.8)

Perhaps the problem is not so much what Lear's mood is, as what Shakespeare expects us to make of it. How far are we meant to see Lear's fantasy as being mere delusion? After all, he has good reason by now to know what his other daughters are like, so it is evasive for him to think that imprisonment is all they have to face. But what he says is fantasy in another way too, though less obviously. He is aware of Cordelia, indeed so aware of her that he won't think of anything else; but does he feel her as a *separate* human being with needs and desires that mayn't coincide with his own? Doesn't that indefinitely prolonged imprisonment (itself unlikely) imply a relationship of a pretty one-sided kind? It seems to me in fact that Lear is thinking of Cordelia not as a daughter but rather as a grand-daughter – an idealised child with whom he can spend the rest of his life playing in a golden glow; 'Have I caught thee?' a moment later suggests that Lear is already, in imagination, playing at 'catch', though the word also suggests his possessiveness. It doesn't occur to him to ask Cordelia how she would like to pass the time. His 'awareness' of her, then, is strictly an awareness on his terms. This may seem unsympathetic, but I am emboldened to press the point because William Empson has made it better than I can:

Relatedness with a young daughter in a prison cell may suit a man of eighty, but he should not assume it will suit her; if he has become so truly related, he might remember that she has just been married for love. The reason why she cries, however, is from sympathy with his shame if he ever becomes sane for a moment; because they are going to be killed anyhow. She feels he has merely got into another delusion . . . [1]

This is extreme, no doubt; nevertheless it is a necessary protest against the odd Quietism that some modern critics mistake for Christianity: the notion that spiritual health is in inverse proportion to engagement and commitment and in direct proportion to the degree of one's opting out. There is a flash of something different in Lear's final words in this episode:

> Upon such sacrifices, my Cordelia,
> The gods themselves throw incense. Have I caught thee?
> He that parts us shall bring a brand from heaven
> And fire us hence like foxes. Wipe thine eyes;
> The good-years shall devour them, flesh and fell,
> Ere they shall make us weep! We'll see 'em starved first.

According to commentators, it is 'renunciation of the world' that is the sacrifice the gods throw incense on; but I don't know what we are to suppose that Lear has renounced. He gave up his throne right at the beginning and indeed in theory gave up everything except 'The name and all th' addition to a king' (i.i.135); so what has he left? The 'world'? Well, but that seems to have given *him* up, pretty conclusively. We notice too that he is assuming Cordelia is as ready as he is to make the 'sacrifices', whatever they may be, although she is still a Queen in a much fuller sense than he, since the first scene, has been King.

The problem then that arises from Lear's mood here is this: we saw that in the mad scenes he became progressively less in touch with his surroundings and couldn't grasp people as people; the 'great rage' is certainly 'killed in him' now, but is the personality we see a fundamentally different one? Are his present intentions fundamentally different from what was implied in this? –

[1] William Empson, 'Next Time, A Wheel of Fire' (review of a book by Maynard Mack), *Essays in Criticism*, January 1967, p. 100.

> I loved her most, and thought to set my rest
> On her kind nursery. (I.i.122)

Lear is himself no longer thinking of killing people who
hurt him, but the implication of

> He that parts us shall bring a brand from heaven
> And fire us hence like foxes

seems to be that he will leave the killing to heaven – in
other words his notion of justice is still sternly retributive.
If an ugly egotism is (as we should all agree) the central
failing in Lear, it seems to me to be still very much alive.
Egotism, after all, has a great many ways of manifesting
itself, and some of them needn't, at first glance, be wholly
unattractive.

We can take these thoughts along with us to the last
episode of all, when Lear is mourning over Cordelia's corpse.
The main issue here is what sort of hope, if any, we should
feel. Some people have no difficulty in thinking enormously
comforting thoughts. Professor Irving Ribner, for example,
says that Lear

> has attained an ideal of Christian stoicism through acceptance of
> human love, which is a reflection of the love of God and of the perfec-
> tion and harmony of the universe – all of which in his madness he
> had denied. After such renunciation, which sets its seal upon the after-
> life of heaven, there is no possibility other than death, and in this
> instance a reunion in heaven for Lear with the Cordelia who has
> preceded him there. If Lear's final belief, as his heart breaks, that
> Cordelia lives is contrary to fact, this is of small significance, for
> Shakespeare's audience could not doubt that she dwelt, in fact, where
> her father soon would join her.[1]

We note how naturally the slackness of the prose consorts
with the assumption about Shakespeare's audience and

---

[1] Irving Ribner, *Patterns in Shakespearean Tragedy* (1960), p. 130. It is worth
remarking that in Shakespeare's day, and indeed until the early nineteenth
century, hanging killed a person not by dislocating his cervical vertebrae
but by slow strangulation; therefore, if the victim was cut down in time he
might be revived. This has two consequences for *King Lear*: (i) Lear isn't
merely deluded in hoping that Cordelia may come round; (ii) Cordelia's face
should be deep purple.

with a view of salvation which is in every sense facile – a view which seems to evacuate all significance from the religion it endorses. L. C. Knights gives a much more sensitive account of the play's close, as might be expected, but its tendency is similar:

…love is that without which life is a meaningless chaos of competing egotisms; it is the condition of intellectual clarity, the energizing centre from which personality may grow unhampered by the need for self-assertion or evasive subterfuge; it is the sole ground of a genuinely self-affirming life and energy. But – it may still be asked – how does this apply to Lear when he prattles to Cordelia about gilded butterflies, or when, thinking his dead daughter is alive, his heart breaks at last?…the question, ultimately, is not what Lear sees but what Shakespeare sees, and what we, as audience, are prompted to see with him. At the end, however poignantly we may feel – Lear's suffering is one of the permanent possibilities, and we know it – we are still concerned with nothing less than the inclusive vision of the whole; and it is that which justifies us in asserting that the mind, the imagination, so revealed is directed towards affirmation *in spite of everything*… For what takes place in *King Lear* we can find no other word than renewal.[1]

I feel very much less sure about that 'inclusive vision' than Professor Knights does; and in any case I rather doubt whether, at the end, we are able to bear anything in mind beyond Lear's agony. If the play ends, not with affirmation or renewal, but with disintegration and annihilation, then that, it seems to me, is what we are left with, however many hints of something better we may have had earlier on.

I need to justify my proposition about what we are left with at the end of *King Lear*; and the easiest way to do so is to compare its close with the ends of other Shakespeare tragedies, particularly with the mood the hero seems to be in as he dies. There is contemptuous defiance as in Coriolanus:

> O that I had him,
> With six Aufidiuses or more – his tribe,
> To use my lawful sword!

There is Cleopatra's abandoned self-surrender:

---

[1] Knights, op. cit., p. 101 (Knights's italics).

> Peace, peace!
> Dost thou not see my baby at my breast,
> That sucks the nurse asleep?...
> As sweet as balm, as soft as air, as gentle –
> O Antony!...
>   What should I stay –

Neither Coriolanus nor Cleopatra has been broken by suffering: in their deepest selves they are still untouched. On the other hand, the Macbeth we met in Act I has, by the end, long since been dead; yet the man who now finds life totally without meaning, a tale told by an idiot, can finally cry out

> Lay on, Macduff;
> And damn'd be him that first cries "Hold, enough!"

Othello, too, has been through a total inner collapse and the disintegration of his feeling for Desdemona has made his life meaningless too; but in his last speech (which I hardly need quote) he tries, most successfully, to pick up the pieces of himself and reassemble his shattered personality. By the time he commits suicide he has got back into what is for him a significant relation to his world. So has Hamlet: in his last moments he is quite consciously acting not merely as Crown Prince of Denmark but as King with the right to nominate his successor –

> I do prophesy th'election lights
> On Fortinbras, he has my dying voice.
> So tell him, with th'occurrents more and less
> Which have solicited – the rest is silence.

Different as these ends are, we can't imagine any of them suiting the spirit of *Lear*. The King is not concerned to cut a figure or be defiant or set the record straight. He can just recognise Kent, but is quite uninterested in Kent's role as 'Caius'; of Edgar and Albany he knows nothing; and when he is told

> Your eldest daughters have fordone themselves,
> And desperately are dead

all he can find to say is 'Ay, so I think'. His old vituperation flashes out once –

> A plague upon you, murderers, traitors all!

and there is the pathetic boast

> I killed the slave that was a-hanging thee . . .
>   Did I not, fellow?
> I have seen the day, with my good biting falchion
> I would have made them skip.

– but his being is centred on Cordelia, in a way that I think
no other tragic hero's is centred upon something outside
himself. In saying that I may seem to be endorsing Knights's
account of the end: if a man's being is centred upon another,
then there is clearly at least the possibility of affirmation and
renewal. I want to argue, though, that this possibility
depends on the *quality* of Lear's love for Cordelia. Obviously
my reading of the opening of v.iii is crucial: if I was right to
find a highly visible streak of egotism in Lear's devotion
there, I don't see any way of showing that it has since been
purged away. (Of course if the reader doesn't accept my
interpretation of the start of the last scene he will be unable
to follow me here either.) The quality of feeling that speaks
in lines like

> This feather stirs – she lives! If it be so,
> It is a chance which does redeem all sorrows
> That ever I have felt

can't be gainsaid; but what we are responding to is the
agonised *intensity*, not (or not necessarily) the *disinterested-
ness*, of the feeling. I don't want to belittle the close of
Lear; I do very much want to be quite clear about what
Shakespeare is undertaking to show us and what he isn't. I
think he shows us a love of rending intensity but is silent
on whether Lear feels it because Cordelia would be
answering his needs. He is as silent on this matter as he is
about what Lear can be supposed to see on Cordelia's lips
when, in his last words, he says:

> Do you see this? Look on her! Look – her lips!
> Look there, look there![1]

---

[1] In the Quarto the line 'Break heart, I prithee break' is spoken by Lear and
is his last utterance. All modern editors follow the Folio in giving the words
to Kent.

We all know what Bradley made of that and it has been repeated a great many times; I think the motive for saying that Lear dies of joy on believing Cordelia to be alive is that it's felt to be vaguely unsatisfactory if, instead of a final insight, we are left with a question; if, instead of coming at last to feel that Lear's suffering has been valuable and purifying, we are left with the question, Has it been?

The play doesn't end there, though. The last fifteen lines again contrast violently with the close of any other Shakespeare tragedy I can think of. There is little or no sense that the state – and how little Britain matters here compared to Scotland or Denmark or Rome! – will struggle on somehow:

> Our present business
> Is general woe

says Albany; and Kent says he is going off to die. The play's world seems to be running down: think how disastrous it would be if the King of France were produced here, like Fortinbras at the end of *Hamlet*, to carry on state affairs. Think, too, of the tone and dragging movement of the very last lines – the nearest we have to an epitaph for Lear – when Edgar says:

> The weight of this sad time we must obey;
> Speak what we feel, not what we ought to say.
> The oldest hath borne most: we that are young
> Shall never see so much, nor live so long.

Compare:

> Good night, sweet prince,
> And flights of angels sing thee to thy rest!

Whatever you may make of that in its context, anything remotely approaching it in *Lear* would sound irrelevant, not to say irreverent. It seems to me to be this play's peculiar strength that (contrary to what is commonly made of it) it refuses to offer consolations, let alone answers. What Lear has grasped in the reconciliation scene is at once snatched away not simply by the outcome of the war but also by the immediate disintegration of his mind – not, this time, into

raving mania but into a different kind of delusion which
takes the form of an incapacity for further experience, a
slipping into something approaching senility. As Empson
finely says, the best Lear can henceforward do is to relive
the wonderful moment over and over again. What he
grasped is almost impossibly difficult to keep and only too
easy to lose.

VI   SOME CRITICAL CONSEQUENCES

What I have been trying to do so far is to show that *King
Lear* should not, and indeed cannot, be read along redemptivist lines. The many accounts of the play elaborated during
the last seventy years which propose a redeemed Lear and
an edifying play are simply ignoring the evidence – though
I realise that in this context 'evidence' is a tendentious
word.

I don't pretend, however, that my reading disposes of any
of the critical problems about *King Lear*: the reading was
offered not in order to solve problems but merely as being,
in my view, more accurate. And the major problem that is
raised by my account will now be obvious to everybody. If
Lear doesn't exhibit some kind of clear forward progression
– if the storm and mad scenes don't show the King to be
getting anywhere in particular – what is the play's *rationale*,
and why does Shakespeare give us no fewer than four
storm/mad scenes? What is the point of showing us a Lear
who in III.ii is saying to the Fool

> Come on, my boy. How dost, my boy? Art cold?
> I am cold myself   (68)

while three scenes later he is shouting

> To have a thousand with red burning spits
> Come hizzing in upon 'em!   (III.vi.15)

– or, in other words, if Lear's mind is not achieving insights
but merely going round and round, why is that interesting
or significant? (This is a question that I think George Orwell
and William Empson should have asked themselves.)

Two answers, or kinds of answers, seem possible: either we must explain the significance of the play quite differently from the way in which the conventional accounts explain it; or else the significance of the play is not merely other than, but actually inferior to, what is commonly assumed – that is, *King Lear* is much less successful than people have thought. Now this, I believe, is why the redemptivists have appeared to put such a strong case that they have carried all before them: because everyone can sense, even if unconsciously, that once you abandon the idea of moral progression as the organising principle of this play, there is little likelihood of your being able to find another principle which appears to explain anything like as much or which is remotely as satisfying – satisfying, that is, if you go to works of art for the working-out of patterns. And it might as well be admitted that, once we start looking at the parts of the play I have hitherto ignored, we find all sorts of things that are difficult to integrate into any reading of it. No doubt we can, in general terms, see the point of the sub-plot; but when we descend to the particular, and start asking questions about, say, the point of the intrigue between Edmund and the daughters, or Gloucester's mock-suicide, or the fight between Edgar and Edmund, we are likely to emerge either with answers that are far from reassuring or with no answers at all.

Take, for instance, the Edmund–Goneril–Regan affair. A common way of justifying it is to say that morally it provides a pretext for Lear's Adultery speech and that dramatically it ensures the deaths of the two sisters at the end. The trouble about the first of these claims is that the whole affair is carried on in a tone which is too light to justify anything as savage as the Adultery speech. Edmund soliloquises like this:

> To both these sisters have I sworn my love;
> Each jealous of the other, as the stung
> Are of the adder. Which of them shall I take?
> Both? One? Or neither? Neither can be enjoyed
> If both remain alive: to take the widow

> Exasperates, makes mad her sister Goneril;
> And hardly shall I carry out my side,
> Her husband being alive. Now then, we'll use
> His countenance for the battle, which being done,
> Let her who would be rid of him devise
> His speedy taking off. (v.i.55)

'Nonchalant' is Bradley's word for the tone of this, and my entire agreement with him leads me to ask what on earth nonchalance is doing at this point in the play – these are the accents of a Richard III at the beginning of his career when all the options seem open. Even if we could justify Edmund's flippancy on the grounds that he is that sort of character, we would still be hard put to it to find, in this speech or any of the others concerning the intrigue, sufficient engagement on Shakespeare's part for us to feel that sexuality is pressing on him here as intolerably as it does on the mad Lear. That, it may be said, just goes to show how little we should take Lear as registering fundamental truths; but then that brings us back to my previous point – if Lear isn't proclaiming basic truths or insights, what *is* he doing and what is its interest? We may of course have some kind of justification for Lear's feelings in Albany's outburst when he sees through his wife:

> If that the heavens do not their visible spirits
> Send quickly down to tame these vile offences,
> It will come
> Humanity must perforce prey upon itself
> Like monsters of the deep. (iv.ii.46)

But the context shows that Albany is thinking of the sisters' 'madding' of their father, not their affair with Edmund; and in any case, his belief in 'visible spirits' and even in the heavens themselves has been so thoroughly undermined that the lines are almost pathetic in their ingenuousness. The same is true, I think, of his reflection a little later on hearing of Cornwall's death:

> This shows you are above,
> You justicers, that these our nether crimes
> So speedily can venge! (78)

Again the context is important, because what comes immediately after makes nonsense of the comfortable sentiment:

> But, O poor Gloucester!
> Lost he his other eye?

'Both, both, my lord', answers the messenger, and Albany's
'justicers' dissolve on the spot.

As to the dramatic function of the adulterous intrigue,
one can freely admit that it gives Shakespeare an opportunity to dispose of Goneril and Regan without too much
fuss in the last scene; but that seems to me a singularly weak
explanation of what comes to look like a mere pretext. It
seems pretty excessive to invent a whole three-sided relationship, which Shakespeare doesn't do much with *as*
a relationship, merely in order to ensure a tidy ending; and
anyway the whole business of the intercepted letter (see IV.
vi.259 and V.iii.154) is so clumsy that 'tidy' stops looking
like the right word. When the knot is finally untied (or
should I say 'cut'?), the contrivance is awkward almost to the
point of ludicrousness: the dagger is

> hot, it smokes;
> It came even from the heart of – O, she's dead! . . .
> Your lady, sir, your lady: and her sister
> By her is poisoned; she confesses it.   (v.iii.222)

Edmund's comment doesn't improve matters:

> I was contracted to them both; all three
> Now marry in an instant.

Isn't there too audible a click, as of the last piece fitting
into a predetermined pattern? Isn't this kind of planning,
and writing, a matter of will and conscious contrivance
which for that reason look shabby in a play whose most
striking moments erupt from much deeper?

The same kind of uneasy questions arise, I think, when
we consider the duel between Edgar and Edmund. Mr
H. A. Mason makes a useful comment when he says that
what offends him even more than the 'absurd bombast' of
Edgar's challenge (v.iii.126f.) is 'the wrong decision

Shakespeare gave in the knightly ordeal'.[1] After all, it is
Edmund who has throughout been presented as aggressive
and who has kept in trim as a fighting-man; so that at the
meanest level of plausibility it seems improbable that the
gullible and impractical Edgar, whose military exploits
have been confined to killing the feeble Oswald, would win
the fight – unless, that is, we are being invited (as Mr
Mason also suspects) to find the finger of Providence just
where a decent man would expect it to appear. Even more
disturbing, if possible, is the trick – I really can't find any
more dignified word for it – by which Edmund is made to
hold back for ninety lines the information that he has
ordered Lear and Cordelia to be killed. This would be a little
less obviously contrived if what went on in those ninety
lines were interesting or even relevant; but Edgar's account
of his father's death and of Kent seems to me so much word-
spinning, especially in a play which, over the Fool, has
shown a sovereign carelessness about dismissing an important character. The only memorable remark in the
whole episode is Edgar's suspiciously gnomic

> The gods are just, and of our pleasant vices
> Make instruments to plague us:
> The dark and vicious place where thee he got
> Cost him his eyes. (169)

Is Shakespeare momentarily giving in (as he does with
Albany) to the temptation to find *some* moral value or order,
however unrelated to the brutal facts of the *Lear* world,
as a stay against nihilism? Perhaps; but I fancy that such
pronouncements, in this context, are self-cancelling, and
certainly shouldn't be taken as offering a positive that one is
meant to accept in a play where the opposite constantly
turns out to be the case. Again, if we ask what reason
Edmund could be supposed to have for wanting Lear and
Cordelia out of the way, all we can find is this:

> As for the mercy
> Which he [Albany] intends to Lear and to Cordelia,
> The battle done, and they within our power,

1 Mason, op. cit., p. 221.

> Shall never see his pardon: for my state
> Stands on me to defend, not to debate   (v.i.65)

– an explanation which seems to me to explain very little. (Bradley was rightly sceptical about the way in which Shakespeare produces the final catastrophe.)

Even if we could ignore these lapses as being venial, the problem of Gloucester would still remain. Whether we see him in Act III as a subordinate or (following Mr Mason) as a main figure, it is still hard to tell exactly what Shakespeare is doing in the episode of his mock-suicide. The orthodox account is that Gloucester has fallen into the sin of despair, and that Edgar, by preventing him from taking his own life, preserves him both physically and morally:

> Why I do trifle thus with his despair
> Is done to cure it   (iv.vi.33)

says Edgar, and we are meant (or so people claim) to take such words at their face value. What is more, when Gloucester recovers himself after having, as he thinks, fallen hundreds of feet, Edgar in his new role describes the Tom o' Bedlam who let him fall as a loathsome devil; this clearly indicates what our attitude should be. Gloucester is cured of his despair and says that he will henceforth 'bear affliction'. What could be plainer than Shakespeare's intention here, and what could be more straightforwardly moral?

I am inclined to retort that it is all *too* straightforwardly moral for a play which has continual doubts about the very foundations of morality; and that in any case I am very much less certain about whether or not this was in fact Shakespeare's intention. Take, for instance, Edgar's description of the beggar-devil:

> As I stood here below methought his eyes
> Were two full moons; he had a thousand noses,
> Horns whelked and waved like the enridgéd sea.
> It was some fiend.   (69)

This seems to me pretty absurd – the diabolism is of the folklore kind we found in Tom's speeches in the scenes on the heath, and the lines obstinately and (as it were) defiantly refuse to compose any imaginative picture, despite their being couched in strongly visual terms. 'He had a thousand noses' pushes what Wilson Knight called 'the comedy of the grotesque' into the realms of farce. The effect of this passage must therefore be to call into question the gravity of the temptation embodied in the 'fiend'; and logically it should also make us uneasy about the emergence from that temptation represented by

> Henceforth I'll bear
> Affliction till it do cry out itself
> 'Enough, enough,' and die. (75)

Now, it is easy enough to defend this and similar episodes by saying that what look like weaknesses are precisely the point; that the play is holding up to ridicule the notion that a 'despair' as utter as Gloucester's could, or should, be cured by a pantomime trick like Edgar's; that the consoling strength Gloucester derives from not dying is a shabby fake. And from this view we could generalise about the last couple of Acts of *Lear* and claim that, whenever consolation appears to be offered, we and/or the characters are always being grossly deceived – particularly in the last scene when from time to time it looks as though things might still work out well for the good characters. Solutions are offered only to be snatched away again: hence the frequent recurrence of peripeteia. Gloucester's mock suicide is immediately followed by Lear's last mad episode, and (we may argue) in the light of that insane nihilism the easy consolations offered by Edgar and accepted by Gloucester melt away. Edgar is Shakespeare's Houyhnhnm and, like Swift's, is carefully 'placed'.

The problem is, though, that even if the mock suicide were not followed by the Lear episode, the consolation would still seem too easy, and if we followed Gloucester in grasping the offered straw we would only be convicting ourselves of having read the verse incompetently. More-over, even if the consolation stands self-condemned, and doesn't need Lear to dispose of it, the way in which it is offered seems curiously slack. *King Lear* is not a play that, in view of the tremendous vitality of the storm scenes, for example (though how far that vitality is consistently directed is another question altogether), can afford a slackening of urgency. It is simply not good enough to have the diabolical temptation 'placed' by the devil's being described in reductive terms, because our sympathies are affronted and indeed outraged by the way in which Gloucester is cheated of peace. Immediately after Edgar's words about the supposed devil, he says:

> Therefore, thou happy father,
> Think that the clearest gods, who make them honours
> Of men's impossibilities, have preserved thee.   (72)

In view of what the play has been implying about the gods, Edgar's remark seems almost pointlessly naive, and it wouldn't be strong enough to offer due resistance to those implications even if it were not at once followed by 'No, they cannot touch me for coining; I am the king himself.'

The point I am making about this episode can be generalised to include a good deal of the last two Acts. Apart from episodes that concern Lear and/or Cordelia, is there much in Acts IV and V that anyone finds especially memorable? Doesn't Mr Mason point out an obvious and awkward truth when he says that some critics, in order to get the 'moral pattern' to work out right, mark up a lot of rather poor writing?[1] Is it reasonable to suggest that the double plot became for Shakespeare, after Act III, more of a liability than an asset – and not merely a 'theatrical' liability, a moral and imaginative one too?

Nevertheless, the judgment that in matters which aren't strictly crucial Shakespeare's touch falters doesn't necessarily mean that over matters which are crucial – what concerns Lear, primarily – we have to express similar doubts. Yet, as I was implying before, I cannot help feeling reservations about the significance of what is supposed to be happening to Lear in his madness; most of all in IV.vi.

[1] Mason, op. cit., p. 220.

Since I seem to be almost alone in finding any major problems here, I must conclude that I am likewise alone in finding much of what Lear says wholly repellent: not merely the reverse of enlightening but such that I can only reject it vehemently. That, of course, may be Shakespeare's point; but it is in practice hard to feel that we are being *invited* to do anything as detached as 'placing' Lear, much less turning our backs on him. The accents are those of total engagement not only on Lear's but also, one feels, on Shakespeare's part – so much so that I wonder whether Middleton Murry wasn't on the right track when he suggested that what we have here is something personal to Shakespeare and that this is why Lear's thoughts don't seem to arise naturally and inevitably from the dramatic context. Certainly when I think of the Adultery speech in comparison with 'Tomorrow, and tomorrow, and tomorrow ... ' or 'O what a rogue and peasant slave am I ... ' or 'Soft you, a word or two before you go ... ' (to take three examples from roughly contemporary plays that happen to come to mind) I cannot see that Lear's words are extruded, forced out of him, in the same way – that there's nothing else, at this point, he *could* say.

One consequence of thinking along these lines is that we would have to accuse Shakespeare here, and perhaps elsewhere in the play too, of using the Lear persona somewhat as Yeats does Crazy Jane: Lear, because of his admitted madness, comes to represent for Shakespeare an almost irresistible temptation. If you write about a madman you are *ipso facto* dispensed from ordinary canons of sense, sequaciousness and relevance, and that being the case it takes a truly heroic effort to sustain them. I think Shakespeare when he wrote Lear was not, or not consistently, capable of this effort: whatever seized his imagination also seized on private disgusts which remain obstinately private. I know that this is very much a minority verdict; but I must say that when I read and re-read the critics, I look in vain for some comment on Lear's madness which doesn't start from the assumption – almost the axiom – that he is continually discovering painful *truths*: truths which are at their most painful, but also at their truest, when he talks about sex and authority. In any case, the problem isn't only that there is nothing which endorses the 'truths' in my experience (which may be deficient), but also that, as I've said, the play itself hardly seems to support them.

Perhaps I can now come back to the question I started this essay with: was George Orwell right to say that 'Lear dies still cursing, still understanding nothing'? From what I've been saying, it will be obvious that I think this implies a much more accurate account of the play than the redemptivist ones. My objection to it is that it is too definite. I don't think that except in the reconciliation scene we ever find out how much Lear has really 'understood'; and the critical point this observation leads me to make is that throughout the piece there are continual teasing suggestions that he has understood a very great deal – suggestions which the redemptivist critics have, therefore, some excuse for having followed up and made into the point of the play. No-one of course will deny that at some points Shakespeare's imagination is working very intensely indeed – at times in a way that makes us feel *King Lear* is different in kind from any other Shakespeare play (except perhaps *Macbeth*). But to talk about the astonishing local vividness of realisation is not necessarily to imply that the local vividnesses compose a properly held and felt whole; and the judgment that Shakespeare in *Lear* is sometimes at his very greatest doesn't of necessity mean that the play is all of a piece.

In fact, as I have been saying, I don't think it is all of a piece: the moving things in the last two Acts seem to me increasingly hard-won victories – and I don't only mean victories over the general tendency towards collapse and meaninglessness but also assertions of creativity and imagination over the increasing dominance of will and a panicky urge to get the play finished somehow, even at the cost of imposing ethical *ideas* on the characters. And having said that, I must briefly return to an issue I discussed at the end of section III, where I was talking about the change in Goneril and Regan as between the end of the second Act and the end of the third. I concluded there that the change from egotists to demi-devils didn't matter, because it was at least plausible and served purposes which were arguably quite respectable; but I remarked (without following it up) that, when we glance back at the first half of the play from the second, it looks all wrong to call the sisters merely egotists and Lear at least as much sinning as sinned against. Now, pondering the doubts I have about the last couple of Acts, I wonder whether there isn't a disturbing shift of emphasis and sympathy as regards the King himself. If we are meant to respond wholeheartedly to his mad anguish, or indeed to respond with any fullness at all, don't we have to forget almost completely what sort of figure he was cutting in Acts I and II, and don't we have to replace the notion that he left his daughters out of angry pride by the vague feeling that he was bodily thrust out? This is at any rate one way of taking the significance of the sorts of claims made by Kent, Gloucester, Cordelia, and Lear himself. And perhaps, too, this is a reason for the sudden disappearance of the Fool: after Act III, Lear must no longer be subject to such stringent and pointed criticism. Then we notice how skilfully Shakespeare manages the role of Albany so as to give apparently disinterested confirmation to Lear's view of Lear. We don't see Albany at all between I.iv (the quarrel with Goneril) and IV.ii, so that he plays no part in the quarrel of Act II or the horrors of Act III; and when he finally reappears he says to his wife

> What have you done?
> Tigers, not daughters, what have you performed?
> A father, and a gracious agéd man,
> Whose reverence even the head-lugged bear would lick,
> Most barbarous, most degenerate, have you madded.
>
> (IV.ii.39)

Here words like 'gracious' and 'reverence' are forcibly insinuating a view of Lear as being like King Duncan – a view which it is hard to reconcile with pretty well anything we have seen of him but which is necessary if we are to respond appropriately to remarks like Edgar's

> I would not take this from report. It is,
> And my heart breaks at it. (IV.vi.140)

It seems to me that Albany is used in the last two Acts so chorically that we aren't encouraged to speculate about his significance; even when what he says is naïvely moralistic, as in his comment on the death of the sisters –

> This judgment of the heavens, that makes us tremble,
> Touches us not with pity (V.iii.230)

– we don't, I think, push our doubts about his reliability back to what he said about Lear: he is, simply, a good man who would like to believe in the justice of the cosmos.

The idea that is imposed on Lear (and on us) is therefore, I think, Lear's idea of himself –

> I am a man
> More sinned against than sinning.

This is another reason why the end of the play seems so questionable as a working-out of the situation set up at the beginning: unobtrusively (but, on critical reflection, unmistakably) our sympathies are shifted towards Lear. If they weren't, the final episode with the dead Cordelia wouldn't seem unendurable; and I think my earlier speculation, about whether Lear's being is centred on Cordelia because she would answer his needs, is irrelevant – not called for by the text of the play at that point: but it is very much called for if we read the last episode with a full sense of the *whole* play, not merely of Acts IV and V. I can represent the process by a quibble of my own: what we see is Lear *undergoing*, but what we are being asked to infer is Lear *understanding*. One may feel inclined to call this sleight-of-hand; I should prefer to think of Shakespeare as an artist who habitually discovered what he was doing as he went along but, when he got to the end of a play, usually didn't trouble to go back and rewrite earlier material that in the light of his final feelings would have seemed irrelevant or misleading. This may well have happened, in *Lear*, over the storm/mad scenes and the other things in the play that I've found artistically worrying.

At all events, I hope that if the reader shares some of my worries about the play I have given him some critical grounds for them. But I also hope I have suggested that *King Lear* is a very much more disturbing, and indeed lacerating, play than modern accounts of it usually concede. In fact some of my criticisms of (say) the mad scenes may very well be felt to cut the other way: the notion that we are being asked to see Lear understanding may be Shakespeare's way of saying 'hard though this is, real learning is still harder'. The spectacle of Lear learning in these scenes would, after all, flatter our complacencies; the spectacle of his *not* learning anything much till he kneels to Cordelia, and of what he then grasps being taken away at once, is nearly intolerable. It is not for nothing that Johnson was 'shocked'.

5. Antony and Cleopatra

I

ANTONY AND CLEOPATRA has often provoked questions such as:

Is [it]...a tragedy of lyrical inspiration, justifying love by presenting it as triumphant over death, or is it rather a remorseless exposure of human frailties, a presentation of spiritual possibilities dissipated through a senseless surrender to passion?[1]

While there are several terms here that one would want to question in any case ('spiritual', for instance), the main trouble is that the offered alternatives leave out of account what is surely, on any reading, a large part of the play. We can scarcely avoid noticing that parts of it are very funny (the galley-scene, for example, or Cleopatra and the messenger), but Mr Traversi's terms would exclude humour altogether as being at best peripheral and at worst totally irrelevant. Yet if the humour is really there and is functional rather than merely decorative, we have to ask what sort of play it is that can somehow combine humour with suggestions of love triumphant over death, and both of these with hints (if no more) of 'remorseless exposure'. It sounds already as though *Antony and Cleopatra* isn't a play that will yield itself to attempts to read it which depend on conventional assumptions about lyricism or about 'exposure' – or, come to that, about humour. Nor does it seem as though beliefs or assumptions about the nature of Shakespeare's art which we may have taken away from the earlier tragedies we have been looking at in this book will be of much use (even supposing, that is, that we have managed to arrive at any such assumptions). Whatever we may finally make of *Hamlet*, *Othello* and *Lear*, no-one, I imagine, would deny that in them Shakespeare is in deadly earnest: he is completely possessed by his interests; his art is

[1] D. A. Traversi, *An Approach to Shakespeare* (3rd edn, 1969), II, 208–9.

upsetting and frequently unnerving. But does anyone ever leave the theatre, after seeing *Antony*, feeling bruised? I doubt it; and while I wouldn't for a moment imply that *Antony* is no more than a *jeu d'esprit*, I want to suggest that 'seriousness' is a very different thing in *Hamlet* or *Lear* from what it is in *Antony*. The questions we have to ask, then, are about the *mode* of this play.

I think its mode is suggested at the very outset, in the well-known speech of Philo:

> Nay, but this dotage of our general's
> O'erflows the measure: those his goodly eyes,
> That o'er the files and musters of the war
> Have glowed like plated Mars – now bend, now turn,
> The office and devotion of their view
> Upon a tawny front: his captain's heart,
> Which in the scuffles of great fights hath burst
> The buckles on his breast, reneges all temper,
> And is become the bellows and the fan
> To cool a gipsy's lust. (i.i.1)

There is much wit here, but it isn't Philo's: the unknown soldier's hero-worship sounds idolatrous, perhaps only because he has an axe to grind in that he very badly wants to convince Demetrius *quantum mutatus ab illo*. Perhaps there may be something in Antony which could genuinely have inspired such devotion once upon a time, but Philo is skirting absurdity when he tells us that Antony's heart burst 'the buckles on his breast'. In fact, right at the start we are getting a view of Antony which is shared by most of the characters, including Antony himself – but it is a view to which no human being could possibly conform.

Though we may feel on our own account that Philo's praise is impossibly extreme, we have to wait for Antony's appearance to decide whether the charge of 'dotage' (foolish affection *and* senile folly) is just. Here I take it that the appearance of the eunuchs 'fanning' the 'strumpet' (whose 'fool' Antony is said to be) is pretty decisive, especially since the 'fanning' takes up Philo's word –

> the bellows and the fan
> To cool a gipsy's lust.

As the first scene develops it becomes clear that there is a
good deal in what Philo said about his master's decline, and
that we therefore can't dismiss his judgment as malicious;
so that the opening of this play is very unlike the opening,
say, of *Othello*, where it becomes plain very early on that
Iago has a grievance which explains his tone about *his*
master. In fact I can't think of any other Shakespeare play
where the first few lines so completely inhibit our sympathy
towards one of the main characters. Yet to speak of an
'inhibition' is to suggest that the opening is something like
that of *Troilus and Cressida*, where the wars and lechery
are placed by the Prologue with mordant dismissiveness,
and we can never thereafter feel any generosity of spirit
about what happens at Troy. In *Antony* the case is less
simple. Our mood is rather one of detachment, but a
detachment that is more amused than censorious: we are
not to be continuously involved with these people, so that
we can very easily afford to let them entertain us. I think
this means that the play isn't a tragedy, but it has its own
peculiar sort of desolating clarity about *bovarysme*.

   To talk about *bovarysme* runs full tilt into the quite
common account of the play which offers us the love between
Antony and Cleopatra as something 'transcendental'.
Even those critics who are unhappy about claiming anything so large nevertheless feel that there are continual
suggestions of something of the kind and that Shakespeare,
perhaps, never quite made up his mind what he thought or
wanted us to think. Mr Mason, for example, in his recent
book, is puzzled by the lovers' behaviour in I.iii: 'The two
characters themselves do not quite know where they stand'.[1]
I can see that there is much alternation of tone and mood in
this scene, but to say that the lovers don't know where they
stand would only be a criticism of Shakespeare if we
thought they *should*. I admit that the reason for Antony's
decision to go back to Rome remains pretty obscure, though I
suspect that on the stage the spectacle of several messengers
bringing news of various disasters that make Antony's

[1] Mason, *Shakespeare's Tragedies of Love*, p. 237.

position insecure would make the decision look reasonable enough. Whatever the reason, Antony does make up his mind to go, and the encounter between him and Cleopatra is superbly comic: Cleopatra tries on everything she knows to stop him, and Antony, even though he has his way in the end, mostly dances to her tune. Of course, there are lines which, out of context, look as though they are claiming something very large; for example:

> Nay, pray you, seek no colour for your going,
> But bid farewell, and go: when you sued staying,
> Then was the time for words: no going then;
> Eternity was in our lips and eyes,
> Bliss in our brows' bent; none our parts so poor
> But was a race of heaven . . .   (I.iii.32)

People's memories stop short there. But Shakespeare's heroine adds:

> . . . they are so still,
> Or thou, the greatest soldier of the world,
> Art turned the greatest liar.

Antony is furious, but Cleopatra taunts him still further. He can only stand up to her by addressing her as though she were a public meeting:

> Hear me, queen:
> The strong necessity of time commands
> Our services awhile; but my full heart
> Remains in use with you.   (41)

Commentators gloss 'in use' variously, but I don't see that it *means* very much; it is as verbal a protestation as Antony's remark at the end of the scene,

> Our separation so abides and flies,
> That thou, residing here, goes yet with me,
> And I, hence fleeting, here remain with thee.   (102)

We need only think of Donne to feel the hollowness. It is precisely of this that Cleopatra accuses him when he tells her of Fulvia's death:

> Where be the sacred vials thou shouldst fill
> With sorrowful water? Now I see, I see,
> In Fulvia's death, how mine received shall be.   (63)

She is very skilfully turning Antony's exaltedly plati-
tudinous tone against him (she is a brilliant parodist):
'sacred vials' is pure Wardour Street. Antony doesn't
notice he is being made fun of, though it does strike him
that he is being told off; and again he speaks with a sublimity
so gross as to be impudent:

> Quarrel no more, but be prepared to know
> The purposes I bear; which are, or cease,
> As you shall give th'advice. By the fire
> That quickens Nilus' slime, I go from hence
> Thy soldier, servant, making peace or war
> As thou affects. (66)

Obviously he himself really believes all this, though it is
laughably inconsistent: if Antony's 'purposes' really depend
on Cleopatra's 'advice', then he wouldn't be even thinking
of going away; and as Cleopatra has no apparent desire to
make war, Antony is merely being disingenuous in leaving
her the option. Her summary – 'So Antony loves' – is both
bitter and a simply true summary of what we have been
seeing in this scene and also earlier in the play. Again
Antony's reply seems remarkable for its unconsciousness:

> My precious queen, forbear;
> And give true evidence to his love, which stands
> An honourable trial. (73)

What sort of 'trial' is Antony saying that his love can or will
sustain? Does he mean that it's very trying to have to go to
Rome, or that Cleopatra is putting him through his paces?
In fact he could mean several things, but there isn't much
sense of his *meaning* any of them; all he offers is verbiage.
Cleopatra now makes him look so ridiculous that he threatens
to leave, to which Cleopatra answers

> Sir, you and I must part, but that's not it:
> Sir, you and I have loved, but there's not it:
> That you know well: something it is I would:
> O, my oblivion is a very Antony,
> And I am all forgotten. (87)

Apart from the obvious reproach, the lines make an appeal
to which Antony could have responded without loss of

face; but he is so annoyed by her earlier resistance that he
turns the knife in the wound:

> But that your royalty
> Holds idleness your subject, I should take you
> For idleness itself. (91)

It seems odd that Antony feels free to accuse her of 'idleness'
(frivolity) in view of his own behaviour in i.i. Cleopatra is
left with no weapon but her talent for burlesque and, quite
unnoticed by Antony, she gives in with a perfect take-off of
the noble-Roman pose which he has insisted on assuming:

> Your honour calls you hence;
> Therefore be deaf to my unpitied folly,
> And all the gods go with you! Upon your sword
> Sit laurel victory! and smooth success
> Be strewed before your feet! (97)

Cleopatra is doing this consciously, of course, but there are
plenty of places in this play where people fall into a similarly
heightened mode of speech in the effort to dissimulate (or
simulate) feelings.

When Caesar, for example, greets Octavia, saying he is
cross that she comes so poorly attended, he makes a great
fuss:

> You come not
> Like Caesar's sister: the wife of Antony
> Should have an army for an usher, and
> The neighs of horse to tell of her approach
> Long ere she did appear; the trees by th'way
> Should have borne men, and expectation fainted,
> Longing for what it had not; nay, the dust
> Should have ascended to the roof of heaven,
> Raised by your populous troops: but you are come
> A market-maid to Rome, and have prevented
> The ostentation of our love, which, left unshown,
> Is often left unloved: we should have met you
> By sea and land, supplying every stage
> With an augmented greeting. (III.vi.42)

This sounds all very fine until you realise that it is an
exceedingly elaborate way of blaming anyone but himself
for not having had her suitably met; and in the process he

pushes the idea of a proper welcome for her (whether she is considered as 'Caesar's sister' or as 'Antony's wife') to the point of ludicrousness. As we know from the beginning of this scene, Caesar realises that Antony has rejoined Cleopatra; in the quoted speech he is trying to build up her sense of her own worth so that she may be all the more offended when she hears that Antony 'hath given his Empire/Up to a whore'.

What is also remarkable about this heightened mode of speech in Caesar's welcome is that it seems to be peculiarly well suited to creating feelings of disappointment – creating a sense that the given experience didn't live up to expectations: that there is perhaps an intrinsic disappointment in the very nature of human experience. The verse realises over and over again *what might have been* – the possibility of which the actuality falls so lamentably short. Another speech of Caesar's, much later, looks on the face of it like a handsome, if conventional, tribute to the dead Antony:

> The breaking of so great a thing should make
> A great crack: the round world
> Should have shook lions into civil streets,
> And citizens to their dens. The death of Antony
> Is not a single doom; in that name lay
> A moiety of the world. (v.i.14)

We doubtless feel, on the level of 'character', that with Antony safely out of the way Caesar can afford this verbal generosity, just as Aufidius can afford it when Coriolanus has been disposed of. But the uncomfortable fact remains that what Caesar says is that he is surprised how *little* Antony's death seems to have meant to the world. Again the heightened mode is, paradoxically enough, realising a blankness or hollowness at the heart of things. Doesn't Bradley's striking phrase for our considered response to the play, 'the sadness of disenchantment',[1] have a singular, if unintended, felicity?

Of course the issue raised by Caesar's epitaph is one that

1 A. C. Bradley, *Oxford Lectures on Poetry* (1909), Papermac edn, 1965, p. 305.

confronts us throughout the play and especially when it deals with Antony. Why, one might ask, should Octavius have supposed that Antony's death ought to have caused such disturbances? Here we run straight into the problem raised by Mr Mason:

We are *told* I don't know how many times that [Antony] was a supreme specimen of humanity, so lofty indeed that to indicate the scale it was necessary to suppose that his nature partook of the divine. The Anthony who is presented dramatically never makes us believe in these reports.[1]

I maintain that this problem solves itself if you think that it was all along Shakespeare's intention to insist on the gap between what Antony is said to be and what he really is. No-one in the play ever quite grasps that the Mark Antony of the olden days – the man who at Philippi

> struck
> The lean and wrinkled Cassius

or who drank

> The stale of horses and the gilded puddle
> Which beasts could cough at

– has long been dead and has been replaced by a man who is much more human and therefore much less dependable. And the play's comedy stems, over and over again, from the fact that everyone (except Enobarbus) is a dupe of Antony's reputation – that is, a dupe of words. That is not, of course, an uncommon situation in Shakespeare; but quite often characters come face to face with their verbal evasions and are shattered by seeing that they are merely verbal; whereas in *Antony* that kind of tragic laceration never happens at all. The characters are so insulated from reality that they can't recognise it even when they stumble over it. What Enobarbus says is true:

> I see still
> A diminution in our captain's brain
> Restores his heart

[1] Mason, op. cit., p. 269.

and

Caesar, thou hast subdued

His judgment too

but one could scarcely, without doing violence to the whole tone of the play, maintain that such verdicts were *enforced* in the same way as Goneril's remark in *Lear,*

> The best and soundest of his time hath been but rash; then must we look from his age to receive, not alone the imperfections of long-engraffed condition, but therewithal the unruly waywardness that infirm and choleric years bring with them.

That has its accuracy cruelly enforced by what we have just seen and what we shall soon see again. *Antony and Cleopatra* is a peculiarly non-moral play, in the sense that people don't seem to have any particular convictions that this is the way to behave rather than that; time and again, where we might have expected someone's conscience to be troubling him, all we in fact get is a verbal pose or gesture, or a mere blank. For example, nobody in the play appears to think of the marriage between Antony and Octavia as having any human consequences for her or him: when Antony coolly says of it

> Yet, ere we put ourselves in arms, dispatch we
> The business we have talked of,

Caesar, Octavia's loving brother, finding nothing odd in the phraseology, simply replies:

> With most gladness;
> And do invite you to my sister's view,
> Whither straight I'll lead you.   (ii.ii.165)

From this it is obvious that, though people are the dupes of words, they are equally, when it suits them, masters of words: the trouble is that they keep confusing a mastery over words with a mastery over brute facts. Hence much of the comedy.

II

Once we have the idea in our heads that amusement is a permissible (and indeed essential) response to large tracts of this play, Antony's fury after Actium, his treatment of Thidias, and his row with Cleopatra, come into sharper focus than hitherto. If for example we want to say (as many critics do) that after Actium Antony has lost, finally and irrevocably, his self-esteem not merely in the world's eyes but, more importantly, in his own too, and that his sense of himself – of his identity as man and soldier – suffers an irreversible collapse, we shall be hard put to it to explain how he can switch so quickly from this

> Now I must
> To the young man send humble treaties, dodge
> And palter in the shifts of lowness; who
> With half the bulk o'th'world played as I pleased,
> Making and marring fortunes   (III.xi.61)

to this

> Fall not a tear, I say; one of them rates
> All that is won and lost: give me a kiss;
> Even this repays me.   (69)

The problem is that he doesn't seem to have been through any very important experience, although a few moments before, at the beginning of the scene, he was claiming that

> I am so lated in the world that I
> Have lost my way for ever.   (3)

What we have here is obviously a collapse of much more than what Enobarbus will call 'judgment': it looks more like a total moral evacuation – or at least it would if the play were being as stern about Antony as Enobarbus is. But it isn't; it never is. Its tone is not merely reductive even when Antony, challenging Caesar to single combat, couches his defiance in the high heroic mode:

> tell him he wears the rose
> Of youth upon him; from which the world should note
> Something particular: his coin, ships, legions,
> May be a coward's, whose ministers would prevail
> Under the service of a child as soon
> As i'th'command of Caesar. I dare him therefore
> To lay his gay comparisons apart
> And answer me declined, sword against sword,
> Ourselves alone: I'll write it: follow me.   (III.xiii.20)

Enobarbus is often used to place this kind of auto-intoxication. He comments here:

> Yes, like enough, high-battled Caesar will
> Unstate his happiness and be staged to th'show
> Against a sworder! I see men's judgments are
> A parcel of their fortunes, and things outward
> Do draw the inward quality after them,
> To suffer all alike. (29)

The further irony which Enobarbus doesn't grasp is that Antony is attributing to Caesar a (possible) cowardice that he himself has just shown – at least in the world's judgment – by running away from the fighting at Actium. And if the world should note 'something particular' of Caesar, what is it likely to think of Antony, now that his behaviour is beginning to give the lie to his old reputation? Yet the 'placing' by Enobarbus is more depressed than savage.

The succeeding interview between Cleopatra and Thidias is overtly comic. He tells her that Caesar

> knows that you embraced not Antony
> As you did love, but as you feared him. (56)

Her reply – 'O!' – could hardly fail to produce laughter in the audience whatever tone the actress adopted. Thidias goes on:

> The scars upon your honour therefore he
> Does pity as constrainéd blemishes,
> Not as deserved.

She answers:

> He is a god and knows
> What is most right: mine honour was not yielded,
> But conquered merely.

And Enobarbus is ready with another comment:

> To be sure of that,
> I will ask Antony.

It now looks as though Cleopatra, left alone with Thidias, is thinking about working her passage home, although it is not quite clear how far she is just teasing Thidias and how far there is some seriousness underlying the teasing: when she invites him to kiss her hand she sounds parodic –

> Your Caesar's father oft
> (When he hath mused of taking kingdoms in)
> Bestowed his lips on that unworthy place,
> As it rained kisses. (82)

This sounds ludicrous enough, especially in contrast to her words to another Messenger:

> and here
> My bluest veins to kiss: a hand that kings
> Have lipped, and trembled kissing. (II.v.28)

Perhaps, as with her farewell speech to Antony (at the end of I.iii), she is both satisfying her intelligence and also saying what the other person wants to hear.

Antony's attitude to her *rapprochement* with Thidias is curious. Earlier in the scene, when the Schoolmaster told him of Caesar's offer of 'courtesy' to her 'so she / Will yield us up', Antony had munificently said 'Let her know't' (16). But now, when he comes in at line 85 – Enobarbus having presumably told him that Cleopatra is thinking of quitting – he loses his temper, not with Cleopatra but, on the quite specious pretext of jealousy, with Thidias; and has him whipped. To keep one's dignity while losing one's temper is rather difficult, but Antony tries hard:

> Authority melts from me. Of late when I cried 'Ho!'
> Like boys unto a muss, kings would start forth,
> And cry 'Your will?' Have you no ears?
> I am Antony yet. Take hence this Jack, and whip him. (90)

Commentators don't seem to notice that in his rage Antony is saying the opposite of what he means: for if a 'muss' is 'a game in which small things are thrown down to be scrambled for' (Dover Wilson from *OED*) then what does that make Antony? He tries to belittle the 'kings' but succeeds in belittling himself even more. And we notice that he is now going to prove his powers undiminished by having Thidias flogged. Enobarbus' comment again places Antony's behaviour:

> 'Tis better playing with a lion's whelp
> Than with an old one dying.

But perhaps even this is too complimentary: an old lion

may be spiteful, but we scarcely expect him to be grotesquely sanctimonious, as Antony goes on to be when he rages at Cleopatra:

> You were half blasted ere I knew you...Ha!
> Have I my pillow left unpressed in Rome,
> Forborne the getting of a lawful race,
> And by a gem of women, to be abused
> By one that looks on feeders?   (105)

It is a useful debating-point to call Octavia a 'gem of women', but that's all it is; moreover Antony has never shown the slightest sign of wanting children to carry on the family name. As for the charge about being 'half blasted', Antony goes on to expand it a moment later:

> I found you as a morsel cold upon
> Dead Caesar's trencher; nay, you were a fragment
> Of Gnaeus Pompey's; besides what hotter hours,
> Unregistered in vulgar fame, you have
> Luxuriously picked out: for I am sure,
> Though you can guess what temperance should be,
> You know not what it is.   (116)

It is not merely that Antony has no right to take this kind of tone: it is also that Cleopatra has never set herself up as a moral paragon – she is honest about what she is in a way that Antony never is about himself. During this long outburst Cleopatra has been interjecting brief protests such as 'Wherefore is this?'; after the flogged Thidias has been dismissed she coolly asks 'Have you done yet?' – a question that cunningly combines contempt for Antony with the tacit assumption that all will soon be well and that the relationship will continue much as before. Antony's reply is in character:

> *Ant.*   Alack, our terrene moon
>   Is now eclipsed, and it portends alone
>   The fall of Antony.
> *Cleo.*   I must stay his time.
> *Ant.* To flatter Caesar, would you mingle eyes
>   With one that ties his points?
> *Cleo.*   Not know me yet?
> *Ant.* Cold-hearted toward me?

Cleo.   Ah, dear, if I be so,
    From my cold heart let heaven engender hail...

                                                    (153)

It is a ludicrous contrast between the eclipsed 'terrene
moon' Antony makes of the Queen and the married
shrug with which she waits for the storm to blow itself out.
But with the swerve into pathos in 'Cold-hearted toward
me?' Antony is obviously vulnerable again and, once again,
Cleopatra judges her tone exquisitely:

> From my cold heart let heaven engender hail,
> And poison it in the source, and the first stone
> Drop in my neck: as it determines, so
> Dissolve my life! the next Caesarion smite!
> Till by degrees the memory of my womb,
> Together with my brave Egyptians all,
> By the discandying of this pelleted storm
> Lie graveless, till the flies and gnats of Nile
> Have buried them for prey!

Yes, an exquisitely judged tone; and she must be very sure
of its effect on Antony to allow herself to call her Egyptians
'brave', a term which, in any of its senses, is about the least
appropriate that could be imagined. Yet Antony's reply is 'I
am satisfied'. A good many commentators are also satisfied:
they are too busy talking about the profound significance of
the imagery of fertility in decay to notice that, as she has
done before and will do again, the Queen is talking to her
lover in what we have come to recognise as Antony-
language – an idiom in which sense counts for little and
grandiosity for much. We recall the fifth speech we hear
Antony make:

> Let Rome in Tiber melt, and the wide arch
> Of the ranged empire fall! Here is my space.
> Kingdoms are clay: our dungy earth alike
> Feeds beast as man   (1.i.33)

or a passage I quoted earlier:

>   By the fire
> That quickens Nilus' slime, I go from hence
> Thy soldier, servant, making peace or war
> As thou affects.   (1.iii.68)

A good deal of the verse in the play falls into this kind of idiom: magnificent, buoyant, sonorous, and empty. If Antony were conscious enough of himself he could say

> J'attends l'écho de ma grandeur interne,
> Amère, sombre, et sonore citerne,
> Sonnant dan l'âme un creux toujours futur!

Of course one doesn't want to deny that Cleopatra's speech is good poetry despite its hollowness: it is good because it is funny, but the funniness, though kindly enough (on Shakespeare's part), is ultimately desolating in what it tells us about the engagements the two lovers think they have with each other. Cleopatra knows this is the only way to hold Antony, if indeed she really wants, by this stage, to hold him; while Antony will listen to any nonsense if it restores his *amour-propre*, although the very fact of his accepting it diminishes him still further in our eyes and, for that matter, in Cleopatra's. He goes on, here, to delude himself that 'There's hope in't yet,' and to prepare himself for the coming day's battle by having 'one other gaudy night'. There is nothing for it but to agree with Enobarbus when he calls all this a 'diminution in our captain's brain'; and those who want to make him out to be a nasty cynic, who really can't appreciate the full beauty of the relationship between the lovers, will have to explain why what he says is so often right – not merely intelligent, but accurate too. He usually speaks, in fact, with the voice of the play: which may well make us want to ask what sort of play it is which can afford to have its vision summed up by an Enobarbus – a play to the summing-up of which an Enobarbus is only too adequate. That may seem a harsh thing to say about Antony (and the play); but is there really, in the next scene but one, more to Antony's farewell to his servants than Enobarbus sees?

> Well, my good fellows, wait on me to-night:
> Scant not my cups, and make as much of me
> As when mine empire was your fellow too
> And suffered my command.　　　　　(IV.ii.20)

He says this, according to Enobarbus, 'to make his followers

weep'; of course Enobarbus has himself just decided to seek
some way to leave his master, so his view isn't disinterested;
but then Antony's own explanation isn't very convincing:

> I spake to you for your comfort, did desire you
> To burn this night with torches: know, my hearts,
> I hope well of to-morrow, and will lead you
> Where rather I'll expect victorious life
> Than death and honour. (40)

But it can't have been very 'comforting' for them to be told

> Haply you shall not see me more, or if,
> A mangled shadow. (26)

So that the far from impartial Enobarbus goes straight to the
point.

Yet even he dies deceived. Admittedly, Antony has
heaped coals of fire on his head by sending all his treasure
after him, and it is this that breaks his heart:

> O Antony,
> Thou mine of bounty, how wouldst thou have paid
> My better service, when my turpitude
> Thou dost so crown with gold! This blows my heart:
> If swift thought break it not, a swifter mean
> Shall outstrike thought: but thought will do't, I feel.
> I fight against thee! No, I will go and seek
> Some ditch wherein to die; the foul'st best fits
> My latter part of life. (IV.vi.31)

Yet we should beware of viewing Antony's generosity
exactly as Enobarbus does: after all, we have just been
seeing him make his servants cry, and if that episode has a
point at all it is to suggest that he badly needs to be thought
well of. His words when he hears of Enobarbus' desertion
are significant:

> Go, Eros, send his treasure after; do it;
> Detain no jot, I charge thee: write to him –
> I will subscribe – gentle adieus and greetings;
> Say that I wish he never find more cause
> To change a master. O, my fortunes have
> Corrupted honest men! (IV.v.12)

It all sounds so terribly sweet, but in fact no message could be more calculated to embarrass Enobarbus and make him feel a traitor. (If Antony had been a Christian, he would doubtless have added: 'And tell him I shall pray for him.') The strategy succeeds admirably: Enobarbus hates himself and his heart breaks. The trouble is, as Mr Mason complains, that the Antony we have been seeing is simply not worth this kind of devotion; but then that, it seems to me, is Shakespeare's point. It may also be true that he couldn't afford the dry pragmatism of Enobarbus any longer; he may perhaps have felt that if he was going to make any attempt at all to produce a *tragic* catastrophe, the belittler would have to go. But this would imply that the play is a tragedy *manqué*, and what I've been questioning all along is whether it is anything of the sort. Let us try to test these thoughts against what happens in the final episodes of the play – the defeat and death of Antony in Act IV and the suicide of Cleopatra in Act V.

III

In a way, the movement of IV.xii and xiii repeats that of III.x and xi (the battle of Actium); but whereas in the earlier battle – also lost through the defection of Egyptian forces – Antony needed little persuasion to return to his mistress, he this time has to hear that she is dead, and himself make a botched attempt at suicide, before they are reconciled. Antony's mood, when he sees the battle is lost, is as usual compounded of self-pity, furious indignation, and other pleasant emotions.

> O sun, thy uprise shall I see no more:
> Fortune and Antony part here, even here
> Do we shake hands! All come to this? The hearts
> That spanieled me at heels, to whom I gave
> Their wishes, do discandy, melt their sweets
> On blossoming Caesar; and this pine is barked,
> That overtopped them all.   (IV.xii.18)

Antony is poised between saying that he is very cross with the 'hearts' for having proved disloyal, and that he is contemptuous of them because their loyalty was in any case worthless (like dogs' affections). One wonders how clearly he grasps the ludicrous implications of the image – a sugared Antony being slobbered over by spaniels, dribbling back onto Caesar the melted sugar they have licked off him. He goes on:

> Betrayed I am.
> O this false soul of Egypt! this grave charm –
> Whose eye becked forth my wars and called them home,
> Whose bosom was my crownet, my chief end –
> Like a right gipsy hath at fast and loose
> Beguiled me to the very heart of loss.

Antony is fibbing in saying that Cleopatra 'becked forth my wars and called them home', rather as he did much earlier in the play –

> I go from hence
> Thy soldier, servant, making peace or war
> As thou affects.   (I.iii.69)

It is one of Antony's great talents to be able to convince himself that anything he wants to do is absolutely essential to Cleopatra's well-being. We can't leave the commentary there, however; we can't avoid facing the question, Is there something which substantiates that compelling phrase 'the very heart of loss'? I think the answer is best given by quoting another piece of Shakespeare:

> Why should a dog, a horse, a rat have life,
> And thou no breath at all?

I apologise for the shock. But if this tells us something ultimate about a sense of 'loss', I can only think that Antony's phrase is no more than a phrase, reminding us of that other remark, 'I / Have lost my way for ever.' Furthermore, the implications of 'fast and loose' aren't very flattering; Antony may intend the suggestion of laxity in 'loose' (as well as the whole phrase) to apply only to Cleopatra, but it takes something of a gull to *be* cheated. More generally, I think we are entitled to ask what we are to make of the military genius of a man who, already let down appallingly by the Egyptian navy at Actium, reposes his trust in it again. We don't regard Lord Lucan and Lord Cardigan as anything but figures from *opéra-bouffe*; why should we excuse Mark Antony?

Cleopatra enters with the question

> Why is my lord enraged against his love?

the artificiality and affectation of which must be intentionally absurd. If it is, how seriously can we take what it prompts, the raging of Antony between line 32 and the end of the scene?

> The shirt of Nessus is upon me: teach me,
> Alcides, thou mine ancestor, thy rage:
> Let me lodge Lichas on the horns o'th'moon,
> And with those hands that grasped the heaviest club
> Subdue my worthiest self. (43)

We know that Antony claims Hercules as his forbear, but the parallel isn't very exact: Deianira, Hercules' wife, gave him the poisoned tunic thinking that it would simply keep him faithful to her; whereas Cleopatra (or so Antony has been claiming) deliberately betrayed him. And while it was one thing for the legendary hero to throw his page Lichas into the sea, it is quite another for this big fleshy fellow to bluster about throwing him up high – 'on the horns o'th' moon' adds a disintegrating touch of pure farce. After adding, twice, that he is going to take his revenge by killing Cleopatra, Antony leaves, but returns after a short scene (IV.xiii) devoted to the Queen's deciding to have him told she is dead. But when he does re-enter, after being offstage for only a couple of minutes, his mood has swung from mindless fury to a sense of inner and outer dissolution:

> Sometime we see a cloud that's dragonish,
> A vapour sometime like a bear or lion,
> A towered citadel, a pendent rock,
> A forkéd mountain, or blue promontory
> With tree upon't, that nod unto the world
> And mock our eyes with air ...
> That which is now a horse, even with a thought
> The rack dislimns, and makes it indistinct

As water is in water...
                    ...now thy captain is
Even such a body: here I am Antony,
Yet cannot hold this visible shape...   (IV.xiv.2)

The poetry is so marvellous that there is a temptation (which we should resist) to drink it in without thinking about the implications of Antony's comparison. As soon as we do so, we realise that, thoughout, he is talking about an optical illusion which, in time, becomes obviously just that. The 'towered citadel', after all, was never more than 'air' together with the fanciful daydreaming of the beholder. Can he be saying that *he* has never been more than an illusory hero – a simulacrum substantiated by the admiring lookers-on? Hardly; but that, I think, is what Shakespeare means, and it is the gap between anything Antony can be supposed to intend and what his creator gives him to say that makes the lines comic in a peculiarly delicate way. He goes on to repeat a familiar claim:

I made these wars for Egypt, and the queen –
Whose heart I thought I had, for she had mine,
Which, whilst it was mine, had annexed unto't
A million moe, now lost – she, Eros, has
Packed cards with Caesar...   (15)

Linked with the urge towards self-exculpation ('I did it all for her sake') and the accusation ('it's all her fault') is the intolerable sense of betrayal ('she's let me down'). Such sentiments are understandable; but the moment Antony hears of the Queen's supposed suicide, his mood has changed again:

I will o'ertake thee, Cleopatra, and
Weep for my pardon.   (44)

Self-abasement could scarcely go any further, unless it does here:

Since Cleopatra died
I have lived in such dishonour that the gods
Detest my baseness.   (55)

Why doesn't Antony recall that a major part of his 'dishonour' comes not from Cleopatra's death but from her life?

It may be argued that the dishonour he feels most keenly is wholly connected with his love for her, and that military honour takes second place: he is now at last realising what genuinely matters to him. This would be a stronger argument if there were now the slightest chance that he could ever recover his military honour; if it were by this stage a matter of *choice*. Nor is his resolution to commit suicide new; before he heard of the Queen's death he was saying

> there is left us
> Ourselves to end ourselves. (21)

We know what he thinks will happen afterwards:

> Where souls do couch on flowers, we'll hand in hand,
> And with our sprightly port make the ghosts gaze:
> Dido and her Aeneas shall want troops,
> And all the haunt be ours. (51)

The following comparison is suggestive:

Ils allaient, ils allaient, les bras enlacés, sans parler. Souvent, du haut d'une montagne, ils apercevaient tout à coup quelque cité splendide avec des dômes, des ponts, des navires, des forêts de citronniers et des cathédrales de marbre blanc, dont les clochers aigus portaient des nids de cigognes...On entendait sonner des cloches, hennir les mulets, avec le murmure des guitares et le bruit des fontaines, dont la vapeur s'envolant rafraîchissait des tas de fruits, disposés en pyramide au pied des statues pâles, qui souriaient sous les jets d'eau... Ils se promèneraient en gondole, ils se balanceraient en hamac; et leur existence serait facile et large comme leurs vêtements de soie, toute chaude et étoilée comme les nuits douces qu'ils contempleraient.

(Flaubert, *Madame Bovary*, Part II, chapter xii)

Antony similarly seems to me to be indulging in a beautiful, but quite insubstantial, daydream. It is significant that Shakespeare makes him pick Dido and Aeneas as the spirits whom he and Cleopatra will replace as leaders. Antony, who thinks Cleopatra has just committed suicide, casts himself as the betrayer Aeneas; but we can't help remembering that, before he heard the news, he was thinking of himself as having been betrayed by the Queen, not vice-versa. Either way, the mythological overtones are not very reassuring. Mr Mason, in the book I have often referred to, comments on the speech that 'it makes a terrible draught on the previous scenes of the play', and that Antony, 'instead of living in the present and ending as a full person, ... projects himself into an unreal future'. I quite agree, but while Mr Mason is not sure whether or not Shakespeare knows what he is doing, I am arguing that *everything* we have seen about the lovers (separately or together) up till this point would lead us to expect Antony to evade reality in precisely this way, and that this speech, therefore, far from making too heavy a draught on earlier scenes, is an exact fulfilment of them. Mr Mason goes on to say:

What turns the scale for me is the emphasis on the admiration Anthony thinks they will get from the Elysian spectators. Shakespeare seems anxious to support this conceit by praising Anthony up well beyond any deserts shewn in the play. First, we have the repeated assertion that suicide is noble as well as prudent, and then the various forms of commentary.[1]

But the 'commentary' that Mr Mason goes on at once to refer to is the ludicrous one made by the soldiers when they discover (IV.xiv.106) that Antony hasn't made a clean job of his suicide; the implication of this would surely be that Antony's conceit is *not* being supported by Shakespeare, but undermined. In so far as the various forms of commentary endorse Antony and Antony's view of himself and his actions, they seem merely designed to show how totally his reputation has managed to impose itself on all around him (twentieth-century military history provides some instructive parallels).

Comedy – of a peculiar kind – is what takes the stress, too, in the scene of Antony's death. And if we want a text by which to test the either/or view of the play – the one that insists it is lyrical tragedy or remorseless exposure – we can do no better than listen to the notes struck here. Isn't it at least disconcerting to hear Cleopatra say this? –

> Here's sport indeed! How heavy weighs my lord!
>
> (IV.xv.32)

1 Mason, op. cit., p. 266.

with its echo of

> O happy horse, to bear the weight of Antony! (I.v.21)

And what are we to make of this exchange? –

Ant.	Give me some wine, and let me speak a little.
Cleo.	No, let me speak, and let me rail so high,
	That the false huswife Fortune break her wheel,
	Provoked by my offence.
Ant.	One word, sweet queen.
	Of Caesar seek your honour, with your safety. O!
Cleo.	They do not go together.
Ant.	Gentle, hear me:
	None about Caesar trust but Proculeius.
Cleo.	My resolution and my hands I'll trust;
	None about Caesar. (42)

In North's Plutarch, which Shakespeare is sometimes accused of having followed rather lazily, there is nothing corresponding to these repeated attempts by Antony to get Cleopatra to pay attention to what he is saying, and there is nothing either to suggest that Cleopatra, as usual, keeps on interrupting Antony, taking the words out of his mouth, refusing to follow his advice, and in general making him look a trifle foolish.[1] If we didn't know this was meant to be a solemn moment, could we infer it from the quoted passage? I doubt it; and my doubt makes me wonder just how solemn the moment is really meant to be. No doubt a critic who took the either/or view would want, if he were brought to see that there is an element of humour in Antony's death scene, to assimilate it to the 'ruthless exposure'; but then the trouble is that there is nothing in the least ruthless or exposing about this death-bed comedy, which (oddly enough) seems rather genial and kindly, almost indulgent, and most certainly not censorious or indignant. Nor is Shakespeare being evasive, as he is for example with Bertram at the end of *All's Well*; we don't find Dr Johnson saying, 'I cannot reconcile my heart to Antony'. That moral judgment is not engaged in any such manner in this play means we

---

[1] Cf. T. J. B. Spencer, ed., *Shakespeare's Plutarch* (Peregrine Books, 1964), pp. 280–1.

can't accuse the author of having at any point evaded it.
It simply never becomes an issue: and that seems to me an
important comment on how the play works and at what
level it appeals to us.

Before Antony's death, Cleopatra has been the more
'realistic' of the pair – shrewd, pragmatic, and honest. But
after it, a change comes over her; and we have to ask
whether she too becomes a slave of words. No-one will
deny that the verse she speaks is wonderful; and it is very
easy to see why 'transcendental' is a term that keeps
cropping up in accounts of the play –

> O, see, my women –
> The crown o'th'earth doth melt. My lord!
> O, withered is the garland of the war,
> The soldier's pole is fall'n: young boys and girls
> Are level now with men: the odds is gone,
> And there is nothing left remarkable
> Beneath the visiting moon. (IV.xv.62)

We don't have to agree with her to find the speech moving;
indeed, one reason why it is so moving is perhaps that she is
so completely self-deceived – and what is more, she is self-
deceived in a mode she has learnt from Antony. We again
recall this exchange:

> *Ant.*   Alack, our terrene moon
> Is now eclipsed, and it portends alone
> The fall of Antony.
> *Cleo.*   I must stay his time. (III.xiii.153)

This is what I earlier called 'Antony-language'; and what
happens is that, at the precise moment of Antony's death,
this language becomes the staple of *Cleopatra's* speeches.
Reality having finally become too unpleasant to face, she
takes her dead lover's way of not facing it. You could argue
no doubt that we get something real when she recovers
from her faint:

> No more but e'en a woman, and commanded
> By such poor passion as the maid that milks
> And does the meanest chares. (IV.xv.73)

She says this in reply to Iras' apostrophe, 'Royal Egypt,

Empress!' But we need to remind ourselves how she goes on:

> It were for me
> To throw my sceptre at the injurious gods,
> To tell them that this world did equal theirs
> Till they had stol'n our jewel.

Milkmaids don't have sceptres, nor is throwing one's sceptre a 'chare'. We need to remind ourselves, too, that she is a woman 'whom everything becomes' (and who, one might add, can become anything); that she doesn't decide to follow her lover's example until Dolabella tells her that Octavius is going to put her on show (see v.ii.110 and 197); and that, when she finally does kill herself, she dies not as a mere woman or milkmaid but as Queen and Empress – a point at which, significantly, the unusual word 'chare' crops up again:

> Show me, my women, like a queen: go fetch
> My best attires. I am again for Cydnus,
> To meet Mark Antony. Sirrah Iras, go.
> Now, noble Charmian, we'll dispatch indeed,
> And when thou hast done this chare I'll give thee leave
> To play till doomsday. Bring our crown and all.   (v.ii.226)

That Cleopatra mostly talks Antony-language in the last episodes of the play is confirmed by that dream-Antony she describes to Dolabella. We cannot write it off as merely, or even mainly, a tactic to bedazzle Dolabella so that he will tell her what Caesar intends to do with her, though that element is certainly present.

> His legs bestrid the ocean, his reared arm
> Crested the world: his voice was propertied
> As all the tunéd spheres, and that to friends;
> But when he meant to quail and shake the orb,
> He was as rattling thunder. For his bounty,
> There was no winter in't; an autumn 'twas
> That grew the more by reaping: his delights
> Were dolphin-like, they showed his back above
> The element they lived in: in his livery
> Walked crowns and crownets; realms and islands were
> As plates dropped from his pocket.   (v.ii.82)

I wonder if we are meant, when hearing about the 'rattling

thunder', to repel our memory of Antony's treatment of Thidias:

> Whip him, fellows,
> Till like a boy you see him cringe his face,
> And whine aloud for mercy.　　　　　(III.xiii.99)

or the bluster of

> O, that I were
> Upon the hill of Basan, to outroar
> The hornéd herd!　　　　　(126)

– to take two examples out of many. Likewise, the Antony we have been seeing did not 'grow the more by reaping', but consistently diminished. And in what 'element' did his delights live? A 'sea of pleasures', suggests Ridley, the Arden editor; is the Queen's suggestion, then, that he emerged from it only occasionally, to draw breath? Yes; but the dolphin's rise and fall also suggests love-making. At the same time we are reminded of other fish:

> Give me mine angle, we'll to th'river: there
> My music playing far off, I will betray
> Tawny-finned fishes; my bended hook shall pierce
> Their slimy jaws, and as I draw them up,
> I'll think them every one an Antony,
> And say 'Ah, ha! you're caught.'　　　　　(II.v.10)

When we come to the end of Cleopatra's eulogy, we may perhaps wonder why she is ascribing Antony's loss of 'realms and islands' to mere regal carelessness, when we have the two disastrous sea-battles fresh in our minds. In fact it seems to me that almost everything in this speech refers back to incidents we have seen and heard earlier in the play, and when we make such reference we find that the Queen's words are magnificent fantasy. I nearly said *just* magnificent fantasy, but the privative word is obviously questionable, if only because so many commentators have taken Cleopatra here to be glimpsing through (rather than in) Antony some reality of a transcendent nature. And by glimpsing it in such marvellous verse, Cleopatra creates it not only for herself but also for the play – for us. My rather reductive commentary (it could be argued) is accurate enough in its own way, but its own way isn't good enough. Yet, while no-one can doubt that Cleopatra is laying hold of possibilities that are intensely meaningful to her, we can't help asking, I think, whether these meanings really could emerge without deception from the possibilities that *we* have been allowed to see in Antony. It is understandable at the end of *Lear* that the King should see all value inhering in Cordelia, though, significantly, it is not something he can celebrate. But by the end of this play it seems to me that Antony is too discredited – genially and kindly, no doubt, but still discredited – for us to be able to simply accept what Cleopatra says as anything beyond a truth for her which is poignantly untrue for us. She can only glimpse what she does through Antony by forgetting about the real man altogether – which is precisely the point of my suggesting that much of what she says relates to what we have been seeing *per contra*. Yet Cleopatra herself, we notice a little later in the same scene, is not so convinced by her own vision that she can no longer imagine what other people (in this case the Roman mob) will make of the relationship: and for her to be able to set aside their view is more a tribute to her need than to the authenticity of her transcendental imaginings. The swelling plenitude of the Antony eulogy is surely qualified by the sharp focus and comic vivacity of this:

> saucy lictors
> Will catch at us like strumpets, and scald rhymers
> Ballad us out o'tune: the quick comedians
> Extemporally will stage us and present
> Our Alexandrian revels; Antony
> Shall be brought drunken forth, and I shall see
> Some squeaking Cleopatra boy my greatness
> I'th'posture of a whore.   (213)

Very coarse of them, no doubt, but *how* wrong would they be? Mightn't the Roman mob have contained a potential Veblen or two?

Antony and Cleopatra is not, of course, the story of a drunk and a whore: such a tale would be merely tedious. And in any case the play's vision is not simple and moralistic. But neither is it the piece that Wilson Knight and others make of it, a celebration and justification of transcendental love – Shakespeare's *Tristan und Isolde.* Its mocking clearsightedness inhibits that kind of simplicity too. To say, however, that simple responses of this kind are irrelevant is not necessarily to say, with Mr Mason, that the play is a string of fine moments with not enough organised around them. To read it like this is, I think, to bring to it assumptions about Shakespeare's art derived, perhaps, from earlier tragedies and to take it for granted that the playwright is trying to do the same kinds of things here as one may guess he was at any rate attempting there. The result is that the geniality of Shakespeare's art in *Antony*, its buoyant wit, become merely puzzling, and, having tried to make the play conform to what we think it ought to be, we fail to see what it is, and we criticise it in terms that are beside its point.

Yet what marks off *Antony* (and *Coriolanus*) from the earlier and less perfectly realised tragedies is not something that is wholly to the advantage of the later pieces. I wonder if there isn't after all something essentially rather reductive about the art of *Antony.* That is what I meant by asking, at the beginning of this chapter, whether anyone ever left the theatre, after seeing it, feeling unnerved and emotionally bruised. I am not suggesting that the function of Tragedy is merely to upset us; but a full experience of a tragedy does seem to involve a certain laceration of spirit; and in Shakespeare's darkest plays such mitigation of the pain as there is results from the playwright's contrivance – from his not being able to face the consequences of his insights (the last scene of *Hamlet* shows what I have in mind). No such manipulation is needed in *Antony*, because there is no insight in the play which desperately needs to be evaded. Its vision, as I have been arguing, is too genial for that; and

what I've called its 'desolating clarity' about *bovarysme* is
desolating in the sense of being no more than (if certainly
no less than) poignant. And though, in the gross, more hangs
on the fate of the lovers than hangs on the fate of Lear or
Othello, there is little sign that the future of the Roman
world is something that Shakespeare thought or cared
much about. Isn't there, indeed, a kind of categorising of
experience in *Antony*, so that the play alternates between
the political and the moral (if 'moral' is the right word)
without their ever becoming part of each other, as they
obviously are in *Lear* and *Hamlet*? If so, that means that
the kind of attention we bring to bear has to keep alternat-
ing, too: which is probably one reason why it is so hard to
feel that any account of the play is accurate all of the time.

Further thoughts in this general direction also work to the
disadvantage of *Antony*. For instance, it is all very well for
me to say that we can afford to let Antony and Cleopatra
entertain us, but isn't that a backhanded tribute? Imagine
saying anything remotely similar about Lear or Othello!
Imagine talking about Emma Bovary in connection with
Lady Macbeth! If the reader has gone along with my invocation of Flaubert, he will perhaps agree that we have set up a
strong presumption about Shakespeare's involvement with
his own creatures: whatever the artist's inner life, the
figures in this play are less important, less significant, than
the earlier heroes. The sensibility deployed here, for all its
generosity of gesture, is narrower than what we find in *King
Lear*. It is not that Shakespeare has ceased to see troubling
things, but that they don't trouble him so much.[1] *Antony*
isn't, as it were, written in blood; indeed, the hero uses
an appropriate counter-metaphor:

> That which is now a horse, even with a thought
> The rack dislimns, and makes it indistinct
> As water is in water.

The characters try, not so much to make sense of their

[1] Cf. F. R. Leavis, 'T. S. Eliot as Critic' in *"Anna Karenina" and Other Essays*
(1967), p. 182.

experience, as to find any experience stable enough, grasp-able enough, to look at without its shifting and dissolving into something else, or into nothingness. *Antony and Cleopatra* is like *Four Quartets* without that poem's religious aspiration.

Index

Index

Johnson, Samuel, *Notes* on Shakespeare, 32, 67, 76, 91, 145, 182, 205, 228
Jorgensen, Paul A., *Lear's Self-Discovery*, 144n

Kelly, T. J., *Hamlet*, 56
King Leir (Anon.), 74
Kirsch, James, *Shakespeare's Royal Self*, 144n
Kitto, H. D. F., *Form and Meaning in Drama*, 23, 24, 26–40 *passim*, 43, 48, 79, 80, 82
Knight, G. Wilson, *Wheel of Fire, The*, 23, 34, 38, 42, 33, 77–8, 126, 199, 233
Knights, L. C.
  Explorations, 25
  Some Shakespearean Themes and An Approach to "Hamlet", 23, 24–42 *passim*, 47–8, 49, 134, 144, 181, 189, 191
Kyd, Thomas
  Spanish Tragedy, The, 70
  Ur-Hamlet, The, 62, 68, 74

Lawrence, D. H., *Women in Love*, 31
Leavis, F. R.
  "Anna Karenina" and Other Essays, 234n
  Common Pursuit, The, 3, 16, 22, 57–8, 85–6, 108, 110, 114, 120, 133–4
Lever, J. W., edn of *Measure for Measure*, 15, 16, 20
Levin, Harry, *Question of "Hamlet", The*, 40–1, 52
Lings, Martin, *Shakespeare in the Light of Sacred Art*, 144n
Lovelace, Richard, 80, 81

Mack, Maynard, *"King Lear" in Our Time* (reviewed by Empson), 187n
McKerrow, R. B., 79n
Marlowe, Christopher, *Jew of Malta, The*, 12, 72
Marsh, D. R. C., *Shakespeare's "Hamlet"*, 72n, 73
Marvell, Andrew, "The Garden" (quoted), 76
Mason, H. A., *Shakespeare's Tragedies of Love*, 4, 87, 95–6, 102, 110, 113n, 120, 166–7, 196–7, 198, 200, 208, 213, 222, 226–7, 233

Maxwell, J. C., in *The Pelican Guide to English Literature*, 66n
Moberly, Rev. C. E., 77
Muir, Kenneth, edn of *King Lear*, 144, 149, 166, 173, 175, 178, 181, 182, 183, 185
Murry, John Middleton, *Shakespeare*, 201

Nash, Thomas, 79, 81–2
North, Sir Thomas, 228

Olivier, Sir Laurence (film of *Othello*), 122, 130
Orwell, George, *Selected Essays*, 145–6, 193, 202
Oxford Companion to English Literature, The, 152, 154, 166

Partridge, Eric, 82n
Plutarch, *see under* North
Prosser, Eleanor, *Hamlet and Revenge*, 38n, 61–5

revenge, 6, 24, 61–2, 66, 73–4 (*see also* conventions; Elizabethan attitudes; incest; suicide)
Ribner, Irving, *Patterns in Shakespearean Tragedy*, 188
Ridley, M. R.
  edn of *Antony and Cleopatra*, 231
  edn of *Othello*, 122–3
Robertson, J. M., *The Problem of "Hamlet"*, 73
Robson, W. W., *English as a University Subject* (reprinted in *Critical Essays*), 77–8
Rossiter, A. P., *Angel with Horns*, 19, 38, 110

Sainte-Beuve, Charles, 5
Schoenbaum, S., 79n
Schueller, H. M. (ed.), *The Persistence of Shakespeare Idolatry*, 57
Shakespeare, William
  All's Well, 228
  Antony and Cleopatra, 4, 7, 9, 21, 61, 92, 189–90, **206–35**
  Coriolanus, 88, 189, 212, 233
  Cymbeline, 91, 109
  Hamlet, 2, 6–7, 9–10, 21, **22–84**, 90, 99, 103, 105, 108–9, 111n, 120, 133, 134, 135, 156–7, 180, 190, 192, 206, 207, 233, 234
  Henry IV, 8, 60